POSITIVELY SE

a guide to help your child develop positive approaches to learning and cope with sensory processing difficulty

Amy Vaughan OTR/L, BCP

Positively Sensory! a guide to help your child develop positive
approaches to learning and cope with sensory processing difficulty

Copyright © 2014 Scribble Media, LLC. All Rights Reserved.
Published by:
Scribble Media, LLC
2101 West Chesterfield Blvd, C100 #66
Springfield, MO 65807
Phone: (417) 459-4749
Fax: (417) 763-3168
Email: contact@scribblemedia.net

Illustrations by Sarah Yake
Design and composition by Kylie Wright Design, LLC

ISBN: 978-0-9908952-0-6

Library of Congress Control Number: 2014918088

DEDICATION

This book is dedicated to my own four precious treasures, who make my world a better place simply by being here, and to my husband, John, an amazing partner in this fun and crazy life.

SPECIAL THANKS

Special thanks to Sarah Yake for her amazing illustrations, Kylie Wright for her outstanding graphic design skill, and to my mom, Jean Stark, for her editing expertise and dedication in helping me see this project through to the end. Thanks also to Deb Fusek, Annie and Janet Fritsch, Megan Ruffing, Anna Quigg and Sarah Jones for their contributions and insight. Finally, thanks to all the children and their families who have inspired me to learn and write this book. This book is for you!

CONTENTS

CHAPTER 1: INTRODUCTION...1

The Treasure

The Problem

Positively Positive

Chapter 1 Deeper Journey to Application

THE FIRST SIDE OF THE COIN: BEHAVIOR

CHAPTER 2: BEHAVIOR FOUNDATIONS...9

ABC's of Behavior

Antecedent

Behavior

The Consequence

Tips for Influencing the ABCs of Behavior

Chapter 2 Deeper Journey to Application

CHAPTER 3: FUNCTIONS OF BEHAVIOR..25

The Dancing Girls Principle

Is There a Better Way? How DO I Respond?

The Make it Go Away Approach

Are you Raising a Couch Potato

Chapter 3 Deeper Journey to Application

THE FLIP SIDE OF THE COIN: SENSORY PROCESSING

CHAPTER 4: SENSORY PROCESSING! THE FUN STUFF.........................43

Sensory and Behavior: Two Sides of the Same Coin

The Cell Phone Principle

Chapter 4 Deeper Journey to Application

CHAPTER 5: SENSORY AND MOTOR FOUNDATIONS.............................51

Developmental Learning Pyramid

What Do We Know About Sensory Input

Sensory Processing: Defining the Senses

Betrayed By the Senses

What Do We Know about Sensory Learning?

Chapter 5 Deeper Journey to Application

CHAPTER 6: SENSORY DEVELOPMENT...77

Stages of Sensory Development

A Happy Healthy Learner

Betrayed by the Senses

Finding the Calm-Alert Sweet Spot

Sensory Processing Gone Awry

Over-Responders are Hyper-Sensitive

Under-Responders are Hypo-Sensitive

Chapter 6 Deeper Journey to Application

CHAPTER 7: SENSORY PROCESSING AND LEARNING STYLE.......................99

Global Approach to Learning

Linear Approach to Learning

Chapter 7 Deeper Journey to Application

CHAPTER 8: THE PAYOFF PRINCIPLE.......................107

Expanding Favorite Things

Chapter 8 Deeper Journey to Application

CHAPTER 9: TOOLS: SENSORY PROCESSING STRENGTHS AND BARRIORS.............117

Strengths Based Perspective

A Child is Not Something to Be Fixed

Purpose Driven "Work"

Foundational Principles of Learning

Chapter 9 Deeper Journey to Application

LEARNING STRENGTHS PROFILE

CHAPTER 10: INTRODUCING THE LEARNING STRENGTHS PROFILE.........................129

Learning Strengths Profile

Primary Learning Strengths Profile

Chapter 10 Deeper Journey to Application

CHAPTER 11: USING THE LEARNING STRENGTHS PROFILE TOOL.............................151

Using the Learning Strengths Profile

Applying the Primary Learning Strengths Profile to Early Learners

Chapter 11 Deeper Journey to Application

CHAPTER 12: PROBLEM SOLVING.......................167

Chapter 12 Deeper Journey to Application

CHAPTER 13: SENSORY DIET.......................181

Chapter 13 Deeper Journey to Application

TOOLS.......................187

APPENDIX

REFERENCES

FOREWORD

You have probably found your way to this book from my website, or from a friend or a therapist who suggested reading up on the subject of sensory processing, behavior, or learning style. Whatever your reason, I'm excited to share information with you related to subjects about which I'm so passionate.

I have met hundreds of kids who are struggling with behaviors of all kinds: kids who are aggressive or impulsive, kids who have difficulty paying attention, kids who have severe learning disabilities, kids who have dyslexia, kids who have auditory processing issues, kids with mild to severe autism, kids with developmental delays, kids with post-traumatic stress disorder, kids who have been abused, kids who have an attachment disorder, and kids who are riddled with anxiety and have a high need to control every situation. However, I've never met a bad kid.

I write this guide because I have met hundreds of kids who are hurting, kids who have the potential to blossom and thrive, but are not thriving. I have met hundreds of moms and dads who have tried everything they can think of but have found nothing is enough. They are at their wit's end, the very end of their ropes. I write this book dedicated to those parents, teachers, and professionals who are reading in hope that tomorrow might be better than today for the children they love.

About eight years ago, my husband John gave me a gift for my office. I opened a large framed photograph of a little boy whose face is half-hidden when you look directly at him, but the beginning of a smile can be seen in his reflection from a window beside him. John said, "To me, this is what you do."

At first I was looking at him thinking that the kids I work with (including our own) are moving a lot and are usually highly engaged in activity. Why was he giving me a picture of a reflection of a boy who is pondering thoughts, looking out a window? Then, he said words I will never forget. He said, "When I look at a boy like this, I see part of him. I don't see beyond what stands right in front of me. When you look at him, you see his whole face because you really see him. You see beyond what he is presenting to the world today. You see where he's going and what he can be, not where he is today. That's what you do."

His words captured my heart's desire to see beyond the circumstance of today and the skill set of today and look forward to walking into a better picture tomorrow. Through this book, I am excited to share information that I hope helps you build new strategies to support your child and family walking into that brighter, more complete picture of tomorrow.

If I can help a parent learn one positive new thing to try with a child or another way to see the situation, I have accomplished my goal. May this book provide hope for you in your situation. May it bless you. May it help you. May you be a better parent or provider for reading it.

The purpose of this book is to guide you. This is not a cookbook recipe, a system, or a miracle pill. It will, however, take you through a process that will give you a framework for addressing sensory behaviors. It is my intention to give you the next step you can take to get started in setting your child up for success or to get back to a better tomorrow. I want to help you find the confidence to engage more fully with your child in positive, developmentally stimulating, and helpful activities that could change your child's life forever.

To all of my friends and fellow therapists out there, old and new, thank you for the gift of your encouragement and support. This book is for each child who has touched me in our work together. May I begin to repay you for all you have done in teaching me.

Amy Vaughn OTR/L, BCP

ABOUT AMY VAUGHAN, OTR/L, BCP

Amy Vaughan is a nationally registered and Missouri State licensed occupational therapist. She is Board Certified in Pediatrics through the National Board of Certification in Occupational Therapy (NBCOT) and has practiced as a pediatric therapist for 18 years. She has worked in hospital-based pediatric settings, school-based intervention, school team consultation, community mental health settings, and private clinic practice. She consults and provides training instruction to therapy and teaching teams both for school districts and for out-patient clinic practices. She works with Burrell Behavioral Health in Springfield, Missouri, where she serves on the Autism Center's Assessment Team and has led the development of Burrell's occupational and speech therapy out-patient services. She also serves on Burrell's Strength-Based Assessment Development Team.

Amy is a graduate of the University of Kansas and is certified in Sensory Integration and Praxis Testing (SIPT). She is also certified to use Interactive Metronome tools, as well as Integrated Listening Systems, and is certified in early intervention using the DIR © (Developmental, Individual Differences, Relationship-Based) method of treatment. She has trained hundreds of individuals in pediatric therapy theory and practical application through leading seminars, teaching a college level pediatric course, and as a module trainer for the Missouri First Steps Program. In 2011, Amy was recognized by the Springfield Business Journal for both their 40 Under 40 Award and their 20 Most Influential Women in Southwest Missouri Award.

Amy's most treasured accomplishment and blessing in life is her family. She is the wife of John, her partner in life. She is the mother of four children, who are her delight and inspiration. Amy is passionate about living life to the fullest, children, helping others, sand volleyball and reading.

CHAPTER I

"Children remind us to treasure the smallest of gifts,
even in the most difficult of times."
- Allen Klein

INTRODUCTION

The driving goal of this book is to provide a behavior and sensory resource to help parents and caregivers build a foundation of knowledge that will support them as they work to respond to both overt and hidden issues and raise a thriving child. Most parents notice sensory processing symptoms beginning in infancy and toddlerhood, but they do not necessarily recognize what they are seeing within a sensory processing framework. They become more concerned as the child enters preschool or grade school and begins to struggle more overtly in academic or social areas. Therefore, the heart of this book is directed to helping support parents who have children that are preschool age through late grade school age. This is often the time that many abstract, seemingly unrelated unique behaviors gel together to become a stumbling block to learning or positive social behavior in the classroom or structured learning situations.

Sensory processing difficulty is not confined to a diagnosis. Every child (and adult) will have seasons of more difficulty where the body is stressed and a problem with learning or behavior appears. My goal in sharing the information in this book is to help give parents a resource for framing that problem as it appears, regardless of whether the child has a diagnosis or not. When parents have a broader framework for seeing the problem, they will naturally have a more solid response for supporting that child as his nervous system struggles to learn and adapt to growing expectations.

The process that I will share for framing an issue and responding to it with a solid plan will apply regardless of diagnosis. Sensory processing difficulty is a hallmark issue in almost every childhood mental health. If your child has a diagnosis, you know you need this information. If your child is struggling, but does not have a diagnosis, you also need this information. **A healthy framework regarding the role of sensory processing and how it relates to and influences behavior and active learning is helpful information for raising every child, any child, regardless of whether that child is currently a joy to raise or whether that child presents challenge after challenge.**

THE TREASURE

My children are my greatest treasure on earth. They are worth more to me than all my possessions stacked together. I remember a time when my third son was in preschool and his teacher told me a story about him sitting at circle time on the first day of school. She said that she was greeting each child and said, "Hey! What do you know today?" He replied, "Well, I know I am my Mommy's most precious treasure."

Why yes, he is! Sometimes that's all you need to know to start a great day. Sometimes, knowing that you are a great treasure sets up the perfect catalyst for learning and positive growth.

I don't believe I am the only one who sees her own children as her greatest treasure. We often collectively talk of the fact that "our children are our future." As our treasures, we take seriously the task of raising them, guiding them, challenging them, encouraging them to grow, and cheering when they do. Picture the difference in your enthusiasm when you watched a favorite sports team win a game compared to when you saw your own child make his first "touchdown" physically or academically. It might have been when he took his first steps or read his first word. Notice the greater intensity related to your child's accomplishment. This great feeling becomes exponentially true for those of you with children who have developmental delays and whose first steps weren't a "given." Our children are what matter, and there is no close second.

We seem to take typical development and natural growth for granted until we can't because they are not happening. We often don't even need to understand child development for our children because things are just naturally unfolding the way they are supposed to, and we are rocking happily along. However, sometimes, the bottom drops out of everything, and the child **hits a wall** in development. He bumps up against something bigger than he is and bigger than his skill set, and he gets **stuck**. This can happen subtly or overtly during times of adjustment to life stressors such as moving or when a life circumstance rocks the family unit. This can also happen for no apparent reason. A child is stressed and begins struggling socially or behaviorally or academically, and no one knows why. In contrast, this can be a pattern of a larger picture of overall developmental delay. Either way, this book will help provide a framework to start supporting your child in the situation and start moving forward toward personal growth and progress.

THE PROBLEM

As much fun as it is to brag on our kids and think about the great concept of having kids and how we are going to *rock* the challenge, that's probably not why you started reading this book. **Raising kids is HARD!** They are not predictable, and as soon as we are sure we have them figured out, we find that we don't. The problem is that we live in an increasingly complex world with processed food and different play rules and different challenges than when we were kids. The problem is that developmental delay happens **often**. Sometimes it is subtle, like having some trouble making friends and keeping them, and sometimes it is blatant.

This guide is dedicated to providing you with a framework for **setting the stage** for progress, regardless of developmental level or ability, regardless of IQ, and regardless of past trauma or experience. The most important thing that is needed is a motivated, caring adult who is willing to put in the time to learn the strategies and put them into action. Head knowledge will help frame your natural response to some situations, but head knowledge without any action is like watching a winning touchdown on TV instead of making one yourself. Big difference!

I encourage you to read and learn and apply the strategies in this book to the best of your ability **because I've seen them work over and over**. The strategies in this guide have worked with children in a wide variety of circumstances. This guide is full of time-tested, therapist-utilized, and success-driven methods that I have collected over the past 18 years as a pediatric occupational therapist. Applying these methods will help you set the stage for progress. It is a place to begin.

POSITIVELY POSITIVE

One of the basic premises in life that I live by is that if we look at where we are going, and get excited about what **can** be, we don't spend as much time wandering in the wilderness where we are **stuck**. When we look forward, we can begin to actually move forward toward positive change, sometimes even in spite of ourselves. I find value in self-reflection about past decisions and actions in order to make better decisions and better actions. However, ultimately, **there is nothing more powerful than finding the positive piece in the situation and re-framing the whole situation around that positive piece.**

I understand how parents berate themselves about what they should be doing and their probable or potential mistakes. I understand because I do it myself as a parent. I recognize the high responsibility of raising a child. I recognize the need to feel you are providing the **right** opportunities and experiences for your child to thrive and be successful. I feel it times four.

Understanding behavior and sensory foundations, as presented in the next few chapters, will give you the framework you need to recognize what you are seeing. You will begin to see the situations you encounter with your child through a new lens, and a new perspective can change everything. Once you have a framework for the behaviors that you see, and you are able to recognize the sensory processing elements and the environmental influence to that behavior, you are better prepared to respond to situations. This perspective sets you up to utilize the tools in this book more effectively.

Next, we will look at how you can apply what you have learned about behavior and sensory strategies to harness motivation and enhance everyday learning to create **win-win situations***. A win-win situation is always the goal. It is most helpful when everyone wins. It is not helpful when the adult wins and the child loses. You have compliance, but you lost the war.

Then, we will learn to purposefully shift to a strengths-based perspective. I get excited about strengths-based assessment and intervention because by identifying and understanding your child's strengths, you can encapsulate weaknesses and your child is then defined by his strength, not his weakness. You are not ignoring his weaknesses, but supporting them. You will find that this is one of the most life-changing pieces to positive intervention. It can literally change **everything** when applied correctly to a child and his learning and interaction.

At the end of each chapter, there are questions for your own personal self-reflection or for group discussion. These are titled **Deeper Journey to Application** because they will help you process the information in each chapter more thoroughly and apply it more specifically to your child. The time you devote to getting a handle on the information in each chapter will serve you well as you strive for successful use of the tools in the last chapter (which is why I know many of you picked up the book). The tools provided in the last chapter will give you a practical starting point for applying what you have learned with your child. Each tool is accompanied by a handout that will help you apply that specific strategy.

This book is designed to be read beginning to end so that you will have a working knowledge of the concepts. It is also designed to allow you to easily revisit specific concepts and strategies that are most applicable to your child and situation. There are layers of information in this book. If you are parent visiting this topic for the very first time, it may feel a bit like you are drinking from a fire hydrant. Read anyway. Parents have said that the first time they were introduced to the information, they were overwhelmed but gained a basic working knowledge of the concepts. They report that each time they revisit the concepts, they learn something new. If you learn even one new positive strategy or gain a more positive perspective on your current situation, it can be life changing.

CHAPTER I DEEPER JOURNEY TO APPLICATION

The Deeper Journey portion of each chapter is set up to provide application and reflection questions or to help support group discussion regarding the information in the related chapter.

1. Describe your child's strengths and weaknesses:

2. Is your child currently defined by teachers, parents or himself by his strengths or his weaknesses?

3. What is getting in the way of you or others seeing your child in a more positive light?

4. Who is currently on your team to encourage and support your child's progress in life?

THE FIRST SIDE OF THE COIN: BEHAVIOR

SECTION I

CHAPTER 2

"No matter how calmly you try to referee, parenting will eventually produce bizarre behavior, and I'm not talking about the kids. Their behavior is always normal."
- Bill Cosby

BEHAVIOR FOUNDATIONS

Before we can truly understand sensory processing, especially sensory behaviors, we have to start with understanding a few basic principles of behavior. We start with the **ABC's of behavior** as a framework to understand sensory processing in the right context.

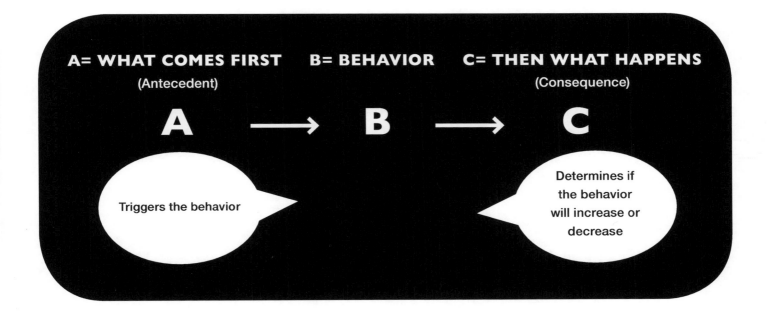

ABC'S OF BEHAVIOR

The (A) antecedent sets up the situation. It is what comes first. The (B) behavior is the actual "doing." The (C) consequence determines whether that behavior is likely to occur again or not. It is what comes next, after the behavior happens. As we will cover later, the consequence is not the same thing as discipline. It is simply what naturally follows the behavior that influences it. (Catania, 2013) (Kazdin, 2008)

ANTECEDENT

As stated above, the antecedent sets up the situation. It includes things that happen to create the setting for the behavior: a person, a place, a time of day, an object (toy or work), motivation, words, hunger, fatigue, etc. The antecedent comes before the behavior happens. It can be a combination of things that together create the "perfect storm" for problem behavior. It can even be the proactive approaches we take to set up positive behavior changes. To understand the antecedent is very powerful because with the antecedent piece, you have the power to change the whole situation.

Notice the examples of the types of things that can be antecedents. You make a difference just by your presence. There are people in your life that calm the situation just by being present. They don't have to say anything because the history of your relationship with them lends the support you need. On the contrary, there are people that irritate you, annoy you, and make you feel uncomfortable or criticized. Their presence starts to rain on your day just because they entered the room.

The same happens for kids.

Before you jump to the conclusion that you really are the problem, look at this a bit deeper. First, kids are just like us. They make lots of assumptions. There have been times when I walk into an assessment room, and a child starts escalating. He doesn't even know me, so it's obviously not based on his previous experience with me. His behavior is not based upon fact at all. The first thing I recognize is that I represent the fear he has of whatever situation we are in. If I want to get the best assessment or make the best progress with him, I must help change his perspective to a positive one before we will be able to get any real work done.

ANTECEDENT: THE "TRIGGER." THE ANTECEDENT IS THE TRIGGER AND SETS UP THE SITUATION.

In addition, we all make mistakes. Sometimes we respond in ways, especially with our own children, that set us up for extra work in the future. When your child behaves like an angel for the teacher or therapist, but "won't do anything for you," yes, my friend, you are the one who needs to change. When you change the way you interact, you will have the power to change the entire direction of the interaction. You hold the key to progress. You hold the key to the work being enjoyable for both of you. You hold the power to wield your influence as a weapon or a positive tool. In short, you have a lot of power to shape your child's experience.

THE POWER OF A PARENT

If you are a parent, you hold even more power over your children than teachers and therapists. You hold the power to inspire a child and be the most influential force in his life. Adversely, you have the power to hinder, squelch and hold your child back from blossoming. I want to utilize the positive power that I have in the lives of my children to support them thriving. Purpose today to check your actions and reactions and make sure they align with the positive role you want to have in your child's life.

Being a parent can be like being on a roller coaster ride with emotional highs and lows. Is there anything more frustrating than when you can't figure out how to help, or when you watch your child struggling against something so much bigger than he is equipped to deal with?

The truth remains: you hold the most power and you are a key to your child's success. No person has greater potential for positive impact in a child's life than a parent. No therapist can replace you. No doctor has a medicine more powerful than you. No one can pay you what your influence in your child's life is worth. Purpose today to make your influence count. Purpose to support your child in discovering a brighter tomorrow and a better day than yesterday. Every day can get better. Each day is new, and today can be the day that you begin to see your child for who he really is and begin to realize just how great it can be to be HIS mom or dad.

BACK TO THE BASICS

You are an antecedent. Actually, you are the most powerful instrument for change in the antecedent group. However, there are other factors that set up the situation: the time of day, the place, a trigger word, an object in the room or the situation, and internal factors for the child, such as hunger, pain, and fatigue.

It is important to look at changing a situation for more success. Take some time to look at the set-up that created the "setting" for the behavior in the first place. Often, one of the best "fixes" for "sensory behavior" is simply tweaking the setup. By providing a supportive routine or an enriched environment for learning, positive interaction is more likely to occur. Don't ignore this piece. Don't ignore the value of the setting and the antecedents that support positive moments for your child. When you manipulate antecedents, you have the power to change the entire situation and set it up to be positive.

---

a note about the antecedent...
Thoroughly understanding the importance of the antecedent is especially important when dealing with sensory-like behaviors. Sensory behaviors are automatically internally reinforced. Therefore, behavior modification and discipline approaches do not readily change sensory behaviors. The key to changing sensory behaviors lies in manipulating the setup (antecedent) of the situation.

BEHAVIOR

The behavior is the "doing" piece. The behavior is simply the thing that the child does, whether it is positive or negative. Labeling a child with "bad behavior" isn't helpful. Labeling behavior as "bad" often communicates your view of the child as "bad." It is negative and means nothing except that the person talking is so frustrated and ill-equipped to deal with the situation that he or she doesn't have better words.

Talking about children being "bad" is reflective on who they are as a person. Furthermore, it's not true. Each of us is wonderfully and delightfully made regardless of our present stressful situation. Just as you don't want to be labeled and judged by your worst moment, neither do children. Mislabeling them is not creating any motivation on their part to make better decisions or change their responses. It also sets other adults up to see whatever they do in a more negative light and can often make the situation much worse for everyone. Being purposeful about the way we describe behavior is a fundamental step.

What if a child does have negative behavior? If we don't call it "bad," what do we call it? We call it what it is. We document for ourselves and for others exactly what the child is doing that is not productive in the situation (i.e. hitting, cussing, spitting, mouthing objects, bumping into peers, tackling peers/ adults, crying, whining, etc.) and we document how often the behavior is occurring. This step gives us better perspective and takes the emotion out of the situation. We will state the facts – just the facts – not how we feel about them.

BEHAVIOR: THE "DOING." THE BEHAVIOR IS THE POSITIVE OR NEGATIVE THING THAT THE CHILD DOES.

Behavior can be positive or negative. Positive, productive behaviors include such things as when a child approaches another peer to initiate play, follows specific requests accurately, rides a bike, draws a picture, or smiles. These are generally things that we are hoping to see the child do again and again. They move a child forward in relationship and skill attainment in a productive way.

Of course, behavior can be negative, too. We hope negative behaviors do not become consistent patterns and habits for our children. Negative behaviors include such things as hitting, kicking, spitting, running away, throwing self to the floor, withdrawing from interaction, tackling peers, biting, head banging, pinching, pouting, screaming, cussing, refusing, crying, throwing, and destroying. Negative behaviors can quickly become a problem or barrier for the child socially and academically. They are especially concerning if they are self-injurious, meaning that they are self-directed to inflict pain to the child from himself. In those cases, parents need to quickly seek the help of a professional team to ensure the safety of the child and obtain help setting up a positive plan for redirecting that behavior.

Sometimes, I get to the end of the day and feel very irritated with my children's behavior toward one another. It can **feel like** they don't know how to treat each other well. For example, when relatives are visiting, I want them to experience kids with great attitudes so fond family memories can form. I don't want them to see the learning that naturally has to take place behind the scenes where a child needs to work through a meltdown or an undesirable attitude. For many parents, this feeling becomes even more magnified in public. For example, when a child has a meltdown as he works through how to ask for (and sometimes not receive) the toy or item he wants while shopping in the store, it feels very intense. Working through teaching a child a better way to respond is simply not easy, especially when you are in public with an audience of critics.

For all of us, taking a moment to define what is actually happening will help us see the situation more clearly. It is an important step because even if you are not a naturally emotive person, you are more stressed by the situation than you probably realize, and you need to reframe it for success.

By defining the behavior you will know what you are up against. You will know how many different behaviors you are dealing with, and you will know how big the problem is, based on how often the behaviors are occurring and how intense they are. This approach can be the beginning of an excellent plan for directly addressing behavior.

TAKE DATA LIKE AN EXPECTANT PARENT

As expectant parents prepare for the birth of their precious treasure, they are often trained and motivated to track details in order to know where they stand in labor and delivery. It is a time in life where we more naturally think to take data. Husbands often diligently track the time between contractions so the couple can know how far labor has progressed and can prepare for what's coming next. Like tracking contractions, paying attention to specific symptoms (behaviors), their timing, and intensity can point to what is coming next. Tracking this information can give you clues for how to prepare for future events. Like labor, most behavior (even sensory behavior) can be predictable.

a note about behavior...

Kids are really smart, regardless of IQ. They are going to use the best tool in their **behavioral backpack*** at any given time to handle the situation they are in and to either make it better or make it feel better. As a therapist, if I encounter a child melting down in the store, screaming, "I want it!" and wailing and kicking his feet, my first thought is, *Wow, that's the best tool he has right now to ask for what he wants!*

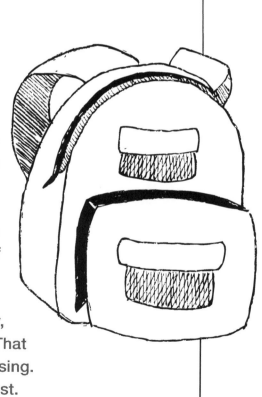

The way the child responds represents his **"go-to"** skills for responding to that situation. That is his current set of coping skills.

Realize that if we want a child to respond in a better way, we have to give him a better tool. It's as simple as that. That tool we teach him has to work better than the tool he's using. He is smart, and he's going to use the tool that works best. If screaming "I want it!" works, that is currently his best tool.

THE CONSEQUENCE

Even the word "consequence" sounds ominous, doesn't it? Do you feel in trouble just reading the word? We have become so used to hearing the word "consequence" in a negative sense that we don't realize it is truly a neutral word to describe what happens after the behavior, determining whether that behavior will increase or decrease. A consequence can be positive or negative. It is simply the "wrap up" that follows the behavior. It can "wrap" the perfect gift or the perfect storm, depending on the situation.

A consequence is the response that follows the behavior and influences whether the behavior will occur again. It **reinforces** the behavior and naturally increases the likelihood of that behavior occurring again. When we are looking at positive behaviors that we want to happen again, we want to reinforce them.

This is a good time to define the difference between a **reward** and a **reinforcer**. These terms are often used interchangeably, but they are actually different. When I give you a **reward**, I am giving you something I think you may like. I am hoping it is reinforcing to you and will increase your use of the positive behavior that I am rewarding. However, a reward is not always actually reinforcing to you. It may just be a reward that I would find reinforcing, but you don't, and so it is not reinforcing to you. A **reinforcer** actually increases the behavior, and so when I want to see a child more consistently perform a behavior, I must pay extra attention to make sure that my rewards are truly reinforcing and powerful enough to influence that behavior, and increase it. (Catania, 2013)

For example, let's say that you are at a public swimming pool and have the opportunity to successfully jump in and save a child from drowning. The parents of the child can't think of a high enough prize for saving their most precious treasure, so the parents offer to give you their child in exchange for saving his life. Wow! Awkward. That reward would cost them much but wouldn't probably be what you were looking for out of the situation, right? You might be much more reinforced by high praise, a thank you card, or a gift card for a dinner out. The reward they are offering may not actually be very rewarding to you.

Remember that a **reinforcer** increases behavior. When I am dealing with a negative behavior, I am looking to remove whatever is reinforcing it. When I think I have been setting up a situation to reshape that negative behavior, and I have attempted to remove what is reinforcing it, and if over time I notice that the behavior keeps occurring, then that means I have actually missed

*My professional colleagues chuckle when they hear parents say, "I found out that's the best tool in his backpack." At this point, they know the family has been hanging out with me. I teach parents to frame what they see behaviorally in terms of tools. The behavioral backpack refers to a child's group of behavioral responses.

what is reinforcing it. The behavior keeps occurring because something is reinforcing it. When this happens, I need to step back and look more closely because I am missing something key in the situation.

As parents, sometimes we tend to relax when our children are behaving well and only intervene when they misbehave, but sometimes jumping in to encourage and notice positive, appropriate behavior and reinforce it is the key to turning around a negative behavior situation. By giving the attention to positive behaviors, those behaviors will begin to outshine negative behaviors and refocus the situation on the best your child has to offer. For children who thrive on parental attention (and all do to some extent), this can be a powerful tool for shaping appropriate behaviors.

CONSEQUENCE: THE "AFTER." THE CONSEQUENCE IS WHAT HAPPENS AFTER THE BEHAVIOR AND DETERMINES IF THE BEHAVIOR WILL INCREASE OR DECREASE.

A consequence can be negative or positive in nature and can set the tone of the entire experience. You might think that a negative reaction will always decrease the likelihood of the behavior occurring again, but that is not necessarily true. In some situations, a negative response simply sets up a negative pattern that is predictable. A negative consequence doesn't necessarily diminish how often a behavior happens.

For example, if a child wants to get out of doing schoolwork, he may know that if he tips his chair over, it will get the teacher's attention, but he discovers that if he throws the chair, the teacher will escort him to the principal's office. The situation is negative, but he achieved his goal of getting out of the challenging school work. The next time he encounters challenging school work, he might follow the same pattern. It is not fun for anyone, but it is predictable and it works to get him out of the challenging school work.

Whether the consequence is hugging or hitting, giving attention or ignoring, making eye contact or avoiding eye contact, praising and encouraging or screaming and reprimanding, giving a toy that is wanted or withholding a toy that is wanted, the consequence has influence.

The key to knowing what consequence will be most positive in a child's life and truly help to shape the behavior into something more productive for the child lies in understanding the motivation for the behavior. This understanding sets the foundation for determining the function of the behavior, which is covered more thoroughly in Chapter 3.

Consequences influence the tone of the entire experience, and so before we dive any further into behavior, let's look at the following two examples illustrating the power of consequences.

THE INDULGENT GRANDMOTHER

Let's suppose that there is a grandmother who cherishes her grandson, Johnny. He is the brightest part of her world, and everything he does is an inspiration to her and something to celebrate. Have you met this grandma?

Now, Johnny is at Grandmother's house and he wanders down to the basement where there are open paint cans sitting on the floor in a variety of great colors. And, SWEET! There are paint brushes too! Johnny looks over to the blank wall and begins to envision what that blank wall would look like if it only had some color. Hmmmm. There's your setup. That's the **antecedent**.

Johnny starts painting. He doesn't stop with one stroke. He doesn't stop with one color. He makes a beautiful mess that is truly inspired. That is the **behavior**. He paints on the wall. A. Lot.

Grandma starts to come down the stairs, and Johnny stands back to see her reaction to his work.

Grandma starts clapping her hands, she sighs, she smiles. She gets a tear in her eye and she says, "Johnny, your art is a gift to the world. You are the next Rembrandt! Let's go get Papa and show him your great work!" As they walk away into the sunset (the paint on the floor is magically cleaned by "The Fairies"), Grandma is muttering, "Fabulous, my boy, just fabulous!" That is the **consequence**: Grandma's attention and positive response.

Consider the next time Johnny walks into a room and sees open paint cans and available tools for painting. One of his basic premises based on his experience will be:

I am good at painting. My grandma is proud of me when I paint and I love that feeling! I enjoyed painting last time. I think I have a gift to give to the world. I'm going to paint!

Do you see the power of consequence? The consequence shapes or reinforces how the situation is framed for the next time you encounter similar circumstances. It influences what you will choose next time.

THE RESPONSIBLE BABYSITTER

Let's suppose we meet a very responsible, trustworthy babysitter. She is attempting to watch four busy children, one of which is crying and in diapers, and one of which is the older brother, Andy. Andy is happily playing in the living room until his little brother starts crying. Babysitter is changing Crying Brother's diaper, and it sure does stink! Andy decides to go play somewhere else.

As he wanders down to the basement, Andy sees open paint cans and some great paint brushes. He looks around, sees a blank wall and decides to keep himself busy and create. After all, he just started school, and they have a great art station in the classroom. He decides to create an art station at home. That's the **antecedent** piece.

Andy paints his masterpiece. He gets inspired and paints a bit on the floor and on himself to add to the greatness. That's the **behavior** piece.

Babysitter gets Crying Brother changed and down for a nap and goes in search of Andy. As she walks down the basement stairs, Andy steps back from his work to see her reaction.

At first she's speechless. The mess is unbelievable. Then she starts crying and screaming at Andy. That's the **consequence**. Babysitter realizes that Andy's parents will be furious because this will be a costly and extensive cleanup, and it has her name and her babysitting cash written all over it. Gone are her visions of the shopping she had planned for the next weekend with her great cash. Now, she is stuck cleaning up this ick after cleaning up the last ick upstairs. Gross! And, he did all of this ON PURPOSE! She's done all this work and now won't even probably get paid! She loses control of her response and gets very angry and harsh, screaming at Andy and getting physical with him. That is the **consequence**: Babysitter screaming and getting physical with Andy.

Bad. Bad. Bad situation.

The next week, Andy rotates into the art center in his classroom at school. He and his partner are supposed to work together to create a picture of what they did at recess. He takes the paint brush (with paint on it), flings it across the room and says, "This is stupid!" while his face turns red, and he holds back tears. His peer tries to encourage him and says, "Hey, Andy, we are supposed to paint about what we did at recess. Come on." Andy turns to his peer, hits him and says, "Painting is for babies and you are stupid. Stop!"

Hmmm. The bad gets worse.

These exaggerated stories show you the power of consequence and that a situation is all in the perspective and the framing. It's all how you look at it.

Consequence is power, my friend.

ALL BEHAVIOR IS A MESSAGE

As we are looking to make positive progress, we have to accurately investigate what is holding a child back. We have to know the **barrier behavior*** we are bumping up against. We need to investigate what is involved in advance of the barrier behavior (the antecedent), what exactly is happening (the behavior), and what is encouraging the behavior to increase or decrease (the consequence). Furthermore, we need to know these things no matter what kind of behavior we are talking about, even sensory behavior. Only then can we most effectively make a plan for a different way. Our goal is creating a better way: a **win-win situation***. The positive win-win situation is even more powerful than the original barrier behavior.

All behavior is a message. It paints a picture of what the child is thinking and feeling and reflects how he or she is processing information from the world. Understanding the reasons behind a behavior can help us **hear** the message more accurately. Often, by analyzing a behavioral situation, we can discover a message that the child is communicating which he cannot articulate. By recognizing and paying attention to the details in the message, we are able to see the situation much more clearly and begin to form a response that will be effective because we see more clearly.

When we are **hearing the message**, we are then ready to understand **functions of behavior**. Understanding **functions of behavior** will give us an additional tool to help us frame situations, including sensory situations, so that we can accurately and positively bring about change, progress, and development.

*I call maladaptive behavior (undesired behavior) barrier behavior. It's not what we are shooting for and it's getting in the way of where we want to go.

*As you can tell by now, I'm all about the win-win.

TIPS FOR INFLUENCING THE ABC'S OF BEHAVIOR

A: Antecedent:

- Change the person teaching or supporting the child in that specific situation

- Change the time of day you are introducing new learning material or the specific activity that is not working

- Change the place you are working or interacting

- Change the object or activity you are requesting the child to engage in – make sure the expectation for performance matches his ability!

- Change your words, reward setup or motivational atmosphere

- Change the lighting, decrease clutter and visual distractions

- Make the atmosphere enticing – would you WANT to work here? If you wouldn't, he might not either.

- Make sure he's rested and fed before work time starts

B: Behavior tips:

- Note all the details you can about the specific behavior: Did he hit/kick/scream/spit/ stick his tongue out/fall to the floor/bite/throw, etc.?

- How intense was the behavior? Mild, moderate, severe?

- How many times did it happen in this episode?

- How long did the episode last?

C: Consequence tips:

- Make notes about what you think is reinforcing the behavior to keep it in place.
    - Attention?
    - Tangibles? Is he getting something he wants?
    - Is he getting out of doing "something" he doesn't want to do or work that is too challenging?

- Does it just feel good to him? If so, what is a better way to get that need met?

Changing the setup (A: Antecedent) or changing the response to the behavior situation (C: Consequence) is the key to changing the behavior.

CHANGING THE SETUP (A: ANTECEDENT) OR CHANGING THE RESPONSE TO THE BEHAVIOR SITUATION (C: CONSEQUENCE) IS THE KEY TO CHANGING THE BEHAVIOR.

CHAPTER 2 DEEPER JOURNEY TO APPLICATION

The Deeper Journey portion of each chapter is set up to provide application and reflection questions or to help support group discussion regarding the information in the related chapter.

1. What "go-to" skills does your child currently have in his behavioral backpack?

Positive Behavioral Responses   Negative Behavioral Responses

These responses listed represent your child's current coping skill repertoire which can be expanded and shaped into a healthier and stronger set of coping skills with each coming day. Getting these response strengths and barriers onto paper is the first step to progress and to recognizing what may already be going well for him that you can capitalize on.

2. List two recent behavioral situations your child has experienced and break them down into their ABC parts:

Situation 1:

A:

B:

C:

Situation 2:

A:

B:

C:

Antecedent: The trigger(s) for the behavior – the setup that creates the perfect storm.

Behavior: The "doing" piece. What, very specifically, is he doing?

Consequence: Remember, this is not the discipline that follows but the response in the environment or with the people that follows. It is what is feeding the behavior to cause it to escalate or continue. What is feeding the behavior?

---

3. **Barrier Behaviors:** What is holding your child back from being all he can be?

4. **Win-Win Situation:** How can those **barrier behaviors** be transformed into a **win-win situation** for your family?

CHAPTER 3

"Most bad behavior comes from insecurity."
- Debra Winger

FUNCTIONS OF BEHAVIOR

The **function of a behavior** is the core reason the behavior is occurring. Analyzing the function of a behavior is an established concept in the behavioral literature. (Kazdin, 2012) When I am looking at a set of behaviors, especially overt problem behavior, and I want to see these behaviors change to something more positive and productive, there is another primary principle that I keep in the forefront of my mind, which I call **The Dancing Girls Principle***.

THE DANCING GIRLS PRINCIPLE

Have you ever visited Broadway or a major live musical drama production? If so, chances are you have realized that there are layers to the entertainment. In the forefront, there will often be eye-catching action, such as dancing girls. This layer is designed to get your attention and draw you in. However, if you never look beyond the dancing girls, you will often miss most of what the production is about because you will probably be missing the story line. The same is true at a football game, where the action unfolds **behind** the dancing girls.

> "Your goal is not truly to just get the problem behavior to go away. Your goal is to TEACH a better way."
> - Amy Tip #6
> Amy's Top 10 Tips
> www.positivelysensory.com

Problem behavior situations happen just that way. The overt problem behavior is like the dancing girls. It gets your attention and draws you into the situation. Sometimes it gets your attention very effectively! If you never focus beyond the problem behavior to the reason behind it, you may spin in circles and become very frustrated. You can ultimately spend a lot of time addressing a behavior ineffectively. At the end of the day, you and your child may end up with negative thoughts and feelings about each other as a result of over-focusing on the **dancing girls** and not the real issues behind the scenes which are triggering that problem behavior. You've missed the storyline.

*The Dancing Girls Principle was one of the first phrases that I coined and is still one of my favorites. We all throw out an awesome dance move or two at times in our lives. They sometimes make for the best stories later in life.

Look beyond the hitting, kicking, cussing, spitting, whining, etc. to the **function of that behavior** (Kazdin, 2012), and then you find the keys to changing that behavior, because you are investigating the real storyline. By looking that one layer deeper, you will be more likely to handle the situation effectively and productively. Ask yourself, "What's the story here?" and choose to look beyond the *dancing girls.*

Burrhus Frederic (B.F.) Skinner is one of the most famous behaviorists in history. He was an American psychologist who wrote much of the foundational work that is used in applied behavioral work with children today. His innovative work with how to apply reinforcement has shaped therapeutic intervention. His work explores the science of behavior, breaking behavior into parts to better understand and shape it.

In the world of behavioral science, every behavior exhibited has a primary function (reason for occurring). Any behavior that you see a child experience has a function or reason. The goal is to identify that function (or sometimes multiple functions) of a behavior, because that tells us what is primarily **reinforcing** the behavior. The **primary reinforcer** is the fundamental thing that supports the behavior remaining in place.

In terms of positive behaviors that we want to continue and increase, we want to identify the thing that is motivating the behavior, and then purposefully continue to build it. Therefore, we increase the likelihood of the desired behavior reoccurring. Think of things like a child initiating play with a friend, writing his name accurately with good penmanship, raising his hand to indicate a need for help, etc. Those are the type of desired behaviors that we want to make sure happen again.

In terms of negative behaviors, the function of the behavior gives us insight into what is maintaining that negative behavior. It will also give us the first clues into what we can do to change the situation to one in our favor. What is the core story behind the behavior? It will be one of these things:

• **Attention: Is the behavior occurring to get ATTENTION from someone? (positive or negative)**

> ➔ Example: A child begins hand flapping to get your attention to begin interaction with you.

> ➔ Example: A child begins screaming to receive comfort and attention after falling down.

> ➔ Example: A child raises his hand and waves it in the air to get a teacher's attention to ask for help with understanding the directions on a worksheet.

→ Example: A child begins dancing in the lunch line in order to make his peers laugh.

• **Tangible: Is the behavior occurring to GET SOMETHING tangible? An "I want" (a toy/ privilege/ food, etc.)**

→ Example: A child begins to hand flap because he wants to play in the rice bucket but doesn't know how to ask you to help him get the lid off to play in it.

→ Example: A child screams in order to get mom to buy a favorite candy in the checkout line at the store.

→ Example: A child touches (or points or waves his hand) to indicate his choice of snack when offered two choices.

→ Example: A child completes his chores to earn his allowance so he can buy the LEGO set he wants.

• **Avoid/ Escape: Is the behavior occurring to AVOID something (work / transition away from a preferred toy/ activity) or ESCAPE a situation that is too challenging or uncomfortable?**

→ Example: A child sees you bring out the rice bucket and begins hand flapping because he is stressed and escalates to avoid playing in the texture.

→ Example: A child enjoys playing in the rice initially, but then becomes overwhelmed by the texture activity and begins flapping to escape the sensory experience he is in.

→ Example: A child begins rocking in his chair and escalates into talking back and cussing at the teacher in order to get sent out of the room (and avoid the worksheet he was supposed to be doing or the challenging subject that was coming next in class).

→ Example: A child whines, telling his mom he is too tired to do his chores in order to avoid doing them.

→ Example: A child toe walks in order to avoid touching the grass with his whole foot (the sensory feeling is uncomfortable).

→ Example: A child sits and spins wheels to calm down when a challenging task is presented (co-occurring sensory and escape functions of behavior).

• **Sensory: Is the behavior occurring because it just FEELS GOOD and it's not about interaction with someone else? Sensory functions must occur across settings. They are internally reinforcing, meaning we cannot manipulate how reinforcing that behavior is to a child.**

→ Example: A child begins hand flapping because he is enjoying the feeling of playing in the rice so much.

→ Example: A child toe walks because it feels good to his leg muscles to be in that position (and gives him better balance information about where his body is in space).

→ Example: A child wiggles his foot in order to help him listen and attend in the classroom.

→ Example: A child twirling his hair in order to concentrate during a problem solving activity.

→ Example: A child hums in order to concentrate and block out the sound of the TV so he can attend to get his homework completed.

Notice that in each set of examples above, the first behavior listed is hand flapping. Hand flapping is typically referred to as a "sensory" behavior. However, shaping the hand flapping behavior effectively will be dependent on accurately identifying the actual function of the behavior, which may or may not be sensory. Why is that behavior occurring? What is reinforcing or maintaining it? That is what is different in each of the scenarios. We will cover sensory concepts more thoroughly beginning in Chapter 4.

During a co-evaluation with our developmental psychologist, a three-year-old girl spontaneously stood up, tensed her whole body, looked toward the ceiling, postured her hands with arms straight out, and wiggled them up and down. Many would label that a "sensory" behavior. It sure appeared so at the time. However, within minutes we recognized that it was actually her spontaneous attempt at requesting "more bubbles." She used it again a few minutes later to request "more balloon." If we had assumed it was a sensory function of behavior and did not look further, we could have developed a treatment plan to extinguish the only spontaneous form of communication that this little girl possessed, delaying her expressive communication development significantly. By recognizing the function of that sensory-looking behavior, we spent fifteen minutes shaping it into a signed request with a vocalization so that it became a tool that worked better for her to communicate.

Many times a child will develop a strong need to control a situation and begin manipulating the "players" in the situation because the reason the behavior is occurring is very strong. For example, if Billy recognizes a pattern where every day after supper (antecedent) it will be time to take a bath and the water and textures of that experience are aversive, Billy may begin to act out during dinner (behavior) to avoid what is coming next. He may become very creative in finding ways to delay bath time or derail the schedule so bath time does not happen. This is a sensory avoiding behavior, and there are both sensory components to the situation and avoidance components.

A behavior that initially happens based on one function of behavior can end up sticking around or morphing into something new due to another function of behavior. Therefore, a behavior initially presenting as one function of behavior may be maintained (or stick around) based on more than one function of behavior secondary to accidental/coincidental learning. For example, let's say five-year-old Elizabeth begins chewing on her toes. She's exploring, and it kind of feels funny. Mom has a strong reaction and responds, "Elizabeth! Nasty! We are not chewing on our toes. That's gross, Sweetie! No toes. Toes out of mouth." She helps Elizabeth take her toes out of her mouth and says, "Good girl. No toes in mouth."

Not such a bad reaction, is it? It is teaching. It is pretty calm. It is helping Elizabeth learn toes don't go in her mouth with a "that's nasty" label for the behavior. It might work.

Let's say Elizabeth really likes Mommy's full attention. She just received animated, full attention. Suddenly, those toes that just tasted funny are morphing into tasting good. Suddenly, a new way to get Mom's attention is to put toes in her mouth. When future sensory stimulation behavior includes Elizabeth frequently putting her toes in her mouth (and refusing to wear shoes as well as taking her shoes off in class or at recess in order to put her toes in her mouth), it is likely that there is a combination of **sensory and attention** functions of behavior that are relevant to maintaining that behavior pattern.

We have to understand functions of behavior to fully find a better way out of the sensory behavior that will work over time. Our goal is to provide more than just a gentle response in that moment. We want our response to reflect a solution that doesn't just work for this moment or today, but one that sets us up for a better tomorrow. We want to identify the core motivation for the behavior so that our response can shape the behavior into a better behavior over time.

Positive behavior plans (Knoster, 2009) capitalize on reinforcing behaviors that you want to happen. Positive plans **teach** the behavior that you want to occur, not just get rid of the behavior that **you don't want**. When you identify the behavior that you don't want, you must first ask yourself, "What do I want him doing instead?" Then, you must explore why he is engaging in the behavior that you don't want and look at what is reinforcing that behavior (the function of the behavior). As we have learned, there is a lot of power in understanding the

ABCs of behavior. We have the power to set up for better success and adjust the consequence piece and determine whether a behavior increases or decreases.

Unfortunately, we sometimes stop intervening after we have a behavior plan in place to stop the negative behavior and extinguish it. We stop too soon. Although we have stopped a behavior, if we didn't look at the function of that behavior we likely will have only temporarily delayed it from morphing into something bigger and more powerful and coming back again. Sometimes, as many of you know, those behaviors come back with a vengeance. If the function of the behavior is not accurately identified and taken into account in the plan to reshape the behavior, the behavior will just keep popping up like a broken record. To effectively and efficiently address problem behavior, especially sensory behaviors, we must not skip the step of looking at the function of the behavior so that our response is fully informed.

IS THERE A BETTER WAY? HOW DO I RESPOND?

There is an essential question that should be asked in each and every treatment plan or positive behavior plan. To make progress and change behavior, you must ask yourself the key question:

"What do I want him to be doing instead?*"

After you have identified the behavior specifically, and after you have looked at what sets it up to happen and what keeps it happening, you have to ask yourself what you actually WANT the child to be doing instead of that behavior. What is appropriate?

I know that sounds obvious. However, it's truly one of the hardest parts of any behavior situation. When you have the answer to what you want the child to be doing, you are halfway to your solution, **because now you know what you need to teach**. You now know what tool is missing from his *behavioral backpack* of responses that he needs for success. In many cases, you now know the coping skill that he is lacking to deal with the big world situation he is encountering.

THE MAKE-IT-GO-AWAY APPROACH

Have you ever been driving in the car when your kids started arguing with you or with each other and you just want to *make it go away**? All you could think about in that moment is that you wanted them to stop (*Make it go away!*) It was hard to come up with how you expected

---

*This is one of the most important concepts in the behavioral information in this book. If you can't answer this question, it really doesn't matter how well you memorize behavioral techniques and methods – they won't work well if you don't know where you are headed. Answer this question well and you don't have to know all the techie stuff-- you're on the right path.

*A family friend recently said he was offended as a kid to read a sign in his mother's kitchen that read: Raising kids is like being pecked to death by chickens. Now that he has kids, he wants a sign, too.

them to be acting because all you could think was, *I can tell you I expect them not to act like this!*

A key to success is **figuring out the better tool**. The tool you need to teach, the tool he does not currently have in his *behavioral backpack* of responses. **Your goal is not truly to just get the problem behavior to go away. Your goal is to TEACH a better way.** If you don't provide a better tool, the vacuum of one problem behavior will simply create room for another problem behavior to take its place.

Your goal is to **replace** the problem behavior with a better way. Teach what you want him to do and then encourage him to use what he knows. After all, this won't be the last time he is tired, hungry, or cranky while riding in the car with others, and his meltdown at age 25 will not be as easy to tolerate as his meltdown today. Today is the best day to start making a positive plan because today is the easiest day to start. Tomorrow the behavior will be more developed and practiced than it is today. Today it will be easier to shape into something positive and appropriate than in another year, and so start today.

Remember that kids will use the **best** tool in their *behavioral backpack* to respond. If they are not responding well, they either don't yet have good tools readily available to use in the situation, or they haven't had enough practice using those new tools.

One last behavior tip before we move on:

Don't offer wanted items, preferred activities or strong attention, food, or other desirables during problem behavior moments. If they are offered or obtained, they will reinforce that "this is a good way to get what I want."

Our tendency in stressful situations, but especially sensory stressful situations, is to start providing a *drop-down menu* of options. For example, Mom sees Nick begin to escalate and so she intervenes saying something like, "Nick, do you want to go to McDonald's?"

He continues to escalate. Mom responds, "Ok, would you like ice cream? Nick, do you need a hug? Nick, do you want a chewy? Do you want gum? Candy? Nick, stop screaming and just tell me what you want! You can have it!"

After more screaming, "Nick, I have your favorite toy in the car. Let's just leave the store, and we'll get your favorite toy." (Inadvertently, Mom has reinforced his avoid/ escape from the store.)

The **drop-down menu*** options can occasionally help in a tense situation to relieve the immediate pressure, but without a better plan for next time the problem behavior will quickly get much more intense, becoming a primary method of behavior in that situation. After all, some pretty great things came from acting out that time. Nick is smart. He will take note of that.

Our ultimate goal is to develop **built-in radar** for tough situations. When the behavior happens the first time, sometimes we just make it through, all the while taking mental notes about the situation and retreat to win another day. Later, we teach a better tool so that when we encounter a similar situation, all Mom has to say is, "Nick, I can see you are stressed. What do you need to do to help yourself?" Nick has a tool to help himself in that situation (and it won't be ice cream or food) because Mom has taught him a better tool to use, such as changing positions in the cart or pressing his hands together firmly or asking to take a break or playing a game of scavenger hunt for the items on the shopping list.

Children who tend to have a lot of difficulty thinking of their options (or who need more support than the verbal question in those situations), may need a visual card with a list of options or pictures that can be used to choose a self-help strategy in the moment. If this is your child, you need to have those cards laminated so they can't be torn up. Have a stash available, one in your purse or pocket, one in his pocket, one in his backpack, one in the car, one in the kitchen, and a stack of replacements in the cabinet so they can be used as needed. You need to have it readily available where he knows to get his card and choose a coping tool when you cue him. A cue might include asking him how he can help himself or simply handing him the card, where the handing serves as the question cue. Either way, you want to do your best to avoid a **drop-down menu response** in a problem behavior situation. There is a big difference between the **drop-down menu** reinforcers and a list of self-help coping strategies. One reinforces the problem behavior. The other reinforces independent self-help and coping skill development.

That being said, there's nothing wrong with offering options to reinforce positive behavior. In fact, that's a bit of what you want to do to help figure out what feels most reinforcing to the child because you WANT to reinforce that great skill or behavior so that it will occur again.

THE POWER OF CONTEXT

One thing I've learned is to never underestimate the power of context. Learning how to use the skills you have, especially social skills, at the right time, with the right amount of finesse is extremely complex.

*If you don't live in America, this will be a harder concept for you to grasp. If you live in America, you have no excuse.

HAVE YOU MET KAYDEN?

Kayden is an elementary student who loves football. He has watched NFL Football for years on television with his dad, and this last Friday night, he attended his first hometown football game. He loved it! He loved the music and the cheering and the uniforms. In short, he had a blast and can't wait until the next home game. On Friday night, he watched the two teams on the field with rapt attention. He noticed that to cheer each other up after a tough play or when they were excited because something great had happened for their team, they would smack each other on the rear end. This seemed to him to be a super cool way to encourage someone on your team.

On Monday when he walked into his classroom, his teacher seemed to be having a tough morning. He walked up and smacked her on the rear end, nodded his head at her and gave her his best "it's going to be ok" face. After all, she is one of the most important members of his learning team...right? you can imagine his surprise when he got to chat about his thinking related to this situation with the principal that morning.

HAVE YOU MET REAGAN?

Reagan is entering junior high in a new school. She recently participated in a series of competitive piano contests where she learned a specific protocol for introducing herself and the pieces she was going to perform. She practiced using the perfect amount of poise and reserve while communicating and her performance was a smash hit!

Though she was able to hang out, laugh, joke, and relax with the best of them, she was nervous on her first day of school and resorted to using her practiced, reserved, and formal presentation for interaction during her first week of school. She was so frustrated that it took her extra time to make friends and she never realized it was that she used her formal introduction skills and not her friend introduction skills that first week or more of school that set her back in her journey to connect with others socially.

Have you ever taken a behavior out of context yourself? Have you ever tried something, thinking it would be encouraging or "cool" or appropriate only to realize how very wrong you were moments later?

It is amazing to realize how many cultural and social unwritten rules there are in our society today. Some children will pick them up subconsciously and gracefully. Others need step by step instruction about how and when to use certain behaviors, and many struggle to keep it all in context.

ARE YOU RAISING A COUCH POTATO?

Let's go back to the scenario in Chapter 2 of being in the car with arguing kids and all you can think about is wanting them to stop. There are many times when it is challenging to figure out what you want a child to **be doing** because all you can think about is that you want the child to **stop** what he is currently doing. However, if your answer is, I want the child to **stop, be still**, and **be quiet**, you may be on course to raise a Couch Potato- literally. Think about it. Do you want to raise a child who is inactive and non-communicative? Probably not. If you are like me, you want to be raising a child who explores, discovers, learns and **acts** in wonderful ways. You want a thriving, go-getter who is actively learning and succeeding. What you are really aiming at is not **less** (stop, be still, and be quiet). Your real aim is for **more appropriate** behavior. Your answer to the question *What do I want him doing instead?* must be an **active response**. After all, you are aiming to see your child do better things, not just do less. Let's look at a few scenarios to show how this principle applies. You will see how the **Make It Go Away Principle** works against you in shaping behavior.

HAVE YOU MET ANGELICA?

Angelica is in third grade. During writing time she rocks back in her chair onto two legs and writes her sentences without correct spelling and punctuation. The teacher identifies these things as "concerns" and sets out to change them. When Angelica rocks back in her chair, there are consequences aimed at encouraging her to **stop**. When Angelica turns in her papers with correct answers and information without correct spelling and punctuation, the teacher counts those answers as incorrect (where Angelica misses the points) because they are not complete answers. She now sits quietly, not bothering other children, but also not working independently (her inactivity puts her at risk of becoming a Couch Potato). Her anxiety is escalating and her engagement in learning while in the classroom is decreasing. This was not part of the teacher's plan!

If the teacher had put some pieces of those behaviors together, she may have discovered that Angelica was rocking in her chair to get attention because she needed help formulating her complete answers during writing tasks (but didn't know how to ask for it) and did not have a tool to help her get beyond her first unedited answer. By teaching Angelica to ask for help and then providing editing tool support to help her develop her complete answer (without negative consequences for the answers that she did provide), it is possible that the rocking would have naturally faded away. (Angelica has more confidence and does not need to seek as much help). Her work production could have been maintained, yet shaped into more of what the teacher was hoping for as opposed to Angelica doing less writing. Angelica's escalated behavior is a result of her coping skill being removed without being replaced and her growing levels of anxiety related to the entire situation. This is why replacing behavior is so important. In the void of replacement, behavior situations morph into something much more complex. Now, Angelica will need supports to redevelop coping skills and reduce anxiety. The teacher has accidentally created more work for herself in order to really help Angelica.

REMINDER: Our goal is not to just get the problem behavior to go away (for it may go away for a short time and come back with worse "friends"). Our goal is to teach a better way. Our teaching will only be effective if we understand why the behavior developed in the first place. What need does the behavior currently meet for the child? Once we know that answer, we can effectively replace it with a better way. This step is worth the effort. This is true for all behaviors, sensory behaviors included.

HAVE YOU MET SCOTT?

Scott is in the fourth grade and he fidgets in class. His teacher has identified this as a behavior that needs to change, and so there are consequences aimed at encouraging him to **be still**. Scott no longer fidgets with his pencil while thinking, but that behavior has morphed into him digging the pencil into his leg, and he has also developed daily stomach aches (that sometimes result in diarrhea), and occasionally thinks he may be having a heart attack due to how fast his heart is racing. The overall result is that Scott is attending less in class and missing more of what is presented, and he continues to be off-task much of the time.

His behavior is now labeled "self-injurious" and so the entire school team is becoming increasingly alarmed and wondering if he might have a diagnosis that they have missed identifying. Therefore, he is referred to the special education department but does not qualify for those support services because he does not have a diagnosis (to obtain a 504 individual support plan), and he does not meet the full criteria for special education planning and individual support.

Scott's fidgeting served the purpose of expending energy and may have been helping him to focus more on what was going on in class by *grounding* him into the moment (instead of letting his thoughts wander into just "thinking"). Scott's fidgeting is an indicator that he has a hands-on learning style where he learns best when he has something to build or manipulate to aid his connection to the learning material (read more about this in Chapter 8).

If the fidgeting was just annoying to the teacher, but not distracting to other students, it may have been in the teacher's best interest to ignore that behavior (because it was serving as a coping skill for Scott to help him attend). She could also have suggested fidgets that were acceptable in her classroom (such as Velcro strips for Scott to rub on the side of his seat, a balloon full of corn starch for him to squeeze while listening, or a bubble cushion to sit on in his chair and play dough to handle between working tasks). Scott's escalated behavior is a result of his coping skill being removed without being replaced. Similar to Angelica, Scott's teacher has just created more work for herself in order to really help Scott learn.

The **Make It Go Away Approach** can be subtle, and we are all prone to falling into that trap at times. Through these examples, I think you can see how a child who is not non-compliant or oppositional, but has behavior that needs to be shaped, can escalate into a child who is struggling to engage actively and productively throughout the school day.

Notice how the teachers in these examples rely on consequences as their only tool to shape the behaviors that they identified. Consequences are powerful as a tool to shape behavior, but often, a more reliable way to influence the situation is to focus on the antecedent first (remember the ABC's of Behavior from Chapter 2?) and re-route the course of the behavior situation so that it is headed in a more positive direction. Starting with the question, "What do I want him to be doing?" helps to outline and create the pathway toward positive behaviors.

HAVE YOU MET AUTUMN?

Autumn is in kindergarten and enjoys talking to others around her. Her teacher has identified that this is a problem and creates consequences aimed at encouraging her to **be quiet**. While the teacher shapes the behavior through consequences, the result is not what she was hoping for. Autumn no longer talks to the students around her about what they are learning in class because she is increasingly disengaged in relationships and school. She does not want to go to school in the morning most days and is struggling to make new friends at school.

Unfortunately, the teacher did not notice that Autumn was often soliciting her peers' opinions related to subjects that they were learning in class and failed to notice that talking to others was an indication of Autumn's verbal and cooperative learning style. The result is that Autumn is talking less, but also less engaged and motivated to learn in the classroom. Therefore, she is not forming a positive opinion about school being fun and a great place to learn. In fact, the opposite is happening. This is not how her mother dreamed of her school career starting and is worried about what is to come over the next twelve years. To complicate the situation even more, this can occasionally be the start to a self-fulfilling prophecy situation where the worry becomes the reality but could have been avoided. Again, her coping skill (learning through talking things out with peers in cooperative learning) was removed without being replaced, which has resulted in less engagement in learning as well as less engagement in relationship development.

BEHAVIOR WRAP UP

In a nutshell, we want to find what is fueling the behavior we are seeing. We either want to add fuel to that fire, igniting a firestorm of progress, or we want to handle the fuel carefully, putting out the fire. Either way, we are dealing with rocket fuel. It is powerful. In some cases we celebrate it, and in some cases we respect its power and handle it very carefully to defuse or redirect it.

In problem behavior situations, we want to carefully and fully identify the reasons for the behavior, shaping it into something productive. Otherwise, there is an accident waiting to happen.

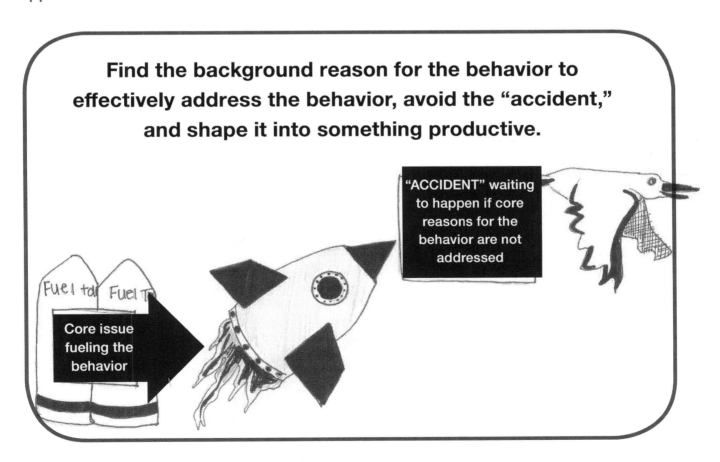

Find the background reason for the behavior to effectively address the behavior, avoid the "accident," and shape it into something productive.

"ACCIDENT" waiting to happen if core reasons for the behavior are not addressed

Fuel ta Fuel T

Core issue fueling the behavior

CHAPTER 3 DEEPER JOURNEY TO APPLICATION

The Deeper Journey portion of each chapter is set up to provide application and reflection questions or to help support group discussion regarding the information in the related chapter.

1. Describe a behavior that your child uses to get your attention: (Remember, this is what is used to seek positive OR negative attention from you):

2. Describe a behavior that your child uses to get something he wants:

3. Describe a behavior that your child uses to avoid or escape a challenging activity or uncomfortable moment:

4. Describe a behavior that your child engages in just because it feels good (it is internally motivated and reinforced):

5. Think of a recent behavior situation where your child was not acting appropriately. List the behavior: (you can use the ABC approach to listing the behavior or just describe the situation):

What was the function of that behavior (attention, tangible, avoid/ escape, sensory)?

What do you want him to be doing instead? (Remember: this answer has to be active. It cannot be passive. It cannot be to "stop" "be still" or "be quiet").

THE FLIP SIDE OF THE COIN: SENSORY PROCESSING

SECTION 2

CHAPTER 4

"A brain that is nourished with many sensations operates well,
and when our brain operates smoothly, so do we."
-Carol Kranowitz

SENSORY PROCESSING! THE FUN STUFF*

Is there a way to learn something without taking in information in some form or fashion? Think about it. Have you **ever** learned something without taking in any information about it to trigger learning?

No. You haven't. You learn through your senses. The brain works with information that the senses bring in to learn and grow. Whether you are learning to dress yourself, learning to respond when spoken to, or learning academic information in a classroom, your brain synthesizes pieces of information brought in by different sensory systems, processes it, and responds. That's how learning happens. The seemingly random pieces of information brought in through the senses form the background for the skills and behaviors that we develop. Just as developing a solid behavioral framework is vital to responding well when a child is struggling, developing a solid sensory processing framework is just as important. They are truly **two sides of the same coin**. Sensory processing is relevant internally to each of us, but measured and overt through behavior.

Let's see if I can make the importance of sensory processing even more relevant for you. Imagine that you are planning your spring break vacation. You've decided to fly, and you have a few unique choices in who pilots you to your destination.

• Pilot #1 has learned how to fly from reading a book. He graduated top of his class in his studies regarding aviation. He has studied flying for 5 years. He is excited to have you aboard to share in his first flight. Though he has never flown before, he has read about over 500 flights.

*Sensory is truly fun to me. It's fascinating. It's powerful. It's relevant. And, yes, it's hard to learn because it's complex. Stick with it. It's worth learning about.

* It hits some people sideways to accept that sensory and behavior concepts are two sides of one coin. True, there is much more research base for behavioral concepts. However, watch the coming research. Sensory research is taking off.

• Pilot #2 has practiced in a flight simulator for 5 years. He's learned protocols and routines and has systematically advanced through 5 levels of flight preparation in his training. He has experienced over 500 simulated flights. He is excited to have you aboard as he conquers his next level of advancement where he is required to have live humans aboard during his first actual flight.

• Pilot #3 has apprenticed as a co-pilot for 5 years. He has co-piloted over 500 actual flights. He is honored to take you to your destination as he moves into the role of captain.

Which pilot seems the most qualified to get you to your destination? If you are anything like me, I am jumping on board with Pilot #3. He's been there and done that and been successful many times. Why would I choose him? Why would most of you choose him? Because we innately understand the value of sensory processing and experience. He hasn't just thought about or read about or played with piloting a plane, he has done it. He has felt what it feels like to take off and land. He knows when it feels sweet, and he knows how it feels when it's not just right. He has likely experienced multiple different wind patterns that create turbulence and even a storm or two. He's experienced in weathering those storms successfully.

His experience with sensory processing has led to skill development and, of those three choices, I would trust him most to get me safely to my destination. There is a reason that our most advanced training programs do not rely solely on book work and intelligence in an area of expertise. There is a reason that field experience and apprenticeship is a long-standing practice throughout history. Though technology has advanced and will continue to advance, I am confident that mentorship and training programs that include fieldwork will continue to thrive. Why? Because sensory processing and experiencing life through our senses is how we are designed to learn and thrive.

SENSORY AND BEHAVIOR: TWO SIDES OF THE SAME COIN

Sensory processing is one of my favorite topics. It is relevant to everything we do, every behavior situation and every part of progress. Sensory processing information is your friend! It is a key to positive change. Even more, it is a key to unlocking happiness, developing coping skills, and responding with grace to a situation*.

Let's start at the beginning. What do I mean by "sensory processing?" Sensory processing is the brain's ability to organize and process input from the senses and to use that information

*Hopefully you are asking how sensory is the key to happiness, coping, and responding with grace, because that information is coming. Stay tuned.

to respond appropriately to a given situation. (A.Jean Ayres, 1979) I love the topic of sensory processing because it is relevant to each one of us. Every day. All the time.

*Imagine a morning where you are tired after you first wake up. You have a huge presentation at work and you are **so not feeling it** today. All the preparation you have done and the hours you have spent compiling the best information possible are suddenly irrelevant because you are not ready and excited to present it. What do you do to help yourself?*

Whether you got yourself coffee, went for a run to clear your mind, or ended up rocking in a corner crying, you utilized a sensory strategy to respond to the situation. The sensory strategy you chose, combined with how well it worked, reflects how well you know yourself and your own needs and how effectively you can help yourself in stressful situations. In this way, the pattern of sensory strategies in your repertoire become part of your coping skill set.

Have you met Sally? Sally is an awesome co-worker. She's bright, in fact, often brilliant. She is a great team player and partner in any project...AFTER she has had two cups of coffee in the morning. It is pointless to talk to her or enter her office before 9 a.m. Real progress on her team only happens after 9:30 a.m. (Good to know!)

By identifying and watching for cues about the sensory patterns of others, it is possible to increase your ability to effectively and efficiently work with that person. This is true whether you are a parent working with a child or a professional looking to partner more effectively with a co-worker.

Do you **care** what you wear on high performance days? If you have to get up and speak to hundreds of people, or even just your team, sometimes it matters what you wear. Perhaps you would shop for the new perfect outfit and new shoes. Instead, maybe you wouldn't dream of wearing anything but the tried and true power suit that has never failed you and the shoes that are well-worn so that your feet don't hurt while you need to concentrate. Either way, you probably pay attention to what you wear when the pressure is on.

Kids are the same. Have you met the child who gets "stuck" wearing the same favorite outfit or two every day for weeks? Yes, I have, too. Have you met the child who has very strong preferences on the types of clothing he wants to buy and how it "feels" to wear them? Yes, I have, too. Kids may have preferences, just like we do, about clothing. They may be just as picky as some of us about what they will wear. Preferences are fine; however, when preferences become so rigid that they impact children's quality of life or ability to live life fully because of the restrictions that they put on themselves, then it is time to intervene with a better plan. Would you pay attention to what you eat or drink before that big presentation? You might grab a donut or candy bar or make sure you had coffee or a Coke to help you feel "ready" and "on your game" for answering the tough questions. Maybe you would never dare to have those things enter your body that morning. You would get up early and make yourself the "tried and true homemade breakfast" and would plan for the most nutritious snack you can think of so that you have "clean" fuel, providing you with clear thinking so you can face the challenge of the day. Either way, you just might have a specific preference for how you get ready to present.

Again, you will find kids are the same. Their methods are not as "tried and true" as ours, but kids will have things they do to get ready for an anticipated situation. Their natural strategies just may not be effectively setting them up for success.

Take a moment and think about what you do to help yourself when:
- You are in a boring meeting and trying to stay awake and listen.
- Your noisy neighbor's dog is keeping you awake in the middle of the night.
- You see a perfect shell, but have to walk across a rocky part of the beach to get it without your shoes.
- You are preparing for a first date or exciting award event.
- You are listening to a detailed list of requests from your boss in preparation for following through on a work project.

Did immediate plans pop into your head? Did you think, "I don't know. I feel my way through situations like that. It just depends. I'd try on ideas until one felt right and then use it." I bet you have met someone (surely, not you!) who responded to one of the above situations with a less than stellar plan that resulted in a mess. My point is that we all take in sensory information constantly, and it influences us. It shapes the way we perform and our attitudes about being "ready" to perform. It influences our responses. Because sensory information influences our behavior constantly, that's why I say the concepts are two sides of the same coin. We separate the concepts to study them, but in a person, they are happening simultaneously and are very intricately interwoven. Basically, the sensory information that we take in about the world around us matters to us. We intuitively use sensory things to set ourselves up for success.*

THE CELL PHONE RECEPTION PRINCIPLE

Sensory processing skill and the ability to receive both accurate and complete information through the senses is a vital first step in forming appropriate responses to a situation. I call this **The Cell Phone Reception Principle,*** because sensory processing is like cell phone reception.

Take notes for a few days on all the ways that you set yourself up for success. The "rewards" you plan for yourself to get through tough situations. I bet it's all "sensory."

Imagine that you are talking on a cell phone to your boss, receiving instructions about critical changes that your boss needs you to communicate to your team at work. Now imagine that you are in a rural area, and the cell reception is poor. Though you catch words, and sometimes phrases, you are missing about 80% of what your boss is saying. Your job, actually the success of your company, is depending on accurate communication of the information your boss is giving you, but you are not fully receiving the message. You will be able to piece together some of the information based on your knowledge of the context and other details you know, but regardless of how intelligent you are, regardless of your rock-star potential as an employee, you may drop this ball and fail. You may hold your own in the situation for a bit, but unless you get better cell phone reception and go over the information again, you won't be helping your boss run

So it is with sensory processing skill.

When the nervous system is wired well and fed well, it is primed for success just like a cell phone with full reception. The messages will be received accurately, and the information has the potential to be fully utilized. When the intake of information is immature or not supported to be accurately and fully received, it becomes increasingly challenging for a person to form an appropriate response to most situations, especially new situations. After all, if you were only receiving a portion of information and that information was in bits and pieces without a full framework to aid your understanding, you would likely revert to your "old" way of doing things and you might become rigid about your routines because that is the context you have that you can depend on; or you might be adventurous, yet very scattered and unpredictable because you are reacting to situations with limited information.

Sometimes, developing a specific sensory skill, such as improving auditory processing, increases a person's abilities. Increasing one sensory ability can be a key to supporting better outcomes and performance overall. After all, you can't complete a mission that you didn't hear and understand. Therefore, it is important to see how sensory and motor developmental foundations, and the synergy that they bring to supporting the ability to form an appropriate response, set us up for better problem solving skills. When you are able to target which senses are not fully and accurately doing their best intake job, then you have identified the areas where therapeutic work can be done to support a better intake, and thus, a better response.

*Each person has varied reception based on their attention, skills, and interest. And, each person has a list of dropped calls that have affected relationships.

COOPERATIVE INTAKE OF INFORMATION

As you learn about the individual senses and their purpose in taking in information, you may begin to identify where some of the breakdown in your child's response begins. At that point, you can begin to research specific activities that will feed the nervous system's ability to take in (and coordinate) information from that specific sense. This will enable you to grow skill and accuracy through that specific sense to make it a stronger part of the intake team. Once you have worked on skills related to that sense (through FUN developmental activities), then you are ready to begin helping that sense coordinate with other senses and work cooperatively on the intake team. That is called multi-sensory processing skill. We need to understand how sensory and motor foundations are vital to our ability to perform well and show what we know.

CHAPTER 4 DEEPER JOURNEY TO APPLICATION

The Deeper Journey portion of each chapter is set up to provide application and reflection questions or to help support group discussion regarding the information in the related chapter.

1. Think through a behavior situation that has recently happened. Describe the behavior and then list any sensory influences you can think of.

2. What do you personally do to help set yourself up for success?

3. Think about your child's sensory processing ability in terms of **The Cell Phone Reception Principle**. How accurately is your child receiving messages? Can you estimate a percentage of the information it currently appears he is receiving?

CHAPTER 5

"The brain, as marvelous as it is,
cannot learn all by itself. It needs information."
-Dr. Carla Hannaford in *The Dominance Factor*

SENSORY AND MOTOR FOUNDATIONS

Carla Hannaford expresses the heart of the idea that sensory and motor development is a foundation for learning, thought, creativity, and intelligence in her book, <u>Smart Moves: Why Learning Is Not All In Your Head</u>. (Hannaford, 1995) She explains how movement initiates and supports mental processes. We often forget that learning, thinking and processing emotions are a whole body activity, not just a brain activity. The brain is solidly attached to the rest of the nervous system (and thus the body) and doesn't function in isolation. Research on this topic has become part of the science behind "whole-brain learning" concepts and multi-sensory teaching practices, such as center-based learning where learning is driven by hands-on experience, as opposed to worksheets alone.

In fact, the constructivist learning theory, widely supported as a best-practice teaching method, is actually a compilation of old-school thinking, dating back to John Dewey's work that has been supported in educational research, as well as cognitive psychology research. (Hein, October 15-22, 1991) John Dewey was passionate about classrooms being full of "meaningful activity," creating an environment where students had a voice in their learning through democracy. His forward thinking was radical, and professionals are still working hard to better apply the principles outlined in his work in classrooms. He saw learning through experience, **learning by doing**, as foundational to a child's development. (Dewey, 1910) (Dewey, 1916) (Dewey, 1938)

We now know that neurons that fire together, wire together. Repeated meaningful experiences and skill practice shape our skill levels and behavior patterns. Meaningful experiences that are created by learning through doing actually change the brain and influence development.

From a developmental perspective, sensory and motor foundations set the stage for better development of higher level skills. One of the most common ways to study development, introduced by Piaget, is arranging information in a developmental pyramid, representing stages of development. (Piaget & Inhelder, 1969) The foundational level represents the early skills, which set the stage for higher progress and more complex skill development. There are many developmental pyramids, but below you will see my version, which I began using years ago to help show a few specific skills and their relationship to sensory and motor processing. When you study this pyramid,* you will see that although behavior principles and framework form the foundation, sensory and motor processing are the building blocks that set up behavioral success. In one sense, you could argue that behavior is the result of how sensory processing skills are coming together.

DEVELOPMENTAL LEARNING PYRAMID

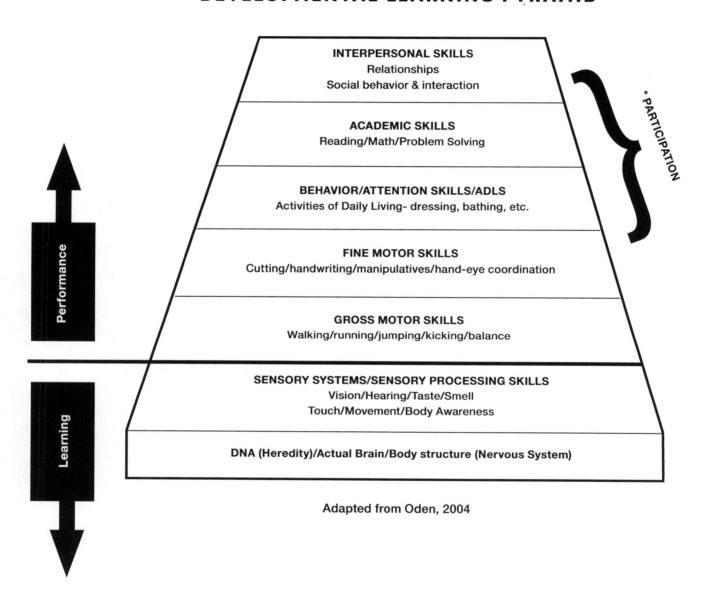

Adapted from Oden, 2004

*You will see an emerging pattern where early development sets the stage for higher level learning to occur. I will introduce it in a global sense, and then I will introduce the pattern in each of the senses individually. Bottom line: foundational skills have to be in place to support extended learning related to that area.

There are three foundational parts that create the base of the pyramid: the nervous system, sensory processing skills, and motor skills. The nervous system represents the DNA and God-given **genetic wiring** that each person develops, beginning in the womb. The nervous system cannot be changed or significantly altered, but it can be influenced through the activities and experiences that we encounter.

Sensory processing skills represent the set of skills that allow us to take in new information about the world. Our **awareness of the world** and of ourselves develops out of this set of skills. I have observed that the interplay between our nervous system and our sensory processing abilities determines our learning style, our rate of learning, and influences our developing cognitive and behavioral abilities.

The third part of the foundational base of this pyramid is motor skills. Motor skills create the foundation for our **response** to the world around us. They are how we show what we know. Whether we are speaking or pointing or moving or typing or running, the most typical way for us to show what we know is through a motor action.

This is why I say motor and sensory processing skills are relevant to everything we do.* The only way to take in information (for learning) is through our sensory processing skills. The most typical way to show what we know is through a motor action. Therefore, sensory and motor abilities are underlying influences to higher level skills, such as behavior skills, cognitive/academic skills, and relationship-building skills.

> I have observed that the interplay between our nervous system and our sensory processing abilities determines our learning style, our rate of learning, and influences our developing cognitive and behavioral abilities.
>
> -Amy Vaughan

The interplay between the nervous system, sensory processing abilities, and motor abilities create the foundation for other skills to begin developing.

*To discount the relevance of sensory and motor processing skills sounds uninformed. Sensory and motor processing skills are relevant...all the time. Because sensory processing is the only way we have to take in information and motor response is the only way we have to show what we know, they are relevant in every human interaction.

In turn, those skill sets create the ability for us to develop the higher level self-help skills needed for **activities of daily living (ADLs)**, a phrase first coined in 1935 by a physical therapist and expanded in 1945 by a physician and physical therapist team. (Reed & Sanderson, 1999) The behavioral patterns we develop and the daily routines that we begin to form are all highly influenced and made possible by our nervous system. The nervous system processes incoming sensory information and forms responses (behaviors) that are carried out through motor actions.

Additional factors, such as those listed below, synthesize to form the basis for attention and learning.
- Hand-eye coordination
- Body awareness
- Auditory processing/listening skills
- Attention and focus skills
- Self-regulation skills

Learning and attention leads to enhanced performance:
- Cognitive skills
- Activities of daily living (ADLs)
- Academic achievement
- Relationship-building skills
- Leisure skills

In the brain, there is a ripple effect where one area of growth and development influences other areas.

Learning is not just about knowing what to pay attention to. It is equally about having the ability to ignore the unimportant, background information. This is called **filtering**. Many children "tune in," but they just tune in to different information than expected. For example, a child who can twirl or flap his hands for an hour at a time is highly focused and tuned in. He's just not tuning in to learning new things. He is tuned in to how great it feels to move like that.

a note about understanding individual differences...

Stanley Greenspan and his wife, Nancy Greenspan, have done a great job of explaining how sensory processing ability is the root system of the body's learning tree, and how what children take in through their roots (senses) results in patterns of thinking (the trunk of the tree). This intake results in their performance abilities (the branches of the tree), such as reading, writing, math, and organization skills. Their book, The Learning Tree, (Greenspan & Greenspan, 2010) thoroughly explains sensory processing and development related to learning ability. It expands on his DIR Floortime* (Developmental, Individual-Difference, Relationship-Based Model) work in the area of understanding individual differences and applying that knowledge in support of a child's individual ability to learn in a beautiful way. Their book, The Learning Tree, (Greenspan & Greenspan, 2010) thoroughly explains sensory processing and development related to learning ability. It expands on his DIR Floortime* (Developmental, Individual-Difference, Relationship-Based Model) work in the area of understanding individual differences and applying that knowledge in support of a child's individual ability to learn in a beautiful way.

Concerning the pyramid of skills, notice the star near the top of the pyramid next to academics, behavior, and relationships. Often parents and teachers and other professionals refer a child to see a professional (psychologist, occupational therapist, physical therapist, speech therapist, tutor, etc.) because the child is struggling with academic performance, or with behavior problems, or with poor social skills. Those are the referral symptoms, but often a big part of what is setting the **perfect storm** for those issues is an underlying difficulty with sensory and motor skill development or maturity.

The development of skills, such as handwriting neatness and coordination, are supported by sensory and motor processing. Sensory and motor processing also support the ability to make a good choice and the ability to initiate play.

The reason that I like this developmental pyramid is that it highlights one of the hardest things that we do in life: engage in relationships. You will find relationships at the very top of this developmental pyramid. One of the hardest, but most important things we do in life, is to connect with other people.

Social learning theory posits that the social environment, through interaction or observation, creates a framework for learning. (Bandura, 1971) That learning is then shaped through

*I highly recommend the DIR Floortime Early Intervention training as well as the Early Start Denver Model training.

rewards and punishments and reinforcement. We are created to be social and to engage in meaningful social experiences. However, underlying differences in the way that individuals are "wired" create individual differences in the abilities and ways that each person connects relationally. In other words, relationships are not a "one size fits all" shoe.

The fact that relating is one of the most important, but most challenging things we do, is one reason why Autism Spectrum Disorders (ASD) can be so devastating for individuals and their families. There is a common myth that the individual with autism does not ever have the desire to connect with others. In my work with individuals with autism, that is simply not true. An individual with autism is simply wired differently.

---

a note about building relationship skills and autism...

Recent work combining the best that we know of applied behavioral analysis with the best we know in relationship-based intervention has recently been published. I recommend Early Start Denver Model for Young Children with Autism: Promoting Language, Learning and Engagement, by Sally Rogers and Geraldine Dawson (Rogers & Dawson, 2009) and An Early Start for Your Child with Autism: Using Everyday Activities to Help Kids Connect, Communicate, and Learn, by Rogers, Dawson, and Vismara. (Rogers, Dawson, & Vismara, 2012) Even though these books focus on toddler and preschool intervention, development and learning, the principles laid out in both books can often be applied and adapted for use with a variety of individuals of different ages. Other excellent work in this area includes The PRT Pocket Guide: Pivotal Response Treatment for Autism Spectrum Disorders, by Robert Koegel and Lynn Kern Koegel. (Koegel & Koegel, 2012)

In an ASD situation, the individual's brain is hardwired differently (from a neurological perspective). (Hadjikhani, Joseph, Syder, & & Tager-Flusberg, 2006) Thus, often the rules and interaction in relationships with an individual with ASD look more concrete than typical situations. Let me be clear. There is not always a lack of desire to connect, but rather a lack of ability to connect.

Sometimes, there is a connection, but it is a misguided connection, such as a closer connection to objects than people. (After all, objects are more predictable than people.) It often takes a team of dedicated professionals to break an individual's unique relationship code and "get in" with that individual for a successful relationship*. Understanding a child's unique sensory preferences can be the key to unlocking progress. However, to be most effective, sensory

---

* I'm here to tell you it can be done. I'm here to tell you it is worth doing. Most importantly, I'm here to tell you that when autism is a word in discussion, sensory strategies can be the best friend that you have.

strategies must be utilized within a good behavior framework, not just utilized in a random pattern or "one plan fits all" approach.

You can look at a sample of our population and realize that those with diagnoses are not the only ones who struggle with maintaining healthy relationships. Divorce would be a non-issue if maintaining a healthy relationship was easy, right? Petty friendship squabbles wouldn't happen, and Facebook wars would not exist. In fact, wars would not exist. Relationship skills rest at the top of the developmental pyramid because so many fundamental skills must be strong to support a positive outcome. A glitch in one's ability to receive and perceive a statement from another person accurately, keep it in context, and then respond in a culturally appropriate way, can topple the whole interaction.

The information that we take in through our senses forms the framework from which we work to understand our world. It is the basis of our learning and understanding. **Our sensory experiences shape who we become.** As Dr. Ami Klin, director of the Marcus Center for Autism, one the leading autism diagnostic and treatment centers in America, said at a conference I attended:

> *"The brain is not only determining who we will be. It is becoming who we are."*
>
> - Dr. Ami Klin (Klin, August 16-17, 2013)

The bottom line is that information taken in through our senses influences our perspective and influences the skills we develop. Sensory input matters.

WHAT DO WE KNOW ABOUT SENSORY INPUT?

We know that enriched sensory environments support increased cognitive development and performance. (Wismer Fries, Ziegler, Kurian, Jacoris, & & Pollak, 2005) (Woo & Leon, 2013) Researcher Mark Rosenzweig, and his colleagues David Krech and Marian Diamond were pioneers in the area of brain plasticity. They began work to prove that early sensory stimulation increases the surface area of the cortex and grows its connectivity. Their work began with rats, proving the increase in the surface of the cortex, increased dendrite connections, and increased volume of neurotransmitters based on sensory stimulation.

That early work has continued, becoming what we know now as the concept of **neuroplasticity.** (Diamond, 1964) Neuroplasticity is the term that describes how the brain is able to change in structure and function, based on what it experiences.

Science tells us that enriched sensory environments stimulate growth and development, and common sense confirms it. Mothers of young children spend time researching the toys that will best stimulate development. Parents begin putting their not-yet-born-babies onto the preschool waiting list of their choice. Legislators and politicians earmark money for early childhood education and intervention. In fact, in the State of the Union Address in January 2014, President Obama called for a national focus on early childhood education and enrichment. Likewise, the Governor of Missouri, Jay Nixon also called for a state focus on early childhood education and enrichment. It is no secret that enriched environment and opportunity matters.

We also know that neglect is detrimental to childhood development and performance. (Ellis, Fisher, & Zaharie, 2004) We have systems in place in America to protect children from environmental neglect and relational neglect because we know that neglect alters the way the brain works. We also know that in cases of neglect, early therapeutic intervention can begin to reverse the negative effects of neglect on the brain. Positive sensory experiences are powerful in their influence on the brain, both to help it grow and thrive and to heal it.

More than ever before, attention and research is focused on defining what sensory activities and enrichment are the very best for brain development and healing. I am watching researchers like those at the University of California, Irvine, who are designing sensory enrichment therapy based on their work related to brain plasticity. They are finding that specific sensory activities, built into a child's daily routine, can have lasting positive effects on that child's development. (Woo, Hingco, Hom, Lott, & Leon, 2010)

SENSORY PROCESSING: DEFINING THE SENSES

It is important to understand how the body takes in information from the environment. What are the senses? How do we take in sensory information to be processed? What systems do we rely on to give us the information we gather about the world?

There is continued debate as to the actual number of senses and what constitutes defining a "sense" in humans and animals (i.e. some animals can sense electrical and magnetic fields or water pressure to a degree that humans do not). (Wikipedia) For the purposes of this book, we will look at five traditional senses and two additional "hidden" senses. These are the most commonly accepted and discussed senses related to human sense-ability.

- Taste
- Smell
- Touch (and Temperature)
- Vision
- Hearing
- Body Position (and Balance)
- Movement

TASTE AND SMELL

Taste and smell are powerful senses that can induce strong reactions. They are considered primitive and are embedded deeply within our brain structure. They work together to create the perception of flavor when eating food. A combination of taste, smell and touch processing often contributes to situations where children have a very limited repertoire of liked foods or when feeding skills are delayed in development. Just as your food tastes differently when you have a severe cold, smells and tastes can be significantly altered and affect eating preferences when this team of senses is not functioning well. Taste and smell help us interpret the chemical world (BrainFacts.org) and influence our perceptions about the food we eat and the world around us.

TOUCH

Our touch system works to register and discriminate incoming touch information through the skin. The touch system tells us **where** we are being touched and gives us information about **what** is touching us. It also serves to protect us by telling us **how** we are being touched. Something perceived as dangerous can trigger a flight/ fright/ fight automatic protection response.

Sensory information that is too harsh or abrupt surpasses the level that the brain can therapeutically process it and triggers the body's defenses, the flight/fright/fight response. (Williams & Shellenberger, 1996) Since the skin is the largest organ in the body, touch processing ability can have a powerful effect, either positive or negative, on a child's ability to fully engage and learn effectively. We know that gentle touch can have a positive, healing effect. We also know that gentle touch can reduce anxiety and positively affect serotonin levels.

Touch processing also influences a child's ability to show what he knows in a performance-learning situation. Touch processing is sometimes a key "player" in motor performance and motor learning situations. Below are two examples of two different children who struggle with touch processing. In both cases, there are additional concerns, but touch processing ability is a primary one.

HAVE YOU MET KYLE?

Kyle craves touching things. It's how he explores and investigates and learns about objects. He tends to hang on people he knows well and chew on his pencil or toys. When he is walking down the hallway, he often runs his hand along the wall as he walks. In the classroom, he can be found fidgeting and engaging in "off task behavior" when the teacher is talking and his job is to be listening. He is at his best when he is building or creating, and he seems to grasp concepts much more quickly when the teacher uses manipulatives and hands-on learning techniques.

HAVE YOU MET CARLA?

Carla startles easily and over-responds to routine situations such as a friend bumping into her in line. She is picky about the fabric and style of the clothing she wears. Even though she likes the look of sequins and asks her mother to buy clothing with sequins, she will refuse to wear the clothing if she puts it on and can feel the sequins through the fabric. She has personal, unwritten rules about how and where she will wash her hands, use the toilet, and drink from water fountains. She also has rigid personal rules about playing with friends and struggles to play cooperatively during recess. She will often have seemingly petty complaints about her friends' behavior during unstructured interaction times. Her perspective is her reality, and so what seems petty to you is real to her.

VISION

The vision system utilizes the eyes to take in information. If our visual acuity is "off" and we need glasses, it obviously impacts how accurately we are able to take in information. Vision is a powerful learning tool. The more proactive we are about making sure that our children see clearly, the more proactive we are in setting them up for successful learning. Eye exams to ensure that a child is seeing clearly are part of setting a child up for a successful reading and visual learning experience. (Taub, Bartuccio, & Maino, 2012)

The visual system allows us to see accurately, process what we see, organize what we see, and then begin to form a response to what we see. In this context, there is a difference between seeing and vision. Seeing, in this learning sense, is actually somewhat passive.

Our eyes either work with good acuity to take in accurate information or they don't. I have heard many stories from my group of parents in treatment over the years about taking their child to an optometrist because they were struggling to learn to read and then finding that the child had 20/20 vision. Many of them get stumped at that point because the eyes are working, right? (Don't forget that reading requires both vision and language skills. We are looking at the visual component most right now, but we will come back to the language processing piece later with a more direct connection to dyslexia symptoms).

Vision in learning situations is a very active endeavor, one that includes the skills of visual perception, visual organization, and visual motor skills. These skills actually give us the ability to understand and respond to what we see. Visual perception is an umbrella term that describes our ability to see and understand what we see. It encompasses our ability to see visual messages or objects, distinguish between similar objects or visual messages, separate relevant objects from a visually busy background, and to recall or comprehend what was seen.

Our ability to accurately process visual information fully can also be affected by how well our eyes work cooperatively to take in information. Our visual-motor performance skills (how we respond to visual information) are also dependent on attention skills, self-regulation skills, bilateral coordination (the ability to coordinate and process information from both sides of the body collaboratively), and filtering skills.

> **a note about vision therapy...**
> An optometrist, behavioral optometrist, occupational therapist, or sometimes a reading specialist in the educational field will have a variety of tools to address vision issues as they are related to learning. For parents looking for a personal account of the impact of vision therapy, I recommend Jillian's Story, a book written by a mother-daughter team about how vision therapy impacted the daughter's life in a positive way. (Benoit & Benoit, 2010)

Below are two examples of students who have difficulty with visual processing skills. In both cases, there are additional concerns, but visual processing ability is a primary one.

HAVE YOU MET DENNIS?

Dennis is a third grade boy who enjoys playing with LEGOS, board games, and playing cards. Though he is bright, he struggles at times showing what he knows accurately in the classroom. For example, he loves math and is able to orally engage in math games, but when he is asked to show his work during written math, he often gets confused or has inaccurate answers, even though the teacher and his parents know he understands the concept.

Dennis loves the idea of playing sports with his friends, but struggles to catch a ball or kick a kickball. He gets embarrassed when he sees that his friends catch a ball and kick a ball well during recess games, while he misses every time. His parents hurt for him as they watch him try and try again during extracurricular ball games. Though he tries hard, he doesn't improve at the same rate as other boys.

His mom decided he might need glasses since he often complains of headaches and seems to be having trouble reading. He skips words or lines, easily misses details in his work (like a number in a math problem), and gets frustrated finding things at home that seem to be "in plain sight." However, he tested with 20/20 vision and did not need glasses, and so Mom is still stumped about what is going on with him.

HAVE YOU MET CASEY?

Casey is a third grade girl. Many mornings when her mother goes in to wake her before school, Casey will curl up into a ball and cover her head with her blanket, screaming, "That light hurts my eyes! Turn it off!" This seems overly dramatic to her mother because the light that is on is not even her room light, but the hallway light outside her room. On those mornings, Casey will cry and lie on the floor periodically throughout the morning, making it challenging to motivate her to get ready for school. Once in school, she excels academically but is often jittery and out of sorts.

She makes friends easily, but sometimes has trouble keeping those friends. Her friends quickly find out she is picky and become alarmed at her intense behavior when she gets upset. For example, if the sun is out, Casey demands that they play house under the platform of the play-set on the playground. She insists on being the "mother" and insists that all the "children" stay in the house. The game quickly becomes boring for the friends, and so most of them decide to leave, avoiding Casey during the next recess.

In the lunch line, she might make a rude comment such as, "Yuck, that food looks gross! Do you see how it is all mixed up! It's like things are moving in it! Who would eat that?" Her friends look at the same casserole, trying to see if there really is something moving in the casserole. Casey "sees" things that they often don't see.

One friend with her during that lunch experience recently went shopping with Casey and her mother. Bright colored jeans were the new style of the season, and Casey's mother thought it would be fun for the girls to each get to choose a new pair of jeans. However, Casey didn't like any of the colors and ended up having a tantrum in the department store, yelling about how ugly the jeans were and how anyone who wears colored jeans "is stupid." Casey's friend has decided that Casey is not the type of friend that she wants because her tantrums seem immature and she is unkind, demanding, and extreme when she gets upset.

As shown through the two examples above, visual processing issues can be subtle, and they present in combination with other issues. Some would argue that treating the visual processing issues in these cases would directly resolve the other (peripheral) issues.

HEARING

Hearing is like vision. Finding out whether your ears work well to register specific sounds is essential. It affects how accurately you are able to get information into the brain to be processed. In a learning sense, hearing is the passive part of listening. Auditory processing skills, auditory perception skills, auditory organization skills, and auditory motor skills give us the ability to understand and respond to what we hear.

Our ability to listen is affected by how well our ears work together to take in information. Are they taking in information equally, completely, and cooperatively? Our ability to listen is also influenced by our attention skills and our ability to "tune in" (auditory focus) to important auditory information. Our listening skills are also affected by our ability to filter out unimportant background noise (auditory filtering skills). Auditory processing skills, just like our visual processing skills, are co-dependent on attention skills, self-regulation skills, and bilateral coordination skills.

We again find that early skills set the foundation for higher level skills to develop. This is the same pattern we have been following in each individual sense as it develops. The following early skills set the stage for listening skills to develop:

- Attention and focus skills (especially the ability to filter out unimportant information and focus on specific requested information)

- Self-regulation skills (the ability to get excited and calm down)

- Bilateral coordination skills (the ability to coordinate information coming in from both sides of the body)

Children with auditory processing difficulty are often easily distracted or bothered by loud noises. They have difficulty following verbal instructions. Often, their performance is better in quiet environments. These children sometimes have difficulty with spelling, learning to read and even speech and language difficulty, such as limited vocabulary or speech articulation issues. The child with auditory processing difficulty may be good at math, but struggle significantly with math word problems. He may often say "huh" or need repetition of auditory information in order to fully process and understand what was said.

Like visual processing difficulty, auditory processing difficulty can have a powerful effect on learning and interaction development. Below are two examples of students who have difficulty with auditory processing. In both cases, there are additional concerns, but auditory processing ability is one of them.

HAVE YOU MET SARAH?
Sarah struggled to learn to read and continues to misspell and mispronounce words frequently. She has been tested for a learning disability, but did not qualify for specific academic support because her IQ is average.

Though she says she wants to make friends and attempts to initiate relationships with other girls in her class, she struggles to successfully maintain a friendship with peers. Her interactions become awkward quickly because she insists on bossing the other girls, demanding that they follow her rules and play the games that she directs. She is not receptive when the other girls suggest a new game or try to change the rules.

She easily becomes rigid in her routines and the unwritten rules that she has about classroom tasks. She begins to escalate when the routine is changed and becomes stressed when a familiar concept begins to build into learning a new concept. She follows directions within regular routines and follows one-step directions well in any context. However, she struggles with following multiple-step directions outside of familiar routines. When asked to get out her history book, turn to page 63, and write her name, but not the date on a cooperative group project, Sarah gets out her book but has it open to the wrong page, and she writes the date, but not her name on the group project.

In the cafeteria, she becomes overwhelmed by the noise level and either begins to escalate into hyperactive behavior or withdraws to play her iPod. Her relational difficulty compounds when peers approach her in the cafeteria, and she ignores them.

Sarah struggles with auditory discrimination; she has difficulty distinguishing between the different letter sounds when reading. That is compounded when she is attempting to spell correctly when writing. Her social skills are impacted by her inability to modulate incoming auditory information and filter out background noise in order to tune into key auditory information that requires her to respond. She struggles relationally to keep up with the conversational pace, which results in her processing information that was presented many minutes ago while her peers have moved on to a new topic. When she tries to insert a comment about the previous topic, it becomes awkward for her and her peers.

HAVE YOU MET DEREK?

Derek has learned to roll with the social flow. He is popular and plays sports well. Derek has always struggled in school, and as he has gotten older, and become more aware, he has learned to compensate in many situations.

Derek will find himself in situations that he didn't anticipate because he does "go with the flow." For example, after a football game, the guys were joking around and making plans. He didn't comprehend the full extent of the conversation, but when asked, "Are you up for that?" he responds with, "Sounds good!" After the group jumps in cars and arrives, he realizes he is in a situation that he would not have agreed to had he understood what the plan really was. Now, he feels stuck, uncomfortable, and unsure about how to navigate the situation.

Derek finds himself the butt of the joke because sometimes common sense things go over his head. For example, last week the guys were joking and one said, "Who is buried in Grant's tomb?" He immediately responded, "President Lincoln?" Then, when he received weird looks, he said, "I don't know. Who?" He still wonders why everyone laughed so long.

Derek struggles with auditory comprehension and reasoning, and he finds himself in situations that he didn't anticipate and to which he doesn't know how to respond. He struggles academically because his auditory memory and comprehension skills don't fully support his ability to engage in abstract reasoning. He struggles to listen and synthesize numerous details efficiently, resulting in poor interpersonal relationship skills.

Below is a quick reference to the senses and common signs of over and under processing in that sense.

BETRAYED BY THE SENSES...

The Visual System:

Located: Eyes, Optic Nerve, Primary Visual Cortex

Job: To help us see and understand what is seen in order to respond

When vision is under-registered and the eyes are under-sensitive:
- Child craves visual input, but has difficulty focusing visual attention for learning.
- Seeks out bright lights, spinning objects.
- Enjoys the glare effect in windows and on metal.

When vision is over-registered and the eyes are over-sensitive:
- Child is overwhelmed by bright lights
- Child is overwhelmed by busy worksheets
- Child has difficulty processing visual instructions
- Child has difficulty making direct eye contact, especially when stressed or in new learning situations
- Child may prefer to use peripheral vision as primary visual source

Visual tools used in therapy: Visual cues (picture or gesture), Visual scheduling, Slant Boards, 3D objects, 2D objects, increase margins and contrast, look at quality instead of quantity for visual teaching. Visual perception work (visual discrimination, visual memory, spatial relationships, form constancy, visual sequential memory, figure ground, and visual closure).

The Movement Position System/Vestibular System:

Located: inner ear

Job: serves as an "umbrella system" and has high interaction with many parts of the brain/ primary processing of gravitational security/highly linked to ocular motor skills. Helps us actively engage in motor movements safely and with functional coordination. Gives us the ability to tolerate and even enjoy movement activities.

When movement is under-registered and the body is under-sensitive:
- Child craves fast movement and often enjoys spinning activities
- Seeks out swinging, rocking, twirling activities frequently and does not get dizzy easily
- "Daredevil" behavior/"Bounces off the walls"
- May love being upside down

When movement is over-registered and the body is over-sensitive:
- Child may avoid movement or being unexpectedly moved
- Displays signs of gravitational insecurity
- Anxious when tipped off balance
- May avoid running, climbing, sliding, swinging activities
- May get seasick or carsick very easily or go straight to sleep during car/boat rides

Movement tools used in therapy: movement (gross motor/swings/scooters), transitions – best to use movement followed by proprioception techniques.

The Touch System/Tactile System:

Located: Skin receptors

Job: Protection/Defense and Discrimination. To help us register and discriminate incoming sensory information through the skin and respond.

When touch is under-registered and the body is under-sensitive:
- Child may have decreased awareness of pain/temperature (very high pain tolerance)
- May push heavily on pencil when writing

- Fidgets with hands/feet (pin rolling with finders, tapping foot, rubbing feet on floor)
- May chew on inedible objects (shirt, cuffs, pencil, fingernails)
- May rub against wall or drag hand along a wall when walking

When touch is over-registered and the body is over-sensitive:

- Child may avoid being touched/is "hurt" often
- May be withdrawn and avoid interaction with others
- May display a "fight or flight" response to getting dirty or an unexpected touch
- Responds negatively to food textures of light touch
- Irritated by tags, hems, seams, textures in clothing

Touch tools used in therapy: tapping, vibration, texture play, brushing protocols; best to use a combination of touch and proprioception techniques.

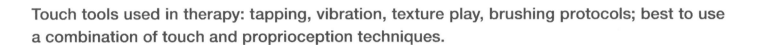

The Auditory System:

Located: Inner ear and Auditory Nerve

Job: To help us listen and understand spoken language and environmental sounds and then respond

When sound is under-registered and the body is under-sensitive:

- Child may frequently be "tuned out" and not respond or be aware of sounds
- Child may not respond when his name is called
- Child may respond to new, novel sounds, but not routine sounds
- Child may easily get confused about similar sounding language (anchor vs. anger / greeting vs. greedy)
- Child may have correlating language delays and/or an auditory processing disorder
- Child may avoid crowds or even small groups because he doesn't easily follow the conversation

When sound is over-registered and the body is over-sensitive:

- Child may avoid specific noises and become very anxious when anticipating noise
- Child may avoid environments (gym/ public restroom) where specific noises are present
- Child is easily irritated by routine noises (people chewing/ hum of appliances/ pencil noise)
- Child has difficulty tuning out unimportant sound information (background noise) and tuning into important information (teacher's voice)
- Child may have correlating language delays and/or an auditory processing disorder
- Child may avoid crowds or even small groups because sound easily overwhelms him and triggers anxiety

Auditory tools used in therapy: favorite music, instrumental music, rhythm games, sound discrimination games. Used tools such as Integrated Listening Systems, The Listening System, and Auditory Processing or Speech Therapy.

The Body Position System/Proprioceptive System:

Located: tendons and joints with heavy input to cerebellum

Job: regulates force and information about body positioning and facilitates coordination.

When proprioception is under-registered and the body is under-sensitive:

- Child displays aggressive/overly affectionate behavior
- Child has decreased coordination/awkward movement patterns
- Child craves sensation and pressure
- Child's movement may be rigid/stiff/tense
- Child may bump into objects, stamp feet, twiddle fingers
- Child may walk on tip-toes

When proprioception is over-registered and the body is over-sensitive:

- Child is often withdrawn, especially in "busy" or group situations
- Child tends to be overly cautious
- Child tends to appear insecure
- Child may be labeled as "lazy"/"couch potato"
- Child slumps, slouches, clumsy or inaccurate could describe positioning
- Child may drag toes or feet when walking

Proprioception tools used in therapy: focus on sustained deep pressure, compression, weigh shifting.

THE HIDDEN SENSES

The "hidden" senses of body position and movement work hand-in-hand "behind the scenes." Body position sense (proprioception) is the body's ability to **know** where each part is in space. It is this system that gives us the ability to move with grace and coordination. This system helps our brain **know** that we still have an arm and how to move it when we aren't looking at it. Body position sense is how we can close our eyes and touch our fingertip to our nose. It feeds information to the brain so that we can coordinate the response between the two sides of the body and move fluidly. The body position sense has deep ties into our sense of well-being, into our sense of security, and into our sense of feeling in **control.** Thus, it is an essential system to help us develop self-control. (Williams & Shellenberger, 1996)

---

a note about stimulating senses for optimal development...

Dr. Jean Ayres wrote about her belief that in order for both motor and cognitive skills to optimally develop, the brain has to receive continual feedback from the senses. She hypothesized that the more the senses began to integrate feedback information to the brain, the more development was optimally stimulated.

She further investigated developmental delay. She began working from the premise that a lack of stimulation to the senses contributed to developmental delay. Therefore, stimulating multiple senses would positively influence developmental progress. She found that giving the senses a **just right challenge** triggered developmental synergy, resulting in progress.

This is not just about flooding the senses with input. This is about creating the just right challenge whereby the senses get the exact stimulation that they are ready for, the stimulation that they can process, and the stimulation that is embedded in an activity that is meaningful to them.

The idea is that the more input to multiple senses that you provide (building from minimal input to more challenging input), the more the nervous system is challenged to synthesize that input together and create enriched processing pathways. (A.Jean Ayres, 1979) Occupational therapists as a profession value learning situations where enhanced sensation is combined with meaningful activity. Our profession is built on the case by case and collective positive outcomes that result.

The movement system (vestibular system) is the system that registers movement. It tells our brain whether we are falling down or standing up, moving or still. This system gives us the ability to become excited and active and then calm back down. Also, it influences our ability to calm down after getting upset. It has very strong ties into our emotions and the limbic system. It is sometimes referred to as an **umbrella** system because it has so much influence over the nervous system as a whole. Because of this influence and the powerful job that the movement system has to do, you will notice that I use "movement system" and "self-regulation" interchangeably at times.

Research tells us that movement positively affects learning outcomes, mood, and overall health. Exercise supports our cognitive development, increases cell repair, increases the flow of oxygen to the brain, promotes more effective glucose metabolism, and protects the body to reverse the effects of stress. Exercise also increases serotonin to the brain and supports improved mood. (Amen, 2005)

We know that our opportunities to take in sensory information affect how we learn. We know that enriching sensory opportunities expands an infant and child's ability to learn, actually increasing his capacity for learning. (Lobo, Harbourne, Dusing, & McCoy, 2013)

There is evidence-based knowledge on the benefits of **multi-sensory classroom instruction.** (Hutcheson, Selig, & Young, 1990 January) (Ogden, Hindman, & Turner, 1989 January) In spite of that evidence, most informed parents and professionals would agree that we often struggle to apply this knowledge effectively in classroom settings.

Lack of training for teachers in this area is one reason teacher struggle to fully apply multi-sensory knowledge effectively in classroom settings, but most teachers desire to provide multi-sensory learning and just lack a method of determining which strategies will be effective for each student. In addition, most teachers have experiential knowledge that "sensory" strategies are not a "one-size-fits-all" solution to gaining attention and accelerating learning. In fact, many have attempted sensory strategies with students, only to have them backfire and result in a student becoming more distracted and less on-task than before the strategy was applied.

There is limited access to occupational therapy consults for teachers. These factors contribute to an atmosphere where the sensory strategies appear minimally effective, leading teachers to abandon the best-practice idea of differentiated, multi-sensory learning because it does not appear to be practical to implement.

Occupational therapists are one of the professionals that could put their knowledge together with the teacher's knowledge to create better solutions for both group and individual success. Lack of resources and staff support to provide multi-sensory activities in group learning creates a disincentive to fully implementing differentiated and multi-sensory learning methods.

> **a note about individual instruction through technology...**
> Technology has provided some promising support for individual instruction in many areas, such as reading skill development. (Torgesen & Barker, 1995) However, technology use must be balanced by active learning in order for the nervous system to thrive. Active learning supports memory and attention development. (Ploughman, 2008)

Cost-effective sensory intervention solutions that can be provided for an entire group of students to support multi-sensory learning are needed. Those intervention solutions must also be socially appropriate where they can be applied to a variety of children without negative social connotation. For example, if only one student is utilizing one of the following supports for learning, he stands out socially as "different:"

- Using a slant board for reading

- Sitting on a ball for a chair or a standing desk

- Accessing a visual schedule taped to the desk

- Checking completed items off an individual to-do list

- Replacing worksheets with hands-on projects as learning indicators

If there are optional learning tools (such as those listed above) for each student in the class and there is instruction on how to utilize them, suddenly using a tool is not a socially awkward experience. It is smart learning.

DETERMINING THE "JUST RIGHT FIT"

Even more important than group access to sensory tools and multi-sensory enrichment is a practical method for determining the "just right fit" for specific sensory supports that enhance learning per student or group. This will reduce the trial-and-error feel of finding the individual supports that will benefit each child to enhance learning, attention, and memory retention.

It has long been accepted that visual and auditory methods of learning are vital to attention, memory retention and cognitive gains. More recent research is lending much credibility to the idea that movement and hands-on learning strategies are just as important as visual and auditory strategies in the classroom.

In this book, we will begin to explore the benefits of sensory learning. We will begin to identify **sensory learning styles**. Sensory learning styles indicate the most accurate and efficient way that an individual child takes in new information through his senses. What we explore in this book will not include all of the facets of cognitive learning styles. For example, musical learning is widely accepted as a learning style and would be classified as a style that falls under sensory auditory learning. Therefore, musical learning is not specifically covered in this book, but the information about auditory learning can be applied to children with musical gifts and talents.

Other styles of learning, including intellectual styles, are not necessarily accounted for in this book. Intellectual styles of learning focus on cognitive processes and are not as intensely focused on accurate and enriched intake of information through the senses to be applied to learning. Therefore, I would direct you to <u>The Handbook of Intellectual Styles</u> by Zhang, Stemberg, and Rayner for more information about intellectual learning styles. (Zhang, Sternberg, & Rayner, 2011)

WHAT DO WE KNOW ABOUT SENSORY LEARNING?

We know that brain plasticity can be triggered by sensory enrichment. We also know that defense mechanisms are triggered when sensory information is too harsh or abrupt, which is counter-productive in learning situations. (Woo & Leon, 2013) (Bengoetxea, Ortuzar, Bulnes, Rico-Barrio, Lafuente, & Argandona, 2012) Therefore, learning is best facilitated in environments that provide gentle sensory enrichment.

We also know that learning must be interesting and related to meaningful activity to be most effective. (Dewey, 1916) (Dewey, 1938) Knowing what a child is already interested in can be an invaluable resource when the goal is increasing that child's rate of learning. Purposeful expansion of that child's liked activities and interests becomes one of the most important goals related to expanding learning potential and ability. You first have to meet the child where he is, which may be a very limited scope of focus, and then you can link into his interests to begin to provide opportunity for that focus and interest to expand.

We know that hands-on learning opportunities improve test scores. (Garrity, 1998) Hands-on learning opportunities improve handwriting and written expression skills. (Case-Smith, 2002) Hands-on learning opportunities improve achievement. (Allen, 2007) Hands-on learning opportunities improve learning and performance according to The No Child Left Behind Blue Ribbon Schools Report.

Knowing that hands-on learning activities engage minds, results in valuing active learning over passive learning. We value activity-based instruction, such as centers that have a learning theme. We value using manipulatives to teach lessons. We value building and drawing and making models and doing projects. We value field trips where we get to go and DO, not just talk about doing.

We know that experiential learning, learning by doing, is foundational to a child's development. (Dewey, 1938) We know that physically active kids perform better academically. (Trost, 2009) (Trost & Van der Mars, 2009) (Keays & Allison, 1995) We know that movement increases learning, memory retrieval, and performance. (Jensen, 2005) We know that movement reduces anxiety and helps a child be available for learning. (Hannaford, 1995) We know that movement stimulates oxygen to the brain to stimulate learning potential and prepare the brain for learning. (Jensen, 2005) In short, it is reasonable to conclude that active learning is more effective than passive learning. **Active learning is sensory learning.**

There is evidence that even 30 minutes of active exercise at least three times per week can have a positive effect on learning, including improved mood and attitude for learning, increased brain mass and brain cell development, improved cognition and ability to connect ideas, and better circulation. (Adlard, Perreau, Engesser-Cesar, & Cotman, 2003) (Churchill, Galvez, Colcombe, Swain, Kramer, & Greenough, 2002) (Markakis & Gage, 1999) (Sutoo & Akiyama, 2003) (Tomoporowski, 2003) (Van Praag, Kempermann, & Gage, 1999)

The movement center (cerebellum) has incredible influence on the rest of the brain. (Middleton & Strick, 1994) In fact, many neuroscientists agree that movement is one of the strongest influences on learning. It supports memory, attention, and spatial perception development. (Jensen, 2005) This lends tremendous support to therapists who are using rhythm and timing work to help stimulate sequencing skills, memory retention, attention and executive functioning skills.

For typically developing kids, this simply means **bringing the fun back to function.** The scales have tipped to where most American children spend more of their day in sedentary, passive consumption of technology (gaming systems, television, etc.) than in active play and engaged learning. To re-engage them in active learning means putting down the tablet, video games, remote to the TV, and handheld gaming devices and making sure that active movement, active play, and active learning outweighs passive engagement during a child's day. In the classroom, this means that we set aside worksheets in favor of more active types of engagement. We prefer projects over worksheets. It means that we use technology to hook interest and begin research and learning on a subject and then we expand that interest in hands-on work or project-based/ center-based learning. Refocusing on sensory learning means that we notice and tune in to what our senses tell us about the world. We take snapshots of moments to store as memories, remembering what the moment felt like, what it looked like, what it sounded like so that our memories are enriched and our learning in that moment is enriched.

Sensory learning means purposefully **being present** in a learning moment in order to form a greater connection to the information. This can be cognitively accomplished by adults and forward thinking students, but the beauty of sensory is that you can use sensory opportunities to help any student more naturally connect to the information. If the sensory experience is pleasant, meaningful, and interesting, you have just enhanced learning about whatever information is connected to that experience. That kind of teaching and interaction is powerful! Understanding what sensory processing is and how vital it is to learning and engaging our brain in performance is the first step toward creating appropriate and enriching learning environments. In their book, **<u>Smart Kids with Learning Difficulties</u>**, Rich Weinfeld, Sue Jeweler, Linda Barners-Robinson, and Betty Roffman Shevitz state:

> *" Our experience has shown that some students who appear to have ADHD will no longer demonstrate the same symptoms, or the same symptoms to the extent that they would be considered a disability, when they are given an appropriate educational environment."*

Their book is focused on providing helpful tips for supporting struggling students who are not yet experiencing success in the classroom environment. (Weinfeld, Jeweler, Barnes-Robinson, & Roffman Shevitz, 2013) The learning environment paired with the presentation style set the stage for whether individual students will have success in the classroom and develop a love of learning.

CHAPTER 5 DEEPER JOURNEY TO APPLICATION

The Deeper Journey portion of each chapter is set up to provide application and reflection questions or to help support group discussion regarding the information in the related chapter.

1. As you read through the different senses and their intake jobs, which sense(s) do you see as your child's strength(s)?

2. As you read through the different senses and their intake jobs, which sense(s) do you see are creating a barrier for your child and not providing accurate or complete information for him to work with in forming his response?

In the barrier area(s) identified, try to figure out if your child is simply not receiving the message accurately or if you see a pattern of over/under responding that applies to him. Describe what you see happening:

3. Now, think through the senses for yourself, personally. Which senses do you rely on most? Which senses trip you up?

Compare your personal information to your child's. What do you see?

CHAPTER 6

"Tell me and I forget. Teach me and I remember.

Involve me and I learn."

-Benjamin Franklin

SENSORY DEVELOPMENT

Just like children use the best tool in their **behavioral backpack** to respond to a given situation, children are only able to "give back" or behave based on the quality of their intake of information. Imagine a computer. If you put faulty information into a computer, you will not get an accurate answer. If you put incomplete information into a computer, you will get a partial (or faulty) answer. So it is with our nervous system. Our sensory system is working at all times to take in accurate information from the world around us so that it can be processed by our brain and central nervous system.

There are three types of neurons that work to receive and respond to our environment. (Bear, Connors, & & Paradiso, 2006) First, there are sensory "intake" neurons. These are the gatherers of information. They work through the sense systems listed in chapter 5 (taste, smell, touch, etc.) to help the brain capture enough accurate information to form an appropriate response.

Often, the information is gathered through multiple different senses to provide a better, more complete picture. Then our response is orchestrated through the synergy between multiple senses to form a graceful response. This synergy happens with the intermediate "talking" neurons as they coordinate information and form a plan of action. The third type of neuron is the motor "output" neurons that carry out the plan and respond.

When occupational therapists or other professionals are analyzing a sensory processing or behavioral situation, they are looking at these three pieces: intake, processing, and output. They are working to find solutions and set up activities that will help grow maturity and connection within each of these three pieces and between each of those processes to help set a child up for success.

STAGES OF SENSORY DEVELOPMENT

The essence of responding appropriately to the environment is the ability to take in the right amount of information in the right context and respond with the right amount of finesse to accomplish the goal. How does that happen? How do you gather the "just right" amount of information, keep it in context and then respond appropriately?

Sensory development happens in stages that build upon one another, much like other skills. Piaget's stages of cognitive development thoroughly teach how individuals form and reform their knowledge of the world based on a result of their interactions with the environment and their perception of those interactions. (Ginsburg, 1987) An increasing awareness and accurate intake of experience with the environment through the senses is, therefore, a critical stage of sensory and perceptive development. Awareness of the environment grows into self-regulation, which grows into controlled responses, and then finally results in the desired skill response.

AWARENESS OF THE ENVIRONMENT

One of the first foundational stages of sensory development is the ability to gather accurate information, as well as enough information about the environment around us. Very early on, we begin to look around, feel around, and notice things around us. We listen for Mom's voice and turn to look and find her. We begin to anticipate when food, comfort, and help might be coming. We look around to notice a bright toy that might be fun to play with, or begin to make eye contact and respond relationally with Mom and Dad.

As our systems continue to mature and work together more effectively, we begin to look around and notice more choices. There are things to explore. Some are very enticing (light sockets, pots and pans to bang on, and small things on the floor), and some are interesting (our newest or favorite toy). We begin to filter information and "tune out" unimportant information (the dog that has been barking since we were conceived) and "tune in" important information (the garage door opening because Daddy is home).

We begin to notice changes in our environment, such as when Mom or Dad took that great toy away! We notice when an important person leaves the house. We notice when a favorite food is cooking or sitting on the table. We notice when bath water is running. In general, we sit up and take notice of what's going on.

We begin to use this information to work for us to get attention, to get things we want, to avoid things we don't want, and to get into situations that feel good and to get out of situations that don't feel good. **We begin to understand that we can change our world**. We begin to understand that we have the power to make things we want happen and avoid things we don't want to happen. You are probably beginning to see how this connects to the behavioral information covered earlier.

SELF-REGULATION SKILL

We get to a point where we begin to get excited and calm down, wake up and fall back asleep, get upset because a toy was taken, and then recover to choose another toy to play with. We begin to regulate ourselves and our responses. (Kochanska, Coy, & Murray, July/August 2001 ; Volume 72, Issue 4) We begin to modulate - where we can give Mom and Dad a strong response or a quiet response - and the dynamics of our responses grow increasingly complex. We become more tuned in to the intensity and the specifics of the situation.

CONTROLLED RESPONSE

As we grow in self-regulation, we grow in our ability to control our responses. We can choose to withhold a response we know Mom and Dad have enjoyed seeing in the past in order to negotiate "a better deal" (such as more attention or a bribed reward). We can handle hearing Mom and Dad say "no" and accept it without having a meltdown. We can listen to the directions Mom and Dad give and then follow those directions to learn something new. We can watch Mom and Dad complete a task and then learn how to do it for ourselves.

We gain a lot of traditional "skill" at this stage because things are coming together for us, and we are making connections that affect outward actions. In the previous stages, behavior was noticeable, but much of the "learning" and "connection" was internal and not as overt. During those early stages, you would have had to notice very specific behavior pieces to "see" sensory skills building. However, at this stage, sensory strengths and weaknesses begin to stand out. This becomes especially true in cooperative learning or social situations. Because cooperative learning and social situations require such a high developmental level of sensory processing skill, these situations are often the first where a child's synthesis of skills will break down. (Pintrich, Zusho, & Eccles, 2002)

SKILLED RESPONSE

The skilled sensory response is what we all strive for every day. The skilled response is when we truly begin to take information in, begin keeping it in the correct context, and begin responding with some finesse to specific situations. This relates directly to our drive to "*be all I can be*" and our motivation to reach our full potential. In other words, this skilled response stage becomes our quest for self-actualization. Self-actualization was first used by Kurt Goldstein in the 1930's to describe an organism's drive to reach its full potential (Goldstein, 1939). Its use was later expanded by both Carl Rogers and Abraham Maslow. (Rogers C., 1961) Maslow's work became what we know of today as the theory of self-actualization. (Daniels, 1982)

The following story is a glimpse into childhood, related to the development of skilled responses, that highlights these principles and reminds us that we are all in different places on the path to reaching our full potential.

HAVE YOU BEEN TO A 6TH GRADE SLEEPOVER?

One way to picture the skilled response is to think of a sixth grade girl's sleepover. Sixth grade girls are at varying stages and rates of development as they move from pre-adolescence into adolescence. Let's imagine that one girl gets her feelings hurt and stomps off, determined NEVER again to speak to any other girl at the party. **Drama-trauma** ensues. She draws a huge line in the sand and steps over it publicly. She gets stuck on the outside of the group because she can't figure out how to "feel better" about the friendships. Eventually, she can't really remember why she's upset with them, but there is a perceived (or real) hurt. To make matters worse, she's hurting even more because not only did she have the initial hurt, but now she's on the outside looking in. She's isolated herself and now feels the effects of being left out. She doesn't have the tools to re-integrate into the group and she's not sure she even wants to. This is what I call **drama-trauma**, where her over-response creates such an extreme situation that it becomes traumatic for her and she gets stuck there.

Now enters the one mature, sweet and sensitive girl (they are few and far between and what you want your daughter to grow into being), who walks over and puts her arm around the girl who has segregated herself. She says something like, "Girlfriend, you are so not staying mad! We are in this together. You and me. You are our friend forever, and we are going to work this out." She successfully orchestrates the graceful re-integration of the segregated one back into the group, AND she gains respect and loyalty from others in the group as she does it. WOW! She's got skills!

I used 6th graders as an example, but you don't have to look farther than Facebook to see hundreds of this sort of example, with both positive and negative outcomes, every day amongst both teenagers and adults.

In life, there are some people who have developed a skilled ability to respond with grace, poise, righteous fury, and gut-wrenching courage. We admire them. We strive to become like them. We watch them in awe or jealousy. We notice their skill and want to emulate it.

What about context? Do you remember the young boy, Kayden (in Chapter 3), in early elementary school who attends his first football game on Friday night with his parents. He is in awe of the Friday Night Lights and the whole experience makes a great impression on him. On Monday morning, he walks in and says hello to his first grade teacher while simultaneously swatting her on the behind. Unfortunately, he didn't get quite the response he was hoping for. After all, the swat on the behind on Friday night meant "We are teammates. We are in this together to win!" It doesn't carry quite the same message in the classroom on Monday morning.

There are many situations where context can trip us up. Therefore, context needs to be on our radar when children begin to struggle. Is part of their struggle that they have picked up some language or behavior that is appropriate in a very casual context but doesn't fit when they try to apply it to a more formal context or, vice versa? If so, it's as simple as teaching context.

Dr. Ruby Payne explains this well in her book, <u>A Framework for Understanding Poverty</u>. (Ruby Payne, 2005) She explains that we are all studying and actively learning something. How you spend your time determines what you are learning and the context of your knowledge. For example, those in poverty have knowledge about agencies and relationships that those spending their time in middle class achievement don't have. How is your child spending his time? The way that he spends his time will largely determine where his knowledge lies.

Dr. Payne goes on to further define context by introducing the five registers of language:
- Frozen – Always the same (Lord's Prayer, Wedding Vows)

- Formal – Standard sentence syntax and word choice of work and school (complete sentences and specific word choices)

- Consultative – Formal register when used in conversation (discourse pattern is not quite as direct as formal register)

- Casual – Friends, 400-800 word vocabulary, general and not specific (dependent upon non-verbal assists/ syntax is often incomplete)

- Intimate – Language between lovers and twins, language of sexual harassment

Words and phrases that one might use in casual, locker-room talk with teammates are not the same words and phrases that we expect to hear in the classroom. Yet, isn't that where many of our children and youth struggle? Yes, context is important. Now, take one more step into this idea and look at context for body language, posture, and behavior as a part of the learning language your child is using. Have you identified that one of the things you need to teach is context?

Dr. Payne states that to survive in poverty, one must rely upon non-verbal, sensory, and reactive skills. To survive in school or at work, one must use verbal, abstract, and proactive skills. I would expand her concept to replace poverty with "stress" for our purposes here. Students with learning differences, or those in extreme stress in the classroom or at home, revert to non-verbal, sensory, and reactive behaviors while we attempt to teach them with verbal, abstract, and proactive teaching. It's not a match that often accelerates their learning or decreases their stress. In fact, often stress in those situations will continue to escalate until someone dares to step in and change things up so that learning is once again relevant and connected to what that child knows and where he is "living" at that moment in time.

Do you know what the biggest game changer is? You might first think that it's going to be a method or a program, but you would be wrong. The biggest game changer is "significant relationship." Significant relationship has power that cannot be under-estimated. One thing I love about Dr. Payne's work is how brilliant she is at analyzing our American education system and proposing new thinking that challenges all of us to make learning meaningful in the classroom, to support and not rescue students, and help children learn to plan and set goals for themselves. If a student cannot plan, he cannot control his impulsivity well.

As you can tell, the skill response is a continuum or spectrum. Some of us form basic skilled response abilities, and some of us stand out like a soaring eagle because we keep cresting summit after summit and breaking new ground. One great example of a soaring social eagle is Mother Teresa. She attained a level of social service and competence that few others acquire. Teenagers and adults fall at different places on this spectrum. Some develop skilled responses resembling grace in social skill interaction, and some struggle and learn lessons the hard way, for most of their life.

A HAPPY HEALTHY LEARNER

How do sensory processing and the sensory stages of development apply to learning? The sensory development information we have covered so far may have provided some insight for you, but how does it apply to today and what's going on for a child in the learning situations? Let's meet the Happy Healthy Learner:

   • Happy Healthy Learner listens and follows directions...because he can accurately

hear what you said and process it fully to respond well.

• Happy Healthy Learner produces his best work...because he can sustain focus and filter out unimportant information and distractions.

• Happy Healthy Learner works well in cooperative learning situations...because he can control his own body and can focus outside of himself to work well with others in a group.

Sensory processing is relevant to every learning situation. It affects and supports our motivation and our performance. Providing multi-sensory opportunities in learning not only helps the Happy, Healthy Learner thrive, but also provides more opportunity than rote instruction for the struggling learner to connect to new information.

BETRAYED BY OUR SENSES...

Sensory skill is based on the primed performance of the nervous system on a specific day. Sometimes children (and adults) who have the ability to form a skilled sensory response will, at times, not. Some days, it's "just not our day." Sometimes the answer is that we retreat to succeed again another day. What happens when we are betrayed by our senses? What happens when things are not rocking along naturally with the developmental process? **What happens when our "off" days are almost every day?** What does this *feel* like?

Some children describe sensory processing dysfunction as feeling out of control and like things are going to hit them in the face and knock them over. Some describe clothing as feeling "spicy" and "scratchy" on the inside. Some describe noises that "drive me crazy." Intense experience is the norm for children who are over-sensitive to specific sensations.

Have you ever experienced a sinus infection to the point that you become nauseous when your head leaves the pillow? Your movement system is aggravated and dysfunctional in that moment. It feels intense. It feels immediate, and life is significantly disrupted.

The illustration of the girls on the beach where there is a body and then the head sitting separate beside it shows what it feels like to be betrayed by your senses and let down by your sensory processing abilities. It feels like your head is literally separated from your body. You are scattered, insecure in your responses, awkward, hesitant, out of sync, and quite simply have trouble pulling it together emotionally, socially, and physically.

Some children describe experiences where specific sensations are diluted, and they simply don't notice what has happened. For example, the child who steps into an overly hot shower and his skin is bright red, but he does not notice until a parent draws his attention to his bright red skin. He then says something like, "Yeah, it might hurt a little. I don't know."

The child with under-sensitivity to specific sensations often engages in higher risk behavior and has more trouble recognizing the risk or the boundary that was crossed. A child may run and bang into others, squeeze others too hard when hugging, or have a lot of difficulty sitting quietly. When asked about the situation, the child will often respond with "I don't know" or something similar, because the child is not paying attention to specific information from the environment. The child is not registering the sensation well.

Most people register noxious or alerting sensory information well, especially a hot, cold, or pain response. When a child's sensory system is not actively receiving and "hearing" messages well from the senses and processing them quickly and efficiently, a child may have a delayed or diluted response to those same messages.

Children and adolescents who struggle with sensory processing will develop a set of coping behaviors. In some, sensory processing dysfunction will present as defiant behavior, opposition, or refusal to cooperate and exacerbate those behavior patterns. Those behaviors may actually develop out of a core need to avoid/escape an over-challenging situation. In that case, it is likely that skills have not developed and learning has been disrupted. Sensory information is not being accurately and fully received. In others, defiant behavior may function as a means to gain attention because the child doesn't know how to ask for help or articulate what he is "feeling" and what is going wrong. In these situations, it is common for children to have difficulty describing what is going wrong for them. After all, the way they are processing is their personal normal, and many of them have no idea that everyone doesn't struggle with sensory processing in the same way they do.

Some children and adolescents will withdraw and show signs of depression. Often, the symptoms of depression continue to morph or reoccur until the underlying sensory processing symptoms are treated. Regardless of the initial behavioral presentation, I have never met a child struggling with sensory processing who is not stressed.

I become a fan of a teacher when I can tell she has true compassion for a child who is struggling with the above symptoms. I respect the teacher (or parent) who can look beyond the irritating, frustrating, embarrassing, upsetting, and difficult behavior to see the struggle that child is living with every day. When I see the compassionate response, I know we are going to soon see supported progress for a child.

Sensory processing difficulty is not always "clinical" and debilitating. We can track these patterns even in children who are developing typically. In typical development situations, these symptoms are often subtle and occur infrequently, with occasional appearances during times of stress or adjustment. In these situations, we can use this information to enhance how we set up opportunities for our children in order to help them become more successful.

However, sensory processing difficulty can be "clinical," affecting a child's ability to perform tasks and interact well with others almost daily. Dr. Lucy Jane Miller is the founder of a specialized sensory processing research program and founder of the SPD Foundation. She has written ground-breaking work such as <u>Sensational Kids: Hope and Help for Children with Sensory Processing Disorder</u> and <u>No Longer A SECRET: Unique Common Sense Strategies for Children with Sensory or Motor Challenges</u>. (Miller, 2006) In her work, she reports evidence that at least one in twenty children suffers from sensory processing dysfunction to a point that it negatively impacts that child's daily learning and performance. If your child suffers from severe sensory behavioral symptoms, I encourage you to read Dr. Miller's work and connect into her resources.

Symptoms of sensory processing difficulty are the outward demonstration of inward struggle with integration of information. They are outward symptoms of an underlying problem. Sensory processing difficulty can be part of a larger disorder or can stand alone to describe sensory processing difficulty that doesn't meet the criteria for another childhood diagnosis.

Sensory processing difficulty is often a descriptor of anxiety, ADHD (Attention Deficit Hyperactivity Disorder), autism spectrum disorders, behavior disorders, obsessive compulsive disorder, social emotional disorders, prematurity, psychotic disorders, mood disorders, attachment and trauma issues, and global developmental delay. Often, behaviors that look "sensory" in nature can be a manifestation of situational or chronic anxiety. It is common for difficulty with sensory processing to be linked closely with anxiety. I find that for many children, once you treat the underlying anxiety, the "sensory" behaviors either disappear or become more manageable.

FINDING THE CALM-ALERT SWEET SPOT

We naturally use specific strategies both to help calm and help alert infants. If we want to help an infant calm, we tend to put soft clothing on them, dim the lights, put on soft music (often instrumental), use calm-soothing voice tones, rock them, pat them and use consistent firm touch with them. If we want to help alert an infant, we tend to provide bright toys, bright lights and light-up toys, varied tone and pitch to make our voices interesting, light touch or tickles, sporadic large movements, and lively active music.

As the nervous system matures, we tend to focus less on providing those deliberate supports because the nervous system naturally begins to modulate more effectively and the child learns to self-calm without as much support from Mom and Dad. However, even the mature nervous system will resort to sensory stimulation to help it modulate. For example, when was the last time you were in the car on a long drive and got tired? What did you do to help yourself? You probably turned on the air conditioning or opened a window, turned the music up to sing to it, stopped to stretch your legs or get coffee, yawned or stretched your eyes wide open or clenched and relaxed muscles to wake them up. Whatever you did, you chose an alerting strategy to help keep you awake so that you successfully arrived home.

When was the last time you got home and wondered, "I don't remember that drive." Your nervous system was working so hard to stay awake and alert that you weren't tuning in to other things. The same thing happens in the classroom for kids. There are some kids that are working so hard to sit still, stay in their seat and stay awake that they miss most of what is going on in the classroom. A majority of their energy is directed toward **self-modulating**, and there's not a lot of energy left for attending and learning. Lasting learning occurs when a student is awake and alert. Low arousal leads to sleep. High arousal leads to reactionary behaviors such as fight, flight, fright responses.

CONTINUUM OF AROUSAL AFFECTS LEARNING

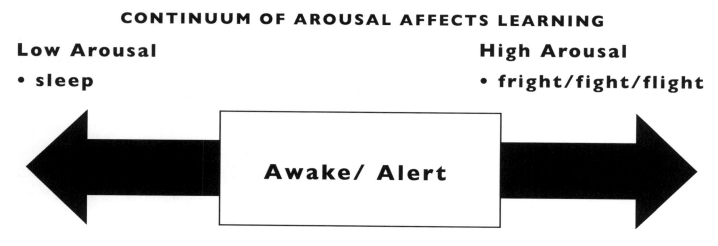

Low Arousal
- sleep

High Arousal
- fright/fight/flight

Awake/ Alert

Lasting learning occurs during Awake/Alert

There is a threshold of sensory stimulation necessary for proper brain function that serves as a minimum daily requirement. **When the brain is deprived on sensory input, it does not actively learn**. Short term sensory deprivation can be relaxing and used in a meditative sense, but severe sensory deprivation is debilitating.

Scientists in the United States and Canada have been studying sensory deprivation since the late 1950s. Isolation (a form of sensory deprivation) is used as a means of torture. (Meyer, 2008) Individuals respond to extreme sensory deprivation by shutting down toward a vegetative state or by hallucinating, providing stimulus to the brain. All of us have a minimum daily requirement of sensory input that must be met for proper brain functioning. When a sensory system is not processing well, it can be debilitating.

There is a part of our nervous systems that is designed as a filter, called the Reticular Activating System (RAS). The filter influences one's level of arousal and alertness at any given time. Its purpose is to filter information as it travels up and down the spinal cord and into the brain stem. Significant information travels up the spinal cord into the brain for higher level processing and "attention." For example, we do not often think about how our clothing, socks and shoes feel on our bodies. We may notice that they feel good or not quite right when we put them on, but we then "tune them out" to focus on other things throughout the day. However, if you get a rock in your shoe or your button pops off of your pants or your clothing rips, your focus returns to what you are wearing.

If the body's filtering system is "out of sync," the child will become over or under sensitive to incoming information. For example, if the filter allows **too much information** through to be processed, the child becomes easily overwhelmed to the point of shutting down. This type of response is often a contributing factor in situations of chronic anxiety and autism spectrum profiles. If the filter **does not allow enough information** through to be processed, the child becomes inattentive, misses information that is in front of him or that he can gather from the environment, and he may begin to entertain himself with his thoughts or day dreaming. This type of response is often a contributing factor in situations of inattention (ADD/ ADHD) profiles.

When a child is not processing sensory input well, he can easily become overstimulated and disorganized in his responses. Classic signs of over-stimulation include: sweaty palms/ back of the neck, dark circles or sheen under the eyes, gagging, vomiting, withdrawal/ sleep, hiccups, nervous laughter, increased respiration, yawning, noise-making, or lip-licking.

Likewise, when a child is not processing sensory input well, he can have an unmet threshold where he is under-stimulated. Classic signs of under-stimulation include: finger tapping, leg shaking, toe tapping, drumming, constant weight shifting, humming, non-meaningful sounds, fidgeting/ moving, or mouthing/ chewing on non-food objects. In a Happy Healthy Learner, self-modulation happens naturally and without a lot of thought. Most high functioning individuals don't spend a lot of time thinking about how to support their nervous systems, but they still provide external supports for themselves intuitively and often.

The Struggling Sensor is the polar opposite of the Happy Healthy Child. One of the most important goals for the Struggling Sensor is to provide supports for them and simultaneously teach them how to support themselves in specific situations. All of us have been in situations where things went awry and we were left feeling inadequate. At those times, if we don't know what to do, we are left in a state of hopelessness and helplessness that is miserable. If we do know what to do, we may still be very uncomfortable, but we do not feel hopeless because we know what to do. The same is true for children.

SENSORY PROCESSING GONE AWRY

Let's review the over and under processing piece again in a different way. As sensory input registers in the brain, it can over-register and become amplified to the individual or it can under-register and become muted to the individual. All of us have slight differences in the way that we perceive our world, which usually makes for healthy and diverse opinions and experiences. However, in some situations, it begins to alter our abilities and our life course.

Sensory behaviors can be signs of anxiety. The behaviors can be situational or global and chronic. Sensory behaviors can also indicate faulty coping skills or lack of coping skills. The behaviors can occur because they feel natural, or because situations feel very uncomfortable, and are "too much."

When the nervous system is not functioning in a neuro-typical way, and the processing is immature, or even atypical, the sensory input registration can "go off the reservation" into over-reactivity or under-reactivity. It is much like a spectrum. There is a natural spectrum of typical response to sensory input that will vary from individual to individual, and then there are the extreme ends of the spectrum that are atypical and consistently interfere with performance and daily functioning.

An individual can be either an over or under responder, or both an under and over-responder. It can happen with any one sense or in multiple senses. Though it is possible to have one sense be the primary sense that is out of balance, it is most common for multiple senses to be out of balance in processing information.

For simplicity, I will briefly outline some identifying behavioral symptoms of specific, out-of-sync processing in each sense. For the purpose of this book, I am most interested in identifying the sensory processing symptoms, but not necessarily looking specifically at diagnosing a sensory processing disorder. For those neuro-scientist moms, you will also notice that I am using general concepts and broad-based overview in order to focus on the different ways sensory input and processing can vary, as opposed to the detailed specific systems and parts of the brain involved in each different "kind" of sensory processing dysfunction.

OVER-RESPONDERS ARE HYPER-SENSITIVE

Over-responders are hyper-sensitive to incoming information in the affected sense(s). Over-responders tend to over-react to the incoming sensory information and are often described as overly sensitive individuals. In some situations, an over-responder presents as fragile. In others, an over-responder presents as picky, difficult to please, touchy, irritable, and rigid.

When a child is hyper-sensitive or **overly sensitive to touch**, the situation is often labeled as "tactile (touch) defensiveness." The child has specific, clear preferences about being touched and interacting with "messy," hands-on-learning activities. There may be a select number of toys or learning methods that the child enjoys, but he does not like to try new things or touch new textures as a part of learning or play.

When a child is hyper-sensitive or **overly sensitive to movement**, symptoms may include a strong preference for sedentary activity. The child may become irritable or even sick during active movement activities such as swinging, sliding, roller coasters, or car rides.

When a child is hyper-sensitive or **overly sensitive to visual information**, the child is experiencing visual defensiveness. This is different than difficulty with visual processing or visual perception skill. This is actual over-sensitivity to incoming visual information. Things feel too bright and too busy to the eyes. The child is often sensitive to direct sunlight or easily irritated in the car if light is reflecting near him or on him.

Many children who are visually defensive struggle with busy presentation of visual information. A full worksheet with small margins and lots of animation can be overwhelming. It can get confusing for teachers and parents to recognize this pattern in some children, because the child may be attracted to a busy, animated TV show or video game, but overwhelmed by school work. In these situations, there are variables that are influencing the pattern, such as motivation, visual processing skill, and performance skill.

Watching TV is a passive activity and is usually for enjoyment. A child may have attention directed toward to TV, but be may not be actively gathering accurate and complete information about what is presented on the TV. In contrast, when a worksheet is presented, there is an expectation of active engagement, and the child's performance responses show when the child is having trouble gathering and making sense of the information.

There is power in being highly motivated. If the child is excited about Skylanders and motivated to learn more about them, he will temporarily overcome his aversion to visual busyness to get a piece of new information about them out of a book or comic. It can appear that he enjoys the busy book and comic because he enjoys the Skylanders subject.

If he is able to successfully find detailed specific information in the busy book or comic, but becomes overwhelmed with "boring" school work, the problem is not a visual processing or over-sensitivity problem, but a motivation/repertoire of reinforcement problem. However, if he is attracted to the Skylanders subject, but only enjoys gathering information that he already knows, and can't successfully gather new information from the busy book or comic, then he may be experiencing visual defensiveness or difficulty with visual processing. In this situation, he will benefit from a friend or parent linking arms with him to learn new information about the subject and pick up details from the visual information presented in the guide. He may be diligent in his quest to discover new information, especially at first, but will become easily discouraged if he is not given enough support to successfully find new information to add to what he knows.

When a child is hyper-sensitive or overly sensitive **to auditory information**, the child is experiencing auditory defensiveness. Again, this is slightly different than difficulty with auditory processing or language skills. This is actual over-sensitivity to incoming auditory information. Unexpected or loud noises hurt.

When a child is hyper-sensitive or overly sensitive **to taste, oral texture, or smell,** the child is experiencing oral defensiveness. This child is often concerned about the textures of foods and is picky about the foods he will willingly eat. Oral defensiveness is often closely associated with touch defensiveness.

I will present both an over-responding example and an under-responding example to help some of these details gel into a more formed picture. However, keep in mind that each child with sensory processing difficulty is unique, and each child's pattern of over-responding or under-responding will be unique to him. Look for the patterns in these examples and the types of issues that the children encounter.

HAVE YOU MET THE OVER-RESPONDER?

Drew is in kindergarten this year, and though most kindergarteners quickly learn to love school and look forward to going the next day, Drew does not. He cries each morning, asking his mother if he can stay home. One morning, she was mortified to have him grab hold of the railing leading to the school door and scream at the top of his lungs, "I'm not going! They don't even like me here and I don't like them. Don't make me go in there! It's dangerous!"

After dropping Drew off in his classroom where there was another round of drama about staying at school, Drew's Mom discussed Drew's behavior with the school counselor. She explained that Drew is bright and the academic work doesn't seem too challenging. In fact, she suspects that he is bored at times during the day. He is not socially awkward and appears to be well-liked by his teacher and the other children, and so his extreme reaction appears out of character.

Upon further investigation, the counselor discovers that Drew is picky about what clothing textures he will wear and that many mornings begin with a battle over appropriate clothing. He would prefer to live in his pajamas, arguing that jeans are not "good learning" clothes! She also discovers that Drew is sensitive. He gets his feelings hurt easily. He cringes and complains of family members "yelling" at him when they were not in fact yelling, and he cries and whines easily if he perceives or really experiences an insult or injury.

Drew is an over responder. He perceives a slap when he is bumped. He feels his ear drums are burning especially when the noise is unexpected or when he is already slightly on edge and irritated. Though he is bright and has some social skills, his difficulty with sensory processing may begin to interfere with his performance during his daily routines. At this age, his peers are very forgiving and may not pick on him for his dramatic behavior each morning at school, but they still notice. By third or fourth grade, their grace for this sort of behavior will be more limited, especially in light of no overt signs of stressors. His parents and teachers may also begin to become weary with the constant battles against unseen insults.

ONE OF MY OWN OVER-RESPONDER AH-HA MOMENTS

About six years ago, I had an intense moment with a family of a child who over-responds to sensory input that changed how I see sensory learning and how it relates to interaction and relationship. We had just opened the Burrell Autism Center, and we were focused on developing a multi-disciplinary screening and evaluation process. A family of a three-year-old came in suspecting that he might have an autism spectrum disorder. During my time with the family, there wasn't a lot of formal testing to be done with the three-year-old because he was not able to cooperate and follow instructions to do formal motor testing, so I found that I had some extra time with them for clinical observation and interaction. I needed baseline developmental information about him, and so I decided to use my Floortime Training*.

We got on the floor, and we played. We had a great time, and I spent time helping his mom interpret his non-verbal cues since he didn't have words. I showed her how to give subtle, inviting cues that she was available to play and helped her recognize when he responded positively (yet subtly) to those cues. I showed her how to read him and back off when he was getting overwhelmed (He was very over-sensitive in most sensory areas), and how to provide very gentle and simple reciprocal play interaction.

She began to learn how much he needed interaction toned down to his level and how sensitive he was to typical toys and play approaches. About 45 minutes into the session, I realized that tears were streaming down Mom's face. Mom said words that will stick with me forever. She said, **"I just realized that I have lived with him for three years, but I think I just met him today."**

She had taken care of him and loved him for three years, but she left that room with a new level of life with him. By learning his subtle cues in responding to the sensory learning opportunities we gave him, she learned that he really does communicate, just not with words (yet) and not in traditional development ways. His language is unique and individual to him, and we just had to learn it to get to know him and give him the opportunity to relate to us more fully.

I am blessed to have a version of this moment repeatedly, where I get to witness parents and siblings getting to know a child better—for who he really is, not the behavior pattern or sensory processing issue that has been overshadowing his true self. There's an anonymous quote that I found years ago that states, **"You have never really lived until you have done something for someone who can never repay you."** I believe it. Tuning in to a person to truly connect with him for their benefit changes you and anyone else who chooses to tune in with you. It's an amazing blessing.

UNDER-RESPONDERS ARE HYPO-SENSITIVE

On the flip side, under-responders are hypo-sensitive or under-sensitive to incoming sensory information. This type of child under-reacts and it takes "more" to get a response.

When a child is hypo-sensitive or **less sensitive to touch**, he will often have issues with accurate pain and temperature registration and may not notice when he is hurt or when the bath temperature is too hot. This child can also begin to present behaviorally as a risk taker or one who is not cautious. His body's natural caution and pain registration are both diluted.

*Floortime is a method of intervention based on development information you gather about a child combined with individual differences that you note about a child (especially sensory processing differences) combined with approaching play from a relationship-based perspective (DIR Method). (Greenspan, SI and Wieder, S., 2006).

This can be an explosive combination.

When a child is **less sensitive to movement**, he will often show signs of hyperactivity and inattention. He may or may not be diagnosed with ADHD. He may crave movement, and one might think he is a moving learner because of how much he seeks movement during his day, but that is not often the case. Generally, when a child struggles with movement processing, he struggles to take in information accurately and efficiently through this system.

Prior to some therapeutic intervention, he may not learn academic information well while moving. In academic situations, he may often get distracted by his own enjoyment of movement and not be able to process both the movement and the academic information. When this is the case, the child will benefit from structured teaching that allows for movement breaks, instead of learning during movement activities. Therefore, a child who craves movement may or may not learn academic information well while moving, and he may or may not learn motor information well when moving. It is possible to have a child who craves movement but is not athletically inclined, as well as a child who craves movement and is very athletically skilled. All children are designed to need a certain level of movement during their day. Some children are designed to need more movement than normal.

When a child is **less sensitive to visual input**, he may crave visual information, but doesn't necessarily learn well from that information. This can be a child who enjoys "vegging out" to TV for long periods of time, or a child who sits and watches a repetitive visual motion such as a spinning object or rolling credits on the TV. He enjoys what he is seeing and is attracted to visual experiences.

When a child is **less sensitive to auditory input**, he may crave auditory information and may begin making his own by vocalizing (humming, singing, repetitive grunting or repeating a specific sound repetitively). This situation gets tricky to problem solve because there are also early learners who begin vocalizing to block out environmental sounds that they don't process well. If in doubt, link arms with a speech therapist or occupational therapist to determine whether your child is actually auditorally hypo-sensitive or just struggles with making sense of auditory information and has therefore developed a behavior (vocalizing) to drown out the confusing input.

When a child is **less sensitive to taste and oral texture or smell**, the child will often over-stuff his mouth during meals. He may also show a decreased awareness of having food in his mouth or exhibit messy table manners. He may crave smelling, licking, biting non-food objects. He may also enjoy pressing objects against his upper lip.

HAVE YOU MET THE UNDER-RESPONDER?

Karen loves to climb, run, jump, and is very active. She does not consistently respond when her name is called, but she does often repeat a random word and phrases that she hears. She likes toys that light up or spin and appears to enjoy toys that are visually animated.

Karen struggles during small group time because she does not sit and maintain her attention during story time and struggles to participate in any discussion about the story. She gets up to wander off from the group when she is not interested in the subject.

Karen doesn't seem to understand the concept of boundaries and will wander out of the classroom. However, if there is red tape across the floor of the doorway and she is prompted that her teachers have taught her to stop when she sees the red tape across the doorway (red means stop), then she does not wander out of the classroom.

Karen is an under-responder. She craves movement and can't seem to absorb enough multi-sensory information to keep her satisfied. However, she has trouble effectively using the sensations that she is constantly seeking out to make quick learning connections. Thus, though she is seeking sensory information, she is not necessarily processing it efficiently for learning. This pattern may be mildly or severely affecting her performance in daily learning and interaction with others.

MY FIRST UNDER-RESPONDER AH-HA MOMENT

In the first few years that I was a therapist, I worked for a small community hospital serving my hometown. I split my time between out-patient adults and out-patient pediatrics, and then I rotated in to do a little of everything else, such as mental health and wellness evaluations.

I remember praying every day on my hour drive to work that I would know enough that day to not do anything stupid that would hurt someone's progress and that I would actually be able to help someone that day. I was spending 60 and sometimes 80 hours per week working to ramp into "knowing" what to do. I spent time in surgery with the adult out-patient orthopedic surgeons that sent me patients straight from the recovery room, and I studied wound care with a highly respected plastic surgeon in the state. I loved working with athletes and adults in rehab, but I was pulled to children and their high needs.

In pediatrics, I worked on a team with a physical therapist and speech therapist who continue to be two of my favorite people and are both very successful pediatric therapists. I was reading every night on sensory issues, the nervous system, and pediatric treatment strategies. I was working so hard to give treatment beyond my "no" years of experience.

One day about a year after I began practicing, I was walking out to meet a six-year-old boy with autism and his mother. As I walked down the hall to greet them, his mother started crying when she saw me. My first thought was, "Oh my, what did I do?" followed by, "He looks physically fine so I don't think I've done anything **big** wrong." (Of course at the time I thought her tears must be a reflection of me because I was so absorbed in doing a good job that I had trouble seeing past me to see her more clearly.)

She said her son had slept through the night **for the first time ever** for the past two nights since I had seen them. She said thank you repeatedly, asked me what I did to make that happen, and asked me (jokingly) to come live with them.

My first thought was, "Whew! It's all good. The crying was a good thing!" followed by, "Oh, wow! What **DID** I do that was powerful enough to help him regulate and sleep well like that?" That moment carried me through many late night hours finding the answer to that question so I could do it again for him and for others.

Movement was his key. He was an under-responder who needed more movement to feed his nervous system. He also craved touch input which was the basis of much of his repetitive self-stimulation behavior. Providing better ways to meet those needs, and building those ways into his regular routines was the key to a better quality of life for him.

My strategies had to work better than his natural tendency to stay up and pace or jump on his bed for self-stimming in order to work. They had to be front-loaded so that his needs were met before he was compelled to help himself by seeking out input. (In other words, we worked hard to change the antecedents to his behavior and set up a better platform for what we wanted to see – sleep). He still had autism, but both he and his parents got sleep. More sleep resulted in less acting out behavior, less irritability, and less sensory-craving behavior patterns. It was a **win-win solution**.

INTERVENTION PERSPECTIVE

The tools section of this book will outline some pre-therapy intervention that can help you get started in addressing any of the above symptoms you might identify in your child. However, this book is intended to provide practical tips for setting up positive sensory learning and is not written specifically to address all activities that can help a child with sensory

"Understanding basic principles of sensory processing and utilizing positive sensory processing strategies can help ALL kids, but those strategies are essential to some."
--Amy's #2 Tip
Amy's Top 10 Tips
www.PositivelySensory.com

processing issues or dysregulation. This book is not intended to be a substitute for therapeutic intervention with a professional, but rather a supplement to that intervention in order to help you even more fully apply what you learn with other professionals. Also, this book is designed to help you more fully apply what you have learned about your child during your treatment journey.

CHAPTER 6 DEEPER JOURNEY TO APPLICATION

The Deeper Journey portion of each chapter is set up to provide application and reflection questions or to help support group discussion regarding the information in the related chapter.

1. Describe your child's natural awareness of his environment:

Is your child's awareness of his environment working to support his success in the classroom? If not, is he over-attending or under-attending to environmental cues?

What can you do support his increased awareness of important cues in the environment while also supporting his ability to ignore non-essential environmental distractions?

2. Describe how your child's natural self-regulation skill has developed. What was it like as an infant and toddler and what is it like now?

3. Describe your child's skill level in responding to situations where he doesn't get his way. Is it purely behavioral or is there a sensory component there also?

4. Describe your child's interaction with peers and his skill in responding with a graceful, coordinated response to the situation. Can you identify any patterns of difficulty that you can model and practice with him so he has a better skill set for those interpersonal interaction situations?

CHAPTER 7

"I am always ready to learn
although I do not always like being taught."
-Winston Churchill

SENSORY PROCESSING AND LEARNING STYLE

Here's the bottom line for our purposes in this guide: **Understanding sensory processing and utilizing positive sensory processing strategies can help ALL kids, but they are essential to some.** Working through this framework and making a plan for positive sensory development support will help each child who has a parent or therapist making a plan for his success.

Sensory strategies have long been enhancing success, regardless of learning style or intelligence. Using visual and touch aids often have noticeable positive effects on learning outcomes, regardless of the student's learning style or preference. In fact, recent research in the physical therapy community confirms that our everyday experiences, including sitting, interacting with objects, and moving, facilitates development and influences cognitive development. (Lobo, Harbourne, Dusing, & McCoy, 2013)

Early delays in perceptual motor development correlate with broader delays throughout childhood. This is one reason that early intervention is so crucial. For example, when infants are supported in their ability to interact with objects (hold, explore and manipulate them), they gain information about the relationship between themselves and the objects and between themselves and the caregivers supporting that interaction. They become motivated to explore more and know more.

Delays in an infant's object interaction are linked to lower IQ scores in middle childhood. Attaining independent sitting skills also opens up an infant's awareness of the environment by improved ability to visually attend and process information. This position supports increased eye control and eye tracking skill and increases the opportunity for the infant to explore the environment by reaching for things and manipulating them. In addition, once an infant becomes mobile through crawling, he begins to use more gestures and realizes that he can effect change in his world by changing his situation (i.e. moving away from something less desired and moving toward something more desired). Supporting an infant's ability to interact with objects and gain mobility serves to support that child's growing cognitive skill development, both in the present and for the future. (Lobo, Harbourne, Dusing, & McCoy, 2013)

Babies grow up, but the truth is perceptual-motor experience and opportunity remains crucial to that child's success. Here's what we know that applies to ALL children, regardless of learning style:

- Brain plasticity (the brain's ability to change in structure and in function based on what it experiences) is triggered by sensory enrichment (Woo & Leon, 2013).

- Hands-on learning opportunities improve test scores (Garrity, 1998), improve handwriting and written expression skills (Case-Smith, 2002), increase achievement (Allen, 2007), and improve overall learning and performance (California Blue Ribbon Project).

- Experiencing the environment—learning by doing—is foundational to a child's development (Dewey, Experience and Education, 1938), and physically active kids perform better academically (Trost S. , 2009) (Keays & Allison, 1995).

Sensory activities help all children engage in learning, but tailoring sensory input for an individual child, specific to his learning strengths and weaknesses, can make all the difference in the world for how effectively he learns the information presented to him.

For some children, tailoring sensory input means streamlining and organizing the information so the sense that is most effectively taking in information is presented with the bulk of the input. Subsequently the other senses can be used in a supporting, secondary role to expand the general use of that new knowledge.

For other children, it means enhancing all teaching in a multi-sensory way so that the child can draw information from multiple senses to gain more context and knowledge. In this situation, the more sensory the presentation, the more quickly and efficiently the child will connect with the information and retain it.

In Chapter 10, I introduce how to utilize The Learning Strengths Profile as a tool to identifying your child's unique learning profile from a sensory processing (sensory intake) perspective. This tool will help you streamline and organize information so that your child is able to most effectively benefit from it.

SENSORY PROCESSING RELATED TO LEARNING STYLE

Though there are numerous resources devoted to explaining and teaching about learning styles, I want to explore learning styles from a sensory processing perspective. Remember, this is not a comprehensive exploration of learning styles. For simplicity, I am introducing *sensory learning styles* that will not include all the facets of cognitive learning styles.

This book presents learning styles from a sensory processing perspective. The way we approach learning and the success we have with the approaches we have tried shapes how our learning style develops. There are two primary **approaches to learning** that we will explore from a sensory processing perspective: a global learning approach and a linear learning approach.

I was first introduced to the concept of these two approaches to learning by Dr. David Pierce, a behavioral optometrist. Since my first discussions with Dr. Pierce, I have found other psychologists who have long held to identifying linear and global learning styles during cognitive testing, and my discussions with those psychologists further honed my own view of linear and global approaches to learning.

How a child takes in information, and whether that process is effective and efficient for the child to accurately gain the information, impacts that child's learning style and approach to learning. I believe the way a child approaches learning gives fantastic information about the way the child is taking in the information, and thus, gives teachers and parents vital information about sensory processing strengths and weaknesses related to learning.

For the purpose of this book, I describe linear and global approaches in sensory processing terms related to learning. These concepts have even more specific application related to cognitive functioning from a psychological perspective than what we will cover here. Some psychologists and researchers classify global sensory learners as being primarily right brain dominant and linear sensory learners as being primarily left brain dominant.

Brain dominance presents the processing preference and style, but when information is not flowing between the two halves of the brain to coordinate information well, a student becomes much more rigid in his learning style and processing abilities, which can end up crippling performance. By understanding a child's processing approach, you gain insight into how to set up a learning environment for that child's success.

GLOBAL APPROACH TO LEARNING

A global sensory learner learns best in a sensory-rich, multi-sensory learning environment. This learner is assimilating information fastest when there is lots of information to be absorbed and it is presented in a big picture way. This learner "walks" through the situation and the experience to understand it better. He will "jump" right into learning and add pieces and details as he goes. He often intuitively knows where he is going. However, he will tend to develop splinter skills or incomplete information if he doesn't work thoroughly with concepts and information. He easily misses details as he is "feeling" his way through to the next idea.

A global learner is action oriented. His action initiates his thinking skill. He recognizes the "big picture" first and then becomes aware of the details as he continues to explore and engage with the materials and information. He usually loves multi-sensory learning and seems to have an attitude of "the more, the better…bring it on!" He often attempts to process large amounts of information at once. He is often not very detail-oriented, but he is physically aware of his environment. His attention easily shifts based on activity within his environment. His teacher may recognize that he is always learning, but he is not always learning the same things as the other children in his classroom. He sometimes thinks more effectively when he himself is moving, but often needs his core trunk muscles engaged to "ground" his thinking skills and likes to balance on a special T-stool or ball chair in the classroom to help him stay focused. He often goes into movement to seek more information, and the information he gathers is then added to his library of sense-information to help process learning.

For this type of learner, providing a movement activity (such as walking or pinching clothespins and pinning them to a clothespin tree) while organizing his thoughts on a subject in preparation for a writing assignment, can prove effective. Some students will also need the aid of a visual chart (mind mapping related details around a main subject) to most effectively organize their thoughts, versus simply generating their thoughts during this activity.

It is rare to find a global learner who already has organizational strategies in place at a young age. This type of learner greatly benefits from organizational strategies and instruction in the classroom in order to be able to show what he knows through his classroom work. However, this type of learner will also push the boundaries of how those organizational strategies are utilized and will often need room to creatively express and organize, loosely based on the original organizational concept, to be most effective.

Rigid performance expectations are rarely successful for this type of learner, but this type of learner almost always becomes highly motivated by positive reinforcement and praise. Success breeds success.

The global learner will become stressed in a classroom situation where sensory input is limited and there are rigid behavioral rules and expectations about movement in the classroom. When this happens, a global learner can become stressed and anxious, feeling hamstrung in learning. This type of learner is constantly fighting against being distracted in the classroom, because he naturally notices movement and peripheral information just as readily as what he has been tasked with doing. When this type of learner becomes stressed or anxious, his natural awareness of movement and peripheral details becomes amplified and sustained to the point where he may become stuck in distraction and begin to display characteristics of a hyper-sensitive, inattentive learner in that environment.

LINEAR APPROACH TO LEARNING

A linear sensory learner is often overwhelmed with too much multi-sensory presentation. He does best if information is presented in a step-by-step fashion, using one sense at a time and adding each building block, one at a time, to form a concept in a piece-by-piece process. Once he understands each piece, then he may enjoy manipulating the concept or the information in a more multi-sensory way to continue connecting it to other things he knows, generalizing it more fully into his repertoire of knowledge.

A linear sensory learner often THINKS before acting. He is often a planner and likes to gather information but sometimes needs help using all the facts effectively. He is often performance oriented. He doesn't like to make mistakes and may withdraw or back away from a task if he even perceives there might be failure. He will shut down quickly if he feels overwhelmed in a learning situation. He is often sequential and detailed in nature. He often conserves his energy for processing. He is not necessarily aware of time when processing a task and may sit "thinking" for longer periods of time compared to other students. Also, he may move things close to his eyes to shut out peripheral information because he intuitively wishes to tune out peripheral distractions and focus in on his target project.

This type of learner is able to focus in and sustain his attention well, sometimes even obsessively when he is motivated. Once this student understands the point of the task and how to successfully complete it, he will often put his head down and work with what he understands. He will be less likely to ask for help because he will think he already has all the tools that he needs to complete the project, and he will creatively apply the limited tools he has before asking for new tools. Therefore, he often responds best to a teacher who layers principles, building a new principle on an older one that is well understood.

When this student finds a way to problem solve or complete specific types of assignments, that way becomes the rule for how to complete them. Even if it is labor-intensive and there is a shorter, faster way to get it done, he will use a tried and true method. In fact, he often will strongly resist teaching methods that teach him "a new way" that is different, or heaven forbid, contradicts the original way. This becomes a hangup in subjects like spelling, reading, and math specifically at various times throughout his school experience.

Though each child often has a primary and preferred method of approaching learning, he may switch the way he approaches learning for specific subjects. He may also switch between approaches when he is stressed or when he is attempting to align his learning to a teacher's style of teaching. Knowing how a child naturally approaches learning is helpful when parents and professionals are attempting to support a child who has become stressed in a learning situation.

ANOTHER STEP INTO LEARNING STYLE FROM A SENSORY PROCESSING AND BEHAVIORAL PERSPECTIVE

Let's take the approaches to learning, learning style and sensory processing connection one step further: **It is helpful for parents and teachers to identify whether a child is flexible or rigid in his approach to learning.** Does your child naturally learn in a linear fashion by preference, but can function in a busy, cooperative learning environment in order to pull out the information he needs to be successful? If so, he's a pretty flexible learner. He may have a preference for visual or auditory or kinesthetic or musical presentation of information, but he can actively learn through a variety of presentations.

If your child quickly gets stuck when information is not presented in "the way he learns," then his style is much more rigid. I bet you already guessed it! One of the common patterns that emerges in children who have a learning disability or disorder is that they develop a very rigid style of learning, and they have trouble adapting when learning situations are not set up according to their specific style.

If that is the case with your child, I first suggest catering fully to your child's learning style and really jumping in to investigate all the details in your child's specific learning style. If your child's name happens to be Uniquely You, you are going to have to identify the **Uniquely You Method of Learning**, because it will be unique, and you may not find another child with that exact learning style. Identify and document the **Uniquely You Method of Learning,** and then find a way to share all that you know about Uniquely's learning style with any teacher or caregiver Uniquely encounters. In the tools section of this book, I share a specific method, **The Uniquely You Method of Learning**, that can be used for gathering the information on learning style and preferences.

Find out exactly what sets your child up for the most success. Indulge his full learning preference and reinforce his learning success until he is on a roll and learning really well. Next, add in a goal to very slowly introduce graded activities and opportunities that will help your child become one step more flexible. Incorporate new activities and learning gently, slowly, and one step at a time.

Before you know it, you will have maintained his learning success (he will still be on a roll). He will be on his way to becoming a more flexible learner, and he will be able to adapt a bit better when things are not set up in his exact preference. There are situations where it takes a team of people putting their heads together to set up a plan for a child, and so don't hesitate to use your resources to pull in the people you need on your team in order to develop the best plan for your child's learning success.

When you are introducing "new learning" information, it is important to intentionally teach to your child's sensory processing strengths and natural learning styles. When you are reviewing old information and forming greater depth to what your child knows, you can begin to work in a variety of ways to help increase learning flexibility.

Investigating whether your child has success in visual learning, and prefers it; auditory learning, and prefers it; kinesthetic learning, and prefers it; musical learning, and prefers it, etc. can be helpful information when you are jump-starting your child's learning progress.

In the coming chapters, you will begin to see how to directly apply your observations about how your child approaches learning and how to better set your child up for learning success by using the Learning Strengths Profile tool. When you are introducing "new learning" information, it is important to intentionally teach to your child's sensory processing strengths and natural learning styles. When you are reviewing old information and forming greater depth to what your child knows, you can begin to work in a variety of ways to help increase learning flexibility.

CHAPTER 7 DEEPER JOURNEY TO APPLICATION

The Deeper Journey portion of each chapter is set up to provide application and reflection questions or to help support group discussion regarding the information in the related chapter.

1. Does your child generally approach learning situations through a linear learning or global learning approach?

2. Think through situations where your child is struggling (especially in learning situations). Is there something about the situation that is not supporting his natural preference for learning (i.e. is the situation set up for a global learner, but he prefers linear learning or vice versa)?

What could you adapt in the situation and the way it is taught to better set him up for successful understanding?

3. In a general sense, is your child a flexible learner, where he is able to take in information no matter what approach to learning is supported in the presentation; or is he more rigid, where he not only has a preference but NEEDS the information to be presented in his preferred way?

This answer gives a parent important information. Your child may simply need you as the parent to provide information to the teacher regarding how your child has had success in learning or what structure helps support his ability to show what he knows. Or your child may need a more formal Individual Education Planning (IEP) process to help support his learning progress in the classroom. The purpose of Individual Education Planning (IEP) is to provide structured consistency for rigid learners who need more support in their ability to take in and respond to information in the classroom. Either way, discussion regarding this question can help you begin mapping out the support to set your child up for more success.

CHAPTER 8

"Interest can produce learning on a scale compared to fear
as a nuclear explosion to a firecracker."
-Stanley Kubrick

THE PAYOFF PRINCIPLE

Think about how few people choose to repeat experiences or continue to engage in activities for a long period of time that are either boring or have no natural reward? If something is boring or has no natural reward, we tend to make a new plan, change the activity so it's more rewarding to us, or stop engaging in the activity. Hard work has to pay off somehow. Many times, the payoff is that it is fun. Behavior analysts have long since described this principle as **behavioral economics**. (Catania, 2013) I think of this idea as The Payoff Principle.

There is a beautiful, small lake with about two acres of mowed grass right outside my office window. I use it to explain **The Payoff Principle** to parents this way: If I told you that I would pay you $5 to mow the lawn around the lake over your lunch hour, would you do it? Not likely. However, if I told you I would pay you $500,000 if you could change your schedule and get the lawn mowed this afternoon, I bet you would think long and hard before you said "no." Most of you would say, "Sign me up!" Why? The payoff. The payoff is the reward that makes the hard work worth it. Money doesn't mean much to children, and so what's the currency for the payoff for hard work? What's the reward? Fun.

Think about a vacation you would like to repeat, or think of any other moment that you wish to repeat. Once you've identified that moment, I bet you can either picture it or *feel* it. Why? Because your senses are activated and they influence how you feel about the experience. Your senses enhance the payoff. Your sensory experience during that experience is so strong that when you think of the activity or moment, your body can seemingly feel it, and you look forward to the reward to repeating that experience. You become motivated to feel that moment again.

Make a list of your favorite things: favorite color, favorite food, favorite indoor activities, favorite outdoor activities, favorite "active" activities, favorite sedentary activities, favorite things to do alone, favorite things to do with friends, favorite things to do out in the community, favorite adventure idea, and favorite vacation.

If you sat down and made a list, I bet there are many things that you would come up with. Most of us can end up having at least 25-50 things or more on that favorites list. Now, think of a list of favorite things in terms of quality of life, happiness and depression.

It is my experience that when a person's set of liked activities (the things that are reinforcing in life to that person) are limited, happiness and motivation begin to funnel into less satisfying, less rewarding, and less enticing extremes. When your senses are not effectively engaged, life becomes boring. Life becomes dull. I believe this contributes to and exacerbates symptoms when a child or adult is battling depression. It is also relevant when considering treatment of behavior disorders, including aggression and defiance. In fact, it is always relevant! (Kazdin, 2012) We just don't often sit and analyze what motivates and reinforces us. We often don't need to know unless something is going wrong.

Let me illustrate with two hypothetical examples. If a person had one love in life, such as watching Wheel of Fortune at 6:00 p.m. each night, that person would look forward to 6:00-6:30 p.m. every night when his favorite show was on. The rest of the 23.5 hours of the day, he would be wishing for Wheel of Fortune, dreaming of it, or simply not engaging fully in anything else.

Now, contrast Wheel of Fortune Guy with the Jake who has 50 liked activities on his list. Jake has more enjoyable activities than there are hours in one day. This means that there are some left over for tomorrow…and next week…and a few he enjoys every day. Do you see my point? Life naturally becomes more rewarding the more our repertoire of liked things expands.

If it is true in our adult lives, it is especially true for children. Children need the payoff, and they are always looking for the fun in life. I believe that we have taken the fun out of academic learning in too many situations, and as a consequence, we often see less interest and motivation to learn. The results? Less learning.

To build a love of life-long learning, we have to be paying attention to how fun and rewarding our activities are. Where is the activity payoff? We have to be paying attention to the sensory aspects of the opportunities and noting what causes the payoff for a child (and then again for ourselves). Almost any activity can become fun or rewarding if you tweak it to make it so! I always joke with my own children saying, "Vaughan kids are fun, so it doesn't matter if the job is boring or hard. We can make it fun because we bring the fun." For more information on rewards and repertoire of reinforcement, I encourage you to read Charles Catania's work on how we learn. (Catania, 2013)

CARROTS PROVIDE PAY

Let's review a bit about reward and reinforcement. A reward can be the key to making something reinforcing, and we remember from our behavioral ABC's that if something is reinforcing, we want to repeat it and we naturally engage. So, in a sense, rewards are like the **carrots** that are waiting at the end of hard work—they are part of the payoff. Just as a rabbit will work very hard to get to his carrot, your child will work very hard to get to enjoy his favorite things.

Identifying the **carrots** that can be used in a situation can be a key to unlocking cooperation and mutual enjoyment of the activity. These **carrots** give the payoff for completing the activity. Furthermore, the size of the rewarding **carrot** should match the challenge of the task. You won't

be successful in paying $5 or a high five for completing something really challenging, but you may be successful with the $500,000 equivalent of screen time (video game, computer, iPod time) to make the challenge worth attempting.

Make sure you have a basket of those enticing **carrots** readily available during challenging learning. Build your number of **carrots**, and make sure you have an inventory of options. Keep lists of your child's favorite things and activities. Ask yourself if this a medium, mild, or an "I'd do anything for this!" brand of **carrot**. Openly and routinely ask your children about their favorite things, observe what your child enjoys, and record your observations.

Another way to explain reward and reinforcement is to expand on a concept I like from Eric Jensen's book, **Teaching with the Brain in Mind**. He writes:

> *Mind and emotions are not separate; emotions, thinking and learning are all linked. What we feel is what's real—even if only to us and no one else. Emotions organize and create our reality. (Jensen, 2005)*

Emotions create the passion we have for a subject and our desire to learn all about it. The passion that we feel for a subject influences how much attention we will give to learning about it. Many of you have children who are able to apply themselves well to learning about all the levels of a computer or video game. Your child can remember the names of numerous characters, the specific details related to each of them and can problem solve how to creatively apply them into play. That is learning!

Our challenge is to connect a child's interests and passions to the learning that is a priority to us. If learning is not naturally a priority to your child, he is not naturally seeing the relevance of the information presented to him. What he sees is that the learning you are asking him to do interrupts the time he would like to be spending on something else. It is when those two worlds collide, and his passionate interest is paired with the priorities you have for him in learning, that it becomes a **win-win situation**. By linking learning activities to things that are interesting and fun and then expanding on them, you naturally support your child's motivation to learn and apply what he has learned. That results in meaningful learning.

You will want to know the things your child is passionate about so you can hook him into learning. You will want to regularly take inventory of his preferences and passions. Expect your child's favorite things to change some over time. Just like you don't like to eat the same dessert every day, your child may not like the same reward every day. Having it every day may naturally decrease its appeal. Also, expect to strategically monitor special favorite things. For example, if the Nintendo DS is not an available option throughout the day to play with, but **is** available as a reward for hard work completed, then it is more enticing. If you tell me that I can read my favorite book if I clean the dishes, but I know I can skip cleaning the dishes and still go read my favorite book...suddenly, I'm not too worried about whether the dishes get done because I get to read my book either way today.

It is my belief that if we spend time identifying and building a repertoire of liked things (for a child or for ourselves), we are not only providing the **carrots** to encourage hard work, but we are building toward a happier, more productive future. We are also proactively combating symptoms of anxiety and depression! It's a **win-win strategy**.

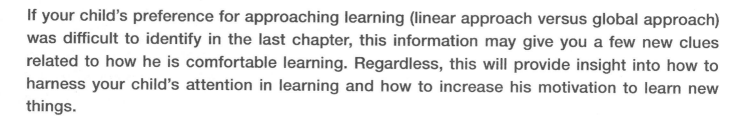

After you have completed the list of your child's current favorite things, look for the sensory pattern. What makes your child's eyes light up? Are many of the experiences that you have identified visual in nature? Auditory? Movement oriented? Touch oriented? Does the pattern show that your child currently chooses multi-sensory activities or one type of specific sensory input at a time in a structured way?

If your child's preference for approaching learning (linear approach versus global approach) was difficult to identify in the last chapter, this information may give you a few new clues related to how he is comfortable learning. Regardless, this will provide insight into how to harness your child's attention in learning and how to increase his motivation to learn new things.

Some of you may be saying. "WAIT! My child only has three to five things on the list! What do I do?" For example, let's say a child has five favorite things: 1) Chicken nuggets 2) Running around the house 3) Holding and snuggling a favorite blanket 4) Screen time and 5) Riding his bike. Even worse, the child who can identify that he likes to watch TV, play Minecraft on the computer, and play LEGO Star Wars on the Wii, and, that's all he enjoys? The problem is all "screen time" is ONE category and counts as ONE activity. He's basically stuck with screen time as his only highly reinforcing activity. You will likely see behavior and attitude issues crop up. He's at risk for regression, difficulty with attitude and attention. Regardless of what that one thing is, the priority is going to be expanding his repertoire of liked activities to find more FUN for him.

If you have a limited repertoire of liked things, you also have a limited repertoire of reinforcement that supports engagement in new kinds of learning. There's a very small reward at the end of any challenging work when there's only one kind of carrot. Your child will either become obsessive about his **carrot** because it is the only thing he has to look forward to, or he will become disengaged and passive, because he ends up with the same predictable **carrot** at the end of the hard stuff as he does at the end of the easy stuff. Why work at anything hard in that case? Reinforcers can lose their effectiveness. (Catania, 2013) A limited repertoire of liked things can set the stage for your child's learning pattern to stall out or even regress. It's simply not enough reward or fun.

A child's repertoire of liked things can also be directly linked to a child's measure of happiness and quality of life. In children who demonstrate symptoms of depression and anxiety, it is vital to spend time looking at their repertoire of **carrots** and how they can be supported in order to grow, both in number and quality.

Remember Jake, who has more than 50 things he can name that he loves to do? Some he is passionate about, some he enjoys, and some are ok but usually pretty fun. Jake has opportunity for things in his life to register on his "happiness meter" throughout his day. He has over 50 options for fun activity in a 24 hour day. Life can start looking pretty great because some of those great things get to roll into tomorrow too! Jake tends to look forward to tomorrow and the fun things that will happen. When you make a goal to increase the number of things a child chooses, expresses enjoying, requests, or indicates that he is looking forward to doing, you have just focused on increasing his quality of life.

Do you see the connection? Those of us who have many things that we enjoy on a regular basis are likely to be living lives that are rewarding, satisfying, successful, and fulfilling. Those of us who have difficulty identifying favorite leisure and liked activities also have low rates of enjoyment in life.

Recently, I was meeting with two teachers about a student who was struggling and disengaged in one class and thriving and engaged in another class. The first teacher described the student as anxious, fragile, disengaged, controlling, and challenging. The second teacher described the student as an active learner, cooperative, independent, self-confident, and doing well in class.

After an hour or more of discussion where the two teachers continued to describe very different experiences with this child, I asked the first teacher to name five things that make this student's eyes light up related to learning. She responded that he likes to learn, but couldn't name anything that make his eyes light up. I turned to the second teacher and asked her to name five things that make his eyes light up related to learning. She named ten and could clearly keep going if needed. I looked at both teachers and explained that their answers to that question were the core reason why the student was thriving in one environment and sinking in the other.

EXPANDING FAVORITE THINGS

The goal is to expand his list of favorite things. You need to expand his repertoire of favorite things in order to make progress in other areas.

- First, note the pattern you see, such as: He likes movement.
- Then, provide structured movement opportunities, such as linear swinging (not twirling yet), riding a scooter, taking a walk or jogging together, jumping on a trampoline followed by hugs inside his favorite blanket, hugs given by him to his favorite blanket, hopscotch, jumping over fun obstacles, etc.
- Track which opportunities he enjoys and then add them to the list. Notice if he likes snuggling, which is a touch/ texture activity.
- Introduce a few texture activities in non-threatening or overwhelming ways. (There is a handout in the Tools section of this book where you can walk through introducing textures into the day).
- Continue to expand the list of things he enjoys until you have at least 10 or more things on the list. Then you can begin some work, because now you have some **carrots** to offer.

CREATING A WIN-WIN SITUATION

Annie came to see me when she was about 9 years old. She was in the 3rd grade (regular classroom with no special supports) and struggling to read. She had been tested for support services and didn't qualify, and yet her mother knew that she was not learning effectively in the classroom. She saw Annie overtly struggling with most reading activities. Annie was also struggling with auditory processing and fine motor/ handwriting skill development. She was struggling throughout the school day and exhausted when she got home, yet she had hours of after-school work because she was not able to get all her work completed during the school day. She was developing self-talk that questioned whether school was her thing and whether she was smart. She was churning academically, not making enough forward progress. She was "stuck," and even had trouble showing what she already knew in class.

When Annie's family came to me, I first had her sit down with her mom and make a list of favorites before her first visit with me. Here is her list:

> Activities
> horse riding
> playing with Jingle
> cooking
> art / crafts
> crochet / knit
> writing
> friends
> dancing
>
> color - purple
> books - Am. Girls
>   Series of Unfortunate Events
> foods - hot / spicy
>   sour candy

After identifying her specific sensory and motor strengths and barriers, we made a plan. We started with the foundational motor (core strengthening) work, using the tools that I will give you in the last section of this book. She engaged daily in tummy time activities where she looked at craft activities she might want to try, or looked at books with pictures of girls riding horses. She completed midline crossing activities daily where she would lay across her wooden coffee table, bearing weight through her arms on the floor prone on hands (a graduated step up from tummy time and working toward dynamic hands and knees balance skills and positioning), sorting pictures or matching school work by reaching across the middle of her body to get the piece that she needed. She worked daily in texture with theraputty, clay or play dough. She would hide coins in the play dough and then work to quickly find the coins, sort them, and count them.

In essence we tied the school work she needed to do into strategic sensory presentation and activity to make it hands on learning, functional and FUN. That's Occupational Therapy! and she was making progress.

But, then I needed her to do eye exercises. If you have ever done or needed to do eye exercises, you know they are boring, but sometimes very necessary. When therapists prescribe them, we are HOPING that a child can be coerced to complete them once or twice per day. Those exercises can feel like torture. They are hard work!

I looked through her list of favorites again and realized that one of the things on her list was her bird, Jingle. She loved that bird, and so I asked her to expand her play routine with her bird Jingle. Thinking that she played with Jingle once or twice per day, I assumed I would get my 1-2 exercises included in her daily repertoire. I asked her to sit Jingle on her finger and then extend her arm away from her, while making eye contact with Jingle and watch Jingle as she moved her arm to her right, to her left, up, down, and then in a slow circle when she played with Jingle each day. I asked her to continue to watch Jingle as she brought Jingle in for a sweet air kiss, and then, play with Jingle like she normally would.

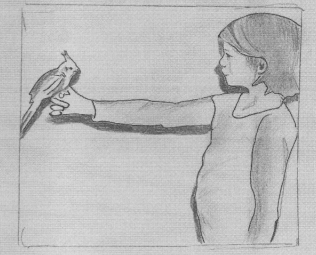

Due to circumstances, I didn't see her for about 3 weeks. When I saw her next I was absolutely amazed. She had made the equivalent of at least 12 weeks of visual processing and visual perception work in 3 weeks. I was truly amazed.

When I asked her, "WHAT have you been doing, girl? This is amazing!" Smiling she said, "I just played with Jingle." Investigating, I discovered that she played with Jingle several times per day by taking her out of the cage, and once she learned to do the eye exercises as a routine when taking Jingle out of the cage, it became natural and she enjoyed the game with her bird. The bird enjoyed the movement and the game too, and so it became a **win-win strategy**. It became reinforcing and fun to do those hard eye exercises...so she did them...often, and she made incredible progress!

Knowing about her love of her bird changed everything, because I could tap into that love and connect it to some of the developmental work she needed to do to jump-start progress. It gave us the opportunity to influence her visual processing progress and her ability to use her eyes in coordination during visual learning.

I was excited last year to cheer for her as she graduated with honors from high school, and chose which **college** to attend! There was a time in 3rd grade when college attendance wasn't a given for her. There was a time when her future was overshadowed by her struggle in the classroom. Now, the future looks pretty bright for sweet Annie, thanks to her hard work and her family's diligent support.

Through Annie's experience, we learned a lot about how Annie learns effectively and efficiently. We studied her sensory processing strengths, her strengths in learning, and we worked on a plan to support her developmental progress.

Annie learned a lot about herself during this time. She began learning how she learns best. She began to identify what she needs to do to help herself when she is struggling to learn something new, how to creatively take new concepts and make them hands-on learning experiences, and how to ask for help when she needs it.

Her hard work and her parents' investment of time, including a season of focused attention on her progress, is still paying off many years later. I know they would tell you learning the information and applying it is worth the effort! May you find the Jingle in your child's life!

CHAPTER 8 DEEPER JOURNEY TO APPLICATION

The Deeper Journey portion of each chapter is set up to provide application and reflection questions or to help support group discussion regarding the information in the related chapter.

1. Start your child's list of favorite things today. Take out a sheet of paper. Make categories and be sure to include:

- Favorite color
- Favorite indoor activity or rainy day activity
- Favorite outdoor activity or outdoor place
- Favorite day trips
- Favorite foods or favorite places to eat (i.e. back porch, picnic, restaurant, etc.)
- Favorite active activities
- Favorite quiet or sedentary activities
- Favorite technology or screen time activities
- Favorite things to do alone
- Favorite things to do with family or friends
- Favorite vacation activities
- Favorite community activities (i.e. swimming)
- Favorite music or favorite things to listen to
- Favorite clothing
- Favorite things to touch
- Favorite things to smell cooking or favorite smells
- Favorite ways to tell you about something important (i.e. writing, drawing, telling, etc.)

Make sure you regularly update your child's list of favorites!

2. How do you think knowing about your child's favorite things can become a key factor in increasing your child's success?

3. Describe one specific situation where you can take one of your child's favorite things and turn it into a carrot that motivates your child in a positive way?

CHAPTER 9

"Every person is gifted, every person is average,
and every person is challenged—not one or the other, but all three."
- Dr. Todd Schaible, CEO of Burrell Behavioral Health

SENSORY PROCESSING STRENGTHS AND BARRIERS

I strongly believe in strengths-based assessment and intervention. The goal of strengths-based assessment is to investigate and find the very best about an individual, his gift to give to the world. Strengths-based intervention capitalizes on identifying gifts, encouraging growth and development of those gifts so that they can be used regularly. I believe a strengths-based perspective reorients a discussion to the positive. It allows quicker movement into a positive framework and practical progress, as opposed to over-focusing on what is going "wrong."

In the book, <u>Strengths Based Leadership</u>, Tom Rath and Barry Conchie write: "If you focus on people's weakness, **they lose confidence.**" (emphasis is mine) Think about that insight in contrast to our existing systems where we must highlight deficit and weakness to establish a pattern of disability for diagnosis. It can be challenging for parents and professionals to be strengths-based in a system designed to identify deficits.

I see too many individuals become defined by their diagnosis and disability.
For better or worse, this system has influenced us. From parents, to teachers, to health care and mental health professionals, many of us have become accomplished at identifying symptoms and watching for them in children. Many have just enough knowledge to identify and misinterpret some of the symptoms they see. In turn, this can lead to mischaracterization of a child, a skewed perception of what is going on with a child, and a natural shift in focus to what is going **wrong** (even if there is a lot going **right**).

The positive side of the increased awareness of symptoms that has developed in the last 20 years is that more and more children are connected into service to help support their growth and development. That is a really good thing! Identifying a diagnostic path for some children is a positive game changer where professionals and teachers can wrap around a child and provide positive supports that help encapsulate weakness in order to allow strengths to again shine. Within each diagnosis, there is strength to be found, and it is imperative to find those strengths!

Let's look at why the system is set up to identify weakness.

One purpose of identifying deficits is that there is money set aside to aid those that struggle significantly more than their peers. We can only measure whether an individual is struggling more than his peers by measuring him against his peers and identifying whether his struggle is significant enough to need access to the specialized services and support available.

Another purpose of identifying deficits is so that caregivers and professionals can use the information to restructure and set a learning situation up for greater success. **The challenge is to identify the deficits as needed to navigate the diagnostic process and pass through eligibility gates, and then to make a purposeful turn toward a strengths-based perspective.** At that point, the deficit finding has served its purpose, and services can now be accessed. **It is essential to make the switch from a deficit focus to a strengths perspective.** It's not easy to make that shift for either parents or professionals, and so it has to be purposeful.

STRENGTHS-BASED PERSPECTIVE

In Strengths Based Leadership, Tom Rath and Barry Conchie identify that employees of organizations that are not naturally strengths-based have a 9% chance of being highly engaged at work. In contrast, employees of organizations focused on strengths have a 73% chance of being engaged at work. Rath and Conchie describe a study initiated in 1979 by University of Florida's Tim Judge and Charlice Hurst. Judge and Hurst studied self-evaluations of 7,660 men and women, following them for 25 years. The men and women with high self-confidence in 1979 started in the workforce making more money than their counterparts with lower self-confidence, making an average of $3,496 more per year. Furthermore, 25 years later, the group with higher self-confidence was making an average of $12,821 more annually!

The research found that not only were income levels affected, but health was also affected. The lower self-confidence group reported three times as many health problems 25 years later, contrasted with the higher self-confidence group, which reported fewer health problems than 25 years prior. That amazing research shows that those who are given the opportunity to identify their strengths in learning and performance are more likely to have increased job satisfaction, confidence, income levels, health and general quality of life. (Rath & Conchie, 2008)

The results of this research have far reaching application in my opinion. One way I apply it to the work that I do is to realize that regardless of an individual's level of function, regardless of his struggle, regardless of his labeled disability, professionals (and parents) must be the tour guides to helping him find his strengths!

WHEN STRUGGLE BECOMES DISABILITY

When speaking to a group of professionals I will often read a poem by Emily Perl Kingsley, Welcome to Holland. This poem describes what it is like to be a parent of a child with a disability. Kingsley explains that it is like going on a trip to Italy, but landing in Holland.

She builds anticipation for a trip to Italy as a life-long dream and then describes the disorienting experience of landing in a completely different place. Holland is a place with a new language to learn, new guide books to buy and a set of new people that you never would have met if you had traveled to Italy. Her point: though most of us dreamed of "normal" as we jotted down our Life Plan that included children, there can be blessing even when that plan is disrupted by abnormal and atypical.

My favorite part of the poem is finding highlights of Holland: "Holland has tulips. Holland has windmills, and Holland even has Rembrandts." For any parent, one with a child with a disability or not, when you compare your child to the stories of the children around you, you will be able to find where your child falls short. You may encounter times when you are jealous of the mom who can say that her child excels in a specific area. That is sometimes very painful, especially if we choose to dwell there. Instead, I highly recommend purposefully shifting back to what is best about your child, the gift that your child has to offer. Find it. Dwell on it. Help support and expand it, for that shift in perspective can be the game changer in your child's life.

Families who have just landed in Holland are often overwhelmed with all the difference and the deficits in this "new world" compared to everyone else's Italy. They must learn a whole new language full of the most complex and difficult words! Our professional language can be an intimidating barrier to actual service and progress! Families will also learn from guide books (like this one), and they will meet new people they never would have met. Professionals have the great opportunity to be the tour guides in this new place. We have the privilege of linking arms with parents to highlight the tulips, the windmills, and the Rembrandts living in their homes.

EVERYONE IS SPECIAL

I believe that all children, if given opportunity and support, can emerge as the uniquely gifted people that they were meant to be. When their needs are met and their development is supported, they are enabled to fully develop their personal gifts. I have been privileged to work on a strengths development team with a group of great minds in the psychology field. Dr. Todd Schaible, CEO of Burrell Behavioral Health in Springfield, Missouri, leads this team. I agree with him when he says, *"Every child is gifted, every child is average and every child is challenged—not one or the other, but all three."*

We often find that children are identified as either gifted, average, or challenged, but it would change the way we approach teaching children if we realized the truth that each child is actually all three—gifted, average, and challenged, regardless of IQ, functional performance skills, or diagnosis.

Another one of the psychologists on the team, Dr. Paul Thomlinson says, *"There is nothing wrong with a child that what's right with him can't fix."* Children's brains are incredibly resilient, the connections are forming and reforming, routing and rerouting. Sometimes children's accomplishments will astound and amaze, often putting theories of "potential" to shame.

I recognize that we live and work in a world where deficits are clearly defined in order to obtain support and services for individuals who are struggling. In addition, I agree with identifying specific deficits of individuals who are struggling so that they get the needed support to succeed. I am well acquainted with that system as I advocate for services for the children I see. However, in that system, a child's unique strengths and gifts often remain in the shadows, under-recognized, under-utilized, and under-developed.

I am passionate about tools that accelerate brain-based learning, setting a child up to discover what's **best** about him. I believe in learning about how our brains are designed to learn so that we teach progressively. Brain-based teaching is helpful to every child, but it is essential to those who are experiencing atypical sensory processing.

A CHILD IS NOT SOMETHING TO BE "FIXED"

The goal in passionately pursuing treatment and support for children that are developmentally delayed is not about "fixing" them. The goal is to support a child in learning so that he blossoms into the unique individual he is designed to be. We investigate how to support the development of the gift he has to give the world. He has a gift to give. He has a lesson to teach us if we engage and "listen" for it.

All children are special, and I want each child to receive individual attention to support individual growth, as well as to discover their own personal, relational, and learning style strengths. I am excited to see professionals continuing to develop various tools to help all the children we love to apply information practically in play situations, learning situations, and in personal relationships. If we continue to develop and think "out of the box," I'm looking forward to a time that we are able to teach each child in the way that he learns. I hope I'm around when we reach that day.

GIFTED AND TALENTED

One of the obstacles with recognizing the value of Dr. Schaible's quote (*"Every child is gifted, every child is average and every child is challenged—not one or the other, but all three"*) is that children who are identified as "gifted," meaning that they have tested in the upper percentages of the population regarding IQ measure, need to be identified and supported in our schools just as much as a child struggling with a learning disability.

Years ago, I was fairly casual about the "gifted and talented" label. Our family shied away from labels. We didn't like the idea of being "set apart." We were in private school at the time and weren't seeking out supports. Once we moved from private school into public school, we became well acquainted with the benefits of being identified as needing special supports.

When most people, especially teachers, look at a child who is struggling significantly with learning difficulty, the natural response is to get those students into more appropriate learning situations. We wouldn't dream of looking at a child struggling with intellectual disability and say, "We will provide you one day of teaching per week that is tailored to your understanding, the way your brain absorbs information, but we need you to tough it out on the other four days per week. Good luck."

We intuitively know that children who struggle to learn must have accommodation, resource, and supports in place daily to thrive. Likewise, those children who are wired to think differently and form connections very quickly, to generalize information and sometimes over-generalize information need daily supports also.

Children who get so absorbed in thinking that they often struggle with organizing their thoughts, filtering their thoughts, and communicating their thoughts, need specialized curriculum and instruction. I have had many mothers tell me that they fought much harder for their high IQ child to be placed in appropriate math instruction than they did for their child with a speech delay to have access to speech therapy.

One of the problems with the label "gifted and talented" is that it misrepresents the struggle that many of the high IQ children that I know face every day. That label assumes that life is easier and that the learner must be naturally more flexible in learning than others when, in fact, it does not feel like a gift at times. Some of our most rigid learners actually have a very high IQ and special needs in the classroom. Just as the professional community recognized that "intellectually challenged" was a better label than "mental retardation," there may be a more appropriate label for our "gifted and talented" population.

PURPOSE DRIVEN "WORK"

Key to the philosophy of supporting children to blossom into their uniqueness is recognizing that every child is created for a purpose and has a gift to give. **We are designed to be naturally purposeful.** I don't care as much about a child's IQ or skill-based achievements as I do about helping him discover his gift to give. Too often, we forget that everyone is unique. We forget that the goal is not to be typical. The goal is not to be "normal." The goal is to be thriving and uniquely **YOU**.

HAVE YOU THOUGHT ABOUT WHAT YOUR CHILD BRINGS TO YOUR FAMILY?

One awesome mom that I have worked with has a physically and cognitively disabled little girl whose personal strengths are her emotional skills. She has two older brothers. The family schedule is often built around this little girl's therapy sessions. Like any family who works to support one with significant delays, life can easily become about therapy, not about quality family time.

One day, as we were delighting in the new baby steps of motor development this young lady was making in therapy, our discussion shifted to her roles in the family. As we talked, I could see that one of the gifts she brought to her family was encouragement. Her mother would describe how her eyes lit up at sporting events as the crowd cheered for her brothers.

Over the next month, we worked to develop her love of encouraging her brothers, clapping her hands, jingling bells to cheer, and getting to wear "spirit wear" that matched their team jerseys. It had already been a role she was playing in the family, but it was amazing how rewarding and positive it was in the dynamics of the family when she was supported to develop her gifts more fully. Her delight grew when she was given the tools to do more with her gift.

Therapeutic focus and intensity are essential at times to help drive self-help skills forward and to improve functional performance. However, if your child is in therapy, I encourage using what you learn in therapy to support holistic development and living fully, not just for skill-based performance. After all, the goal is not to re-qualify and remain in more therapy.

The goal is to get out and live life to the fullest, making authentic connections and using acquired skills to the best of one's ability. That can only happen when families partner fully with therapists to absorb the professional's knowledge about their child and add it to their own expertise. This doesn't happen well if you are not purposefully involved in gathering that information.

If you don't know what your child is working on in therapy and why, then you don't yet know enough. Find out. Most therapists are excited to answer questions about how what they are working on applies to life outside the therapy session. Part of their job is to share functional tidbits about what you can be doing at home to support and accelerate progress. Push for that information, ask questions, and clarify information until you have a practical working knowledge of all things related to your child.

INSPIRING THE JOY OF LEARNING

Norman Vincent Peale said:

> *Become a possibilitarian. No matter how dark things seem to be or actually are, raise your sights to see possibilities—always see them, for they're always there.*

I encourage you to adopt this perspective and hone detective skills in identifying your child's strengths. Make your observations more focused on strength than weakness, especially once you've outlined where you need to most support your child. Take some time to dwell in the land of what's best about him—it will naturally increase the possibilities you see for him.

HIGHLIGHT THE STRENGTH BUT RECOGNIZE THE BARRIER

Defining a child's progress from a strengths-based perspective and utilizing the tools in this book to support a child in development is helpful for any child. However, it is especially helpful when you are raising a child with a disability.

A **Strengths Profile** is the compilation of the strengths information identified in a strengths-based assessment. (Character, 2011) (Roth, 2007) The mission of a **Strengths Profile** focuses on identifying and capitalizing on a child's strengths while recognizing, but encapsulating, barriers in order to best support individuals to become all they can be. Though there are some psychology tests that lend themselves to strengths-based identification, I am not currently aware of a specific test that a professional will use to gather this information about your child. It is primarily a stylistic focus in the way that a professional writes up or presents the information about your child that reflects his own strength-based perspective.

Traditional methods of support and intervention actively respond to identified barriers, ensuring that the barriers are effectively addressed. However, without the strength-based focus for balance, the identified barriers begin to overshadow the individual's strengths in learning, and the balance is lost.

Ancillary wrap-around services, where a team of multiple professionals work together to support a child functionally at home and school, are needed for children who are significantly struggling. Recognizing realistic barriers to learning and relational interaction is the practical balance to focusing on a child's strengths. Supporting identified barriers and highlighting identified strengths are both required for balance.

We all encounter situations that are bigger than our ability to handle well. Whether they are academic and work-related or social and relationship-related, they do not bring out our best. I am finding that those are sometimes the most important times to purposefully refocus on strengths. I hope you have met a child who has a positive learning perspective, one that helps us to prioritize strengths and not be bound by weaknesses, making supportive plans to work on them, without allowing those weaknesses to overshadow the strengths present within the same child. I do this for all four of my children because they all have areas where they shine and areas where they have challenge. All of my children have unique learning styles, strengths and challenges, and together they make life interesting.

I am intrigued by how much one's perspective on a situation influences the actual situation. Our perceptions about ability and disability shape how we respond to children in different situations. Our perceptions about advantages and disadvantages also shape how we relate to others. Malcolm Gladwell's books, <u>David and Goliath: Underdogs, Misfits and The Art of Battling Giants</u> and <u>Outliers: The Story of Success,</u> (Gladwell, 2013) (Gladwell, 2011) are a couple I recommend. He challenges our societal perceptions of disability, coping, discrimination, and success.

There is strength in difference. Different perspectives are valuable in cooperative learning. For children preparing for cooperative learning, teaching an appreciation for learning differences and the positive balance those differences bring to the group is valuable. After all, most of us want to be a magnet for teaming and balance in a group, no matter which classroom of life we enter.

FOUNDATIONAL PRINCIPLES OF LEARNING

I have scribbled a collection of principles of learning on scraps of paper gathered over the past 15+ years. They have come to collectively represent my philosophy of learning. I keep these in front of me to remind me of what I believe about learning when I attempt to teach new skills to children or adults. These are the learning principles that I personally review before attempting to implement a new strategy with my own children or the children I work with:

1. Learning is developmental. Early learning foundations form the basis for future learning and understanding. Strong foundations set the stage for accelerated and consummate learning.
2. Learning involves the whole mind and body. Whole brain learning involves the best of both neuroscience and kinesthetic learning.

3. The best learning techniques make sense from a developmental, medical, educational, and psychological perspective.

4. Facilitating whole brain learning is purposeful. Traditional methods of learning target either language, logic, and sequence; or they target forms and patterns, rhythm, space and imagination, but not often both. Current brain research shows how much more effective whole brain learning techniques are in facilitating well-rounded learning, generalization, and skill development. Whole brain learning techniques create opportunities for the left and right brain to connect together in learning, creating a *learning loop: see it, say it, hear it, do it/write it.*

5. In today's world, *what* students learn can become outdated. But *how* to learn is a skill that will last a lifetime. Focus as much on **how** as **what**.

6. Teach children how to think for themselves and make decisions, not just blindly obey and follow others.

7. Effective learning is relevant, not just facts to be absorbed or memorized. Learning happens when new knowledge or skill is integrated into existing knowledge. Learning is an active creation of new meanings, new neural connection and networks, and new patterns of electro/chemical interactions within a child's brain and body.

8. Learning at its best is interactive and social. Collaborative and cooperative learning is highly valuable in our world. A community of learners engaging in a collective learning adventure is better than talented, but isolated, individuals who lack the ability to engage in community process.

9. Learning takes place on many levels simultaneously. Students who know how they learn best will be more confident in exploring and integrating new information than students who lack insight about how they learn. Students who have opportunities to engage in enriched, multi-sensory learning will develop into more flexible learners.

10. Positive emotions improve learning and comprehension. Feelings determine the quality and, often the quantity, of a student's learning. Negative feelings inhibit learning. Positive feelings accelerate learning. Students do not assimilate new information readily when they are in a state of stress.

CHAPTER 9 DEEPER JOURNEY TO APPLICATION

The Deeper Journey portion of each chapter is set up to provide application and reflection questions or to help support group discussion regarding the information in the related chapter.

1. Describe the personal strengths of your child:

2. Describe the areas where your child is rocking along and doing well, not his personal strength areas that stand out, but also not where he is struggling....the areas where he is "fine."

3. Describe the situations where your child is currently floundering or struggling to succeed:

THE LEARNING STRENGTHS PROFILE

SECTION 3

CHAPTER 10

*"We are each gifted in a unique and important way.
It is our privilege and our adventure to discover
our own special light."*
-Mary Dunbar

INTRODUCING THE LEARNING STRENGTHS PROFILE

I have developed a tool, **The Learning Strengths Profile***, designed to give an overall perspective about a child's approach to learning from a sensory processing perspective. This tool looks at how a child naturally approaches learning and how he best takes in information to use it for learning. It helps identify which ways of taking in information are working for a child and which ways are working against him.

This tool does not replace other formal tools that are used to identify barriers, functional skill performance, or areas of concern. However, it gives a global profile that can be used to probe strengths-based approaches to learning. The Learning Strengths Profile tool can be used by a parent, teacher, or professional as a quick overview tool and does not require any certification or licensure for use. It has been helpful in my practice with parents, schools, and the network of professionals that I work with. I share it with the hope that it proves helpful with the children in your life.

THE GOAL

The goal of the Learning Strengths Profile is to aid parents and professionals in facilitating a discussion about a child's unique approaches to learning, to identify where the child's strengths lie and where they are bumping up against barriers that are affecting their performance. I will explain how you can use the collected information to increase social engagement based on sensory processing strengths that you find in a child's profile. I will also explain how to harness a child's motivation as a catalyst for learning when he seems "stuck." For children who are struggling with memory retention and generalization skills, I will also cover how this information can be incorporated into supporting memory and generalization of information. The Learning Strengths Profile is a flexible tool that can be used to identify patterns of learning that are positive and strengths-based. Strength areas identify a child's most effective

*You will find The Learning Strengths Profile at the end of this chapter and also in the Tools Section of this book.

that are positive and strengths-based. Strength areas identify a child's most effective approaches to learning. It is designed to quickly identify strength areas that can be used when introducing new learning concepts or new social experiences. It also quickly identifies or confirms barrier areas to be avoided in new learning situations. It can also be used to confirm patterns of dysfunctional learning in order to support, teach, and adapt learning situations for better performance and success.

Parents, caregivers or teachers will rate a child on his general performance in a given area. A pattern of strengths and barriers will then begin to emerge. The left columns will begin to identify strength areas. These strength areas should be utilized to support new learning (introduction to new material), expand social interaction, and highlight strengths-based performance. To increase a child's accuracy in learning new material, parents and teachers should build instruction around the identified learning strength areas. To increase a child's motivation (natural reinforcement) for learning, parents and teachers should build learning experiences around the identified strength areas.

Remember *The Cell Phone Reception Principle* in Chapter 4? It is important to identify how a child is best receiving information and to identify whether the child is primarily receiving good information through one sense system or a combination of sense systems. By knowing this information, we can better outline how to reach the child more effectively, because it becomes clear where to start.

Barrier areas will be identified in the columns on the right. Barrier areas identify learning areas that need support or treatment attention. Identified barrier areas indicate that the child is not processing that type of learning effectively and efficiently for new learning purposes and, therefore, should not be used as a primary method of introducing new learning material.

Once a child is experiencing success using strength-based areas, additional areas (including barrier areas) can be introduced to help increase a student's generalization of skills. Barrier areas should be incorporated when reviewing information that is already understood. Expanded practice of a concept using multiple senses is a great way to support generalization skills in the classroom, but is not always an effective way to present new concepts and information.

By identifying the barrier areas, patterns of poor fits between instruction and reception become increasingly clear. For example, if a teacher is giving instructions verbally most of the time and a child has a barrier in the area of auditory learning, it becomes much more clear why that child is struggling to perform in that situation. It has been my experience that many problem behavior situations become much more clear and predictable when a child's learning strengths and barriers are analyzed alongside the behaviors that are occurring. You will remember the importance of identifying the function of behavior discussed in Chapter 3. Analyzing **The Learning Strengths Profile** information alongside behavior specifics can often help you begin to identify the function of that behavior.

The **Learning Strengths Profile** is designed to reflect the general skill levels of children from ages five or six through adolescence (school-aged children). The ***Primary* Learning Strengths Profile** is designed for children who are earlier learners and demonstrate a developmental performance level of 12 months through 6 years.

For typically developing children, using their chronological age will help you identify which profile will be most helpful. However, for children who have experienced significant developmental delays, it is most helpful to look at the approximate developmental performance level (is the child functioning with skills above or below kindergarten levels?) to help determine which profile will be most helpful.

The primary profile will be used for cataloging responses at an earlier performance level than the regular profile. The regular profile is based on the assumption that there is a certain level of academic performance skill. If the regular **Learning Strengths Profile** is used and a student scores only in barrier areas, with no identified strengths, the ***Primary* Learning Strengths Profile** will be the better tool to use with that child to identify strength areas of performance.

There have been rare cases when a very bright and academically capable student has scored with only barriers identified and no emergent identified strengths. In those cases, the profile has been more reflective of the deficit-focused perspective of those completing the form, combined with their level of frustration, rather than a true reflection of the child's abilities. In those cases, it is beneficial to expand the team of people wrapping around the child and to include more objective data, highlighting a child's strengths and barriers with standardized testing supports in order to begin to have a more accurate profile emerge.

The Learning Strengths Profile is able to profile skills for both typically and atypically developing children. One thing I like most about The Learning Strengths Profile is that when you put a typically developing child's profile next to an atypically developing child's profile, you can't necessarily tell them apart, because the tool is based on the belief that we are all unique.

The process of filling out The Learning Strengths Profile will often be enlightening to parents and teachers who realize that they have not presented enough opportunities for different kinds of learning. If a parent or teacher reads the three different levels of performance and doesn't know which fits the child, it's time to investigate. In those situations, it pays off for the team to take a few weeks to explore learning in the different areas with a child and track his response. Once information is presented in a variety of ways, the child's unique style often becomes more apparent.

There are times when a parent or teacher will get stuck filling out the profile because a child responds one way on a "good" day and another way on a "bad" day. In that case, mark both the good day and the bad day. Mark all boxes that apply. The resulting profile will show you the consistency and predictability with which your child performs. Some children are very consistent in each area, and there is one pattern that describes them. Others are very inconsistent and their performance can fluctuate significantly from day to day. This information is also helpful as parents and teachers plan for success.

If a student emerges with a profile that reflects fluctuating consistency and predictability, it often indicates a more rigid learning profile, where the student needs material presented in specific ways in order to generate a positive response. Other times, the profile indicates that there are behaviors directed toward the teacher or parent filling out the profile that are masking the child's learning profile (usually oppositional or defiant behavior patterns).

By having two or more adults interact with the child and fill out the profile, it becomes apparent which scenario applies. If the first scenario applies (where the student has a rigid learning profile), interaction with multiple adults will help to further define the specifics of where the child thrives and where the child struggles with learning presentation. If the second scenario applies (where the student has specific behavior patterns built around interaction with specific individuals), interaction with multiple adults will help to further identify those patterns, as well as true strengths and barriers that can be applied to help alleviate stressful interactions related to learning presentation.

The Learning Strengths Profile doesn't compare a child's performance to peers. It is not designed to compare a student's performance to another student's. It is neither a standardized test nor comparative measure. For that reason, it works well in atypical situations. It is a tool that doesn't require a diagnosis, or even "clinical" symptoms, to be helpful. Parents and teachers can utilize it independently or in collaboration with a therapist.

The Learning Strengths Profile tool focuses on learning from a sensory processing perspective, which gives vital information about how a child takes in information to learn it. When combined with traditional measurements of learning, the synergy of information becomes dynamic and rich and begins to yield insight into how to enhance a child's success and support his challenges.

TARGETED APPROACHES TO LEARNING

The Learning Strengths Profile highlights a child's skill in the following targeted areas related to how he learns and how he approaches learning.

MOTOR IMITATION

Motor imitation is the ability to accurately or functionally copy a motor movement or position. This skill is important to observe and then rate, because it is used as a primary method of teaching in almost every learning situation. A child who shows strength in motor imitation is able to watch and learn well. He will benefit from being **shown** how to complete a task. He is often a "hands on learner."

You need to know whether motor imitation skill is a strength or a barrier for your child. The Learning Strengths Profile quickly identifies if motor imitation is a first intervention priority or a strength area in learning. If imitation is hard for your child, learning is sometimes excruciatingly hard for your child. If this is a barrier area, it is a first intervention priority.

TOUCH LEARNING

Touch learning is the ability to register and discriminate incoming sensory information through the skin and respond appropriately or functionally. A child with touch learning strengths is a hands-on learner who processes touch information well.

Touch learning is an area where a few strong preferences can overshadow a child's love of "doing," pointing directly to both an encapsulated barrier and a learning strength reflected in one specific area of sensory processing. Accurately applying what we learn through touch processing can make or break social and hands-on learning opportunities.

Using this tool to identify specific strength and barrier information can make the difference in whether a child is actively engaging and completing tasks or whether he is subtly avoiding learning situations in the classroom. It will also provide insight into subtle differences in presentation of material that may be derailing his learning process.

Touch learning is often an area where inconsistencies in performance can be identified. For instance, it is possible to have a hands-on learner who does well using math manipulatives to learn math, and yet resists other types of hands-on learning information, such as drawing letters or spelling words in shaving cream. Knowing this information about a child can be very important as parents and teachers strive to help a child develop into more flexible learning pattern where he can thrive in a variety of learning environments.

A child who shows strength in touch processing has a hands-on learning style and needs to touch in order to learn most effectively. The strong touch learner will benefit when manipulatives (hands-on learning objects or materials) are used to introduce a learning concept.

---

a note of caution related to touch learning:

Just as we would never force-feed food to a child, I strongly caution against force-feeding sensory activities. Think about this: I can push you to clean out a pumpkin or eat the stringy innards, but does that build a great memory that you want to repeat? Does it encourage you to repeat it? In most situations, force-feeding sensory experience is equivalent to handing both the child and yourself a piece of tin foil and chomping down on it. It's painful for both of you and doesn't set up a positive reinforced learning track in the brain.

Remember, your goal is to create a positive sensory experience that will build into confidence and a foundational belief that learning is fun and feels good. Otherwise, you both simply endured the experience and, though learning occurred, it is not necessarily the learning that you intended (the child may have learned it is not fun to engage in learning with you).

Learning experiences that are painful are not as likely to be repeated if the child has a choice in how to spend his time. Learning experiences that are enjoyable are more likely to be repeated and expanded when the child has a choice in how to spend his time.

VISUAL LEARNING

Visual learning is the ability to understand and respond to what is seen. A child with visual processing strengths has a visual learning style. This child often benefits from the use of visuals to learn in the classroom and to build relationship skills. This child also benefits from the use of animation and technology to support engaging in life and learning. Many children benefit from the use of tools such as visual scheduling and creating lists, to help them anticipate or plan for what needs to be accomplished next.

Visual aids are key tools in our society, for both adults and children. For example, adults use calendars, to-do lists, and signs as constant visual cues to keep themselves on task and oriented. Children need the same types of cues that are developmentally appropriate.

Think back to the stages of sensory development in Chapter 5. A child who has an under-developed awareness of his environment may not be picking up on the natural visual cues in his environment. Visual supports that are developed and tailored to his awareness may be needed in order to help him be more oriented and productive.

Just as each adult develops a unique style of using visual supports (some of us use paper calendars and write out our to-do list and some of us use technology with no paper in sight), each child will also have a developing style that works best for him. In this age of technology and advancement, one size does not fit all.

Children benefit when adults help them explore the methods that work best for them. I have seen many problem behavioral situations quickly defused by simply switching from auditory instructions to providing a visual list of tasks to check off or a visual list of reminders. It can be a refreshing change to work within your child's strength patterns.

The child with autism, who has a profile of strong visual learning coupled with limited areas of interest and exploration, can be engaged by using technology to support learning and relationship. This is many children with autism! Be aware that without purposeful engagement that is linked to relationship, this child may instead use technology to escape learning and interacting with others. For example, a child may excel in learning via a computer game, but his time on the computer does not often support positive interaction with others. Time spent developing a relationship with the computer is time that is not developing strong social skills or relationships with peers. There needs to be a balance. It is a good idea to support learning using technology for this type of child, as long as it is balanced with purposeful relationship-building time. The goal is that people become as preferred as the computer. When technology that is very attractive to a child supports social skill development, it becomes the best of both worlds.

VISUAL PROCESSING RELATED TO LEARNING ENVIRONMENTS FOR TEACHERS AND HOMESCHOOL MOMS

Is the classroom or learning area visually enriching or just visually "busy?" What is hanging on the walls? Has adequate thought gone into what is there and why?

Classroom themes are good. They entice us into learning. They plant the thought that learning is fun and rewarding. Colorful decorations invite children to learn.

Most of us are able to tune out what is visually distracting so we can focus on work, because we have effective visual processing. However, there are some children that do not have effective visual processing. The following ideas will help you think through setting up an environment from a visual processing perspective. The goal is to support a variety of learning styles (especially children with ADHD), while maintaining a visually inviting atmosphere.

- **By the door**: This is the place to visually invite the student in to learn. Here is where the impression is formed that says "This just might be the most fun classroom ever! FUN learning takes place here!" If there is a theme, this is where it should be highlighted. You are inviting students into your "magic school bus" and asking them visually to take a learning adventure with you.

- **Front of the classroom**: Wherever you stand to teach from most often is the front of your classroom. Attractive visual aids containing information to which you will be referring every day should be at the "front," which is the most visually referenced part of the room. If you don't use it daily, it doesn't go here.

- **Sides of the classroom**: This is where you can put the visual aids that you refer to weekly, but not every day. If you don't use it weekly, it doesn't need to be hanging. Simply pull it out when you need it for a lesson.

If your classroom is set up where students face the sides of the classroom and turn to look at what you consider the "front" of your classroom, just realize that you are planning from your perspective and not theirs. Their "front" is the direction they are facing. Their "back" is behind them, and so in many classrooms the front and back of the classroom from the student's perspective is different for each child.

The children who have very effective visual processing skill will not be thrown off by their position in the classroom (unless it is the auditory throwing them off). However, the students who struggle with effective and efficient visual processing will struggle more with learning if they have to turn their heads to see you to gather information from what you consider the "front" of the classroom.

The reason this issue is relevant is related to reflex integration and motor control issues. If you find that a child is struggling with his physical position in the classroom and your gut tells you he could be in a better place, but you don't know where that might be, consult an occupational therapist, physical therapist or possibly the school counselor to help you problem solve.

The rule of thumb here is that a struggling student needs to be facing the teaching area, and visual information needs to be presented at mid-line for any student who is struggling with learning (the middle of their body, right in front of them on a slant board, for instance, to be most effective).

- **Teacher's desk area**: This is the area where you (the teacher) can indulge your own personal theme and preferences. Set this area as your haven so you can be most refreshed and "on your game." Make this a place where you can focus and get work done efficiently.

---

a note to other professionals entering a teacher's classroom with advice on "set up" or arrangement:

I encourage you to be cautious when attempting to influence another teacher's classroom set up. Giving advice directly to a teacher in a new consulting relationship takes rapport and finesse. A teacher's classroom, like a woman's house, is her personal castle. Since her heart is invested there, she may not welcome a third party who enters that domain, throwing out advice. It could affect your working relationship, and so be sensitive to timing and presentation.

The variety of classroom set-up and teaching styles represented in a typical school setting support a variety of learning needs. Teachers are often intuitive about what their kids need, and their initial set-up doesn't always stay the same throughout the year. They adapt because they assess what their children need. I love to see a room set up to support a teacher's natural style.

Teachers will be at their best when the room supports both their teaching style and a variety of learning styles. Know that most classrooms will have slight differences in set up and that can be very healthy for students. The purpose of analyzing the set-up is to ensure that the environment is working to actively engage children in learning. The goal is to make the classroom set-up work for you when teaching, not have it subtly work against you by distracting the student.

MOVEMENT LEARNING

Movement learning is the ability to actively engage in motor movements safely, with functional coordination. It includes the ability to tolerate and even enjoy movement activities appropriately. A child who has an identified movement processing strength has a kinesthetic, movement learning style. This student may look similar to the hands-on/touch learner in some ways. However, the kinesthetic learner may be distracted by manipulatives. To learn, this learner needs to move, but not necessarily touch. This learner often enjoys something as simple as taking a walk while talking through (or thinking about) a learning principle.

Just because a child moves a lot, and likes to move, doesn't mean that this area is a strength for him. It can be. Many children with ADHD or impulsivity tendencies move a lot, leading you to believe that they are kinesthetic (moving) learners. However, this is not always true. They can grow into moving learners, and often there is a kinesthetic strength to their learning, but simply adding movement doesn't always help a child organize himself for concentration and learning.

There is a difference in moving to feed our bodies and balance energy and having a movement learning style strength. Our bodies are designed to move. Movement is essential to learning for all children. The question is how and when to provide the movement opportunities to set a child up for success and to discern what that movement activity looks like (structured or unstructured).

I am frustrated with the current trend of taking away more recess and physical education opportunities during the school day, while we wonder why our national testing scores keep dropping. We were designed to move and learn.

Movement helps us process information, helps us generalize information, and helps us absorb and reflect on information. It is an essential part of every person's day. Movement is a part of every plan for every child I see. However, have you noticed that many of the children who are struggling the most don't necessarily use their recess time effectively?

Random movement is not usually effective movement to feed and balance the bodies systems. Purposeful and coordinated movement is effective movement. In the situations where I am consulted because there is a problem behavior in a classroom or learning situation with a "sensory kid," I may track some of the behavior patterns and find the child is escalating or less focused following recess time. Often when I track what the child is doing during recess, he is either spinning on swings or the merry-go-round for extended periods of time, swinging for extended periods of time, or spinning in circles by himself on the playground. He is not processing movement effectively, and he can't seem to get his movement cup full no matter how much movement he seeks. Therefore, he continues to escalate into seeking more and more movement which, in turn, feeds his disorganization.

One of the first things I look for when I see a child with disorganized behavior or dysfunctional behaviors is the kind of movement he seeks to engage in most. Often the child is craving movement, but is not naturally engaging in a type of movement that will help him organize himself or "help himself." In those situations, as described above, his craving is working against his success. He needs movement, but also needs support in order to make beneficial movement activity choices that are going to feel good and be lead to progress.

In dysfunctional learning and behavior situations, the first thing I do is to remove the spinning/rotary movements during the day and replace them with upright linear movement opportunities (think straight lines – forward/back and side/side), followed by a *grounding activity*. Grounding activities involve proprioceptive input, "heavy work" and weight bearing to the joints, which helps release natural calming and self-regulation ability. In essence, this creates a movement sandwich with movement being the "meat" of the input and the self-calming/proprioceptive input being the "bread," which anchors the movement experience on both sides.

The goal is to provide movement **at the level that the child's body is able to functionally process it**. Opening up opportunities for more complex movement only as the child is able to maintain the ability to regulate himself while engaged in that movement, will create a positive effect, where his behavior remains organized following his experience.

---

a note on movement development...

We build our movement processing skill in a fairly structured way. In most learning situations we tolerate upright, front to back linear movement well (think walking and swinging), and next upright, side to side lateral linear movement, and next prone (on tummy) and supine (on back) linear movement, and finally, rotary or spinning movement.

I encourage you to be cautious and attentive in atypical development situations. Occasionally, I find that well-meaning adults push developmentally delayed kids into complex movement experiences (i.e. rotary movement) before they are effectively able to process it well. Coincidentally, development becomes static for a period of time, or random behavior patterns pop up on the side. If the adult is not looking at the whole picture, he can miss the fact that the movement, and the child's inability to process it effectively, is part of the trigger for those alternative "stuck" issues.

A child who is a "spinner" but doesn't tolerate linear, slower rocking movement well is likely not processing the movement of spinning well either. He will crave it, but rarely process it effectively and is rarely satisfied/satiated. Thus, the act of spinning is contributing to his disorganization, because he is not effectively processing that movement even though he is choosing it.

A plan that replaces movement that is not being processed well with movement

---

that is easier to process will often serve a struggling child better. The number of special needs kids to whom this applies is surprising. Just as force-feeding food is not the most therapeutic approach, remember not to force-feed movement. Set up the opportunity, and support him through it, but never force it.

SELF-REGULATION SKILL

Self-regulation is the ability to become excited and then calm back down. It is also the ability to calm down following being upset, and the ability to modulate motor, sensory, and emotional information functionally. A child's set of coping skills is closely related to his self-regulation skill.

Coping skills are a child's best survival tactics in a given situation. Cumulatively, they strengthen his self-regulation skills and responses. A child who has self-regulation strengths is able to adapt and "handle" himself when things don't go his way. He flexes when things don't go as he expected. He is able to get ready for an event without external support or excessive preparation, and he is able to calm down following exciting or challenging events.

It's important to note that early trauma affects future self-regulation skill development and global sensory processing skill patterns. Early trauma might include:

- Stress in the womb before birth
- A difficult birth experience
- Medical complications following birth (like GERD or severe reflux or a medically specific acute or unresolved chronic situation)
- Physical abuse or neglect
- An accident-related experience

In these situations, "misbehavior" or "sensory behavior" is almost always masking a cry for help to recover from that early trauma. Treatment that targets both social-emotional and trauma recovery, as well as sensory processing skill, is the best approach to early trauma intervention. This often requires as at least two collaborative therapists, often from different disciplines, such as a psychologist (or counselor) partnering with an occupational therapist. The psychologist (or counselor) will be specifically targeting coping skill development and more effective responses to anxiety, as well as family dynamics and purposeful building of relationship and attachment. The occupational therapist will be a related service, supporting work in sensory processing skill development and strategies to strengthen the functional daily routine. The synergy in this dynamic can be very powerful treatment.

a note about adoption:

For an adopted child there is attachment and sensory processing work to be done. For some parents, this work happens almost unconsciously as they follow their natural instincts to nurture. However, for most adoptive families, a network of support resources and information is a needed link to happy, healthy attachment and development.

AUDITORY LEARNING

Auditory learning is the ability to listen and understand spoken language or environmental sounds and then respond appropriately. It encompasses our ability to hear auditory messages, distinguish between similar sounds or words, separate relevant speech from background noise, and recall what was heard.

This auditory processing piece is important, especially for children who demonstrate any signs of dyslexia. There is some promising work being done and is continuing to be done that is beginning to analyze the link between dyslexia and auditory processing difficulty.

a note about dyslexia:

A significant piece of dyslexia is the inability to naturally discriminate the sounds of the letters within words and language (phonemes). Surprisingly, this language issue is more central to dyslexia than visual processing difficulty. When we can't accurately register the individual sounds in words, we can't move forward with sounding out words or spelling them. Moving to sight word reading and memorization is not always effective. I am impressed with the body of work that has been developed based on the Orton-Gillingham methodology. If you have a struggling reader or a student with any written language, listening, or reading issues, I highly recommend you look into Orton-Gillingham work or Linda Mood-Bell work to find strategies that have been developed based on their work.* In her book, Overcoming Dyslexia, Dr. Sally Shaywitz, a Yale neuroscientist, presents research on dyslexia (Shaywitz, 2005), as well as strategies designed to help stimulate the exact part of the brain that is immature in those with mild to severe signs of dyslexia.

*I have personally used these principles at my house and it felt like magic.

AUDITORY SENSITIVITY

There are a few interesting patterns I often find in children with auditory defensiveness. Their over-sensitivity is sometimes more about the unexpectedness of the noise and the novelty than it is about it being "loud." If the child is not anticipating the noise, it startles him and he flips into a fight/fright/flight mode of defensiveness. The intensity of his response leaves him irritated and "on edge," and the negative experience is extended and becomes a generalized pattern of reaction. This is usually part of a larger anxiety-response pattern that includes more than noise.

Other children with auditory defensiveness tune out much of the regular auditory noise around them, not fully processing it effectively or efficiently. When novel noises occur, the noises trigger their attention and are not tuned out. When they can't tune out specific novel noises effectively, they become distressed when those noises occur.

Another auditory pattern that I see often is the child who begins to engage in vocalization or vocal "stim" because it brings a level of predictability to the auditory/language and communication patterns. Vocalizations can also create a more predictable interaction pattern with others because they tend to influence the way others approach the child to engage in interaction. It becomes more about controlling the predictability of the interaction than the "sensory."

True auditory sensitivity is evident when a child has an amplified ability to hear things that other people can't hear and becomes easily irritated by noises that are not of his own making. At times, this type of learner will respond well to specific patterns and types of music when the volume is adjusted to his preference.

One of the things I do with children experiencing auditory defensiveness is to frame it, first, as an anxiety behavior. I look at developing a plan for coping with the anxiety as a core piece of the treatment planning. Simultaneously, I add treatment planning that focuses on self-regulation skill and provides extra weight-bearing/proprioceptive input. I "beef up" the tools that the child has for calming in a general sense. Next, I focus on developing auditory processing and auditory motor skills, beginning with elementary levels and working toward more complex skills.

NATURAL INTEREST AND MOTIVATION

Do you remember how powerful it is to increase a child's repertoire of favorite things? (If you don't, you can review this information in Chapter 8.) The **Natural Interest and Motivation** section of The Learning Strengths Profile captures information related to a child's range of interests. It can help parents, teachers and professionals predict how much support a child may need to expand his willingness to try new things and explore new ideas. This area highlights whether the child's motivational interest is broad or narrow, which directly affects learning situations. This area will give an indication about whether the child has a full basket of **carrots** or whether you are starting with the **King Carrot*** and need to recruit more **carrots** to form your army of rewards. Time reviewing this area of information and pre-planning your strategy for providing rewarding intervention will be time well spent toward your successful progress with a child.

For typically developing kids, engaging on a campaign to increase their repertoire of liked activities has to be purposeful, but is not really that challenging. There are hundreds and hundreds of options to choose from. Every child benefits from having a full range of interests and motivation.

What about the child who has autism or another developmental delay or diagnosis where limited liked activity is a hallmark symptom? What do you do then? Go back to what you found in the Learning Strengths Profile.

Look at the top two identified strength areas. Start brainstorming activity opportunities and experiences based around those identified strengths and then start introducing them. Make developing strengths-based opportunities and learning experiences your first priority in treatment, because there must be a foundation of liked activities to work from to make most effective progress.

A child with broad interests has a full basket of carrots to motivate him in applied learning situations. He has a number of liked activities that will actively capture his interest and his curiosity. A child with limited interests and only specific carrots that motivate him indicates that teaching situations will probably have to be tailored specifically to his preferences. In either case, the child's list of specific liked things will be needed, in addition to the profile of interests as captured by this area of The Learning Strengths Profile. His specific likes can be utilized in planning to further entice and motivate him into learning by tying them to the material that he needs to learn. This not only increases his interest in the subject, but also makes the information more meaningful and purposeful to him.

*A King Carrot is the ONE big carrot that overshadows all other daily activities. It is often related to a growing obsession with screen time.

LEARNING STRENGTHS PROFILE

Student Name:	Date:
Student's Date of Birth:	Person Completing form:
Grade Level/School:	Relationship to Student:

The Learning Strengths Profile is a big picture method of capturing a student's individual approaches to learning and interacting. A parent/ caregiver, teacher, or therapist can complete a Learning Strengths Profile for a student. The Learning Strengths Profile is most effectively utilized with students who have a developmental performance level of 5-6 years through adolescence.

The Learning Strengths Profile is a flexible tool that can be used to identify patterns of learning that are positive and strength based. Strength areas identify a child's most effective and efficient methods of learning (i.e. visual learning, auditory learning). It is designed to quickly identify strength areas that can be used when introducing new learning or social experiences as well as barrier areas to be avoided in those situations. The Learning Strengths Profile can also be used to confirm patterns of dysfunctional learning in order to support, teach, and adapt learning situations for a student's best performance and success in learning.

Once all areas are completed, a student's learning strengths will emerge. Strength areas should be used to introduce new learning, expand social interaction, and highlight strength based performance. To increase a child's motivation for learning and natural reinforcement for learning, parents and teachers can build learning experiences and instruction around the identified learning strength areas. Barrier areas will identify learning areas that need support and treatment attention. Identified barrier areas indicate that the student is not processing that type of learning effectively and efficiently for learning purposes and, therefore, should not be used as a primary method of introducing new learning material. Barrier areas should be used with "old" learning for review of information that is already mastered. Once a student is successfully using strengths for new learning and is successfully reviewing information using a variety of senses to aid generalization, a plan to increase flexibility in learning can be designed to capitalize on strengths while incorporating weaknesses.

Learning Areas:

MOTOR IMITATION:
The ability to accurately or functionally copy a motor movement or position.

TOUCH LEARNING:
The ability to register and discriminate incoming sensory information through the skin and respond appropriately.

VISUAL LEARNING:
The ability to understand and respond to what is seen.

MOVEMENT LEARNING:
The ability to actively engage in motor movements safely and productively, not escalating into hyperactivity, but remaining self-controlled during movement. The ability to modulate motor and sensory processing information during movement activities.

SELF-REGULATION
The ability to become excited or active and then calm back down. The ability to calm after being upset. The ability to modulate social-emotional information.

AUDITORY LEARNING:
The ability to listen and understand spoken language and environmental sounds and then respond appropriately.

NATURAL INTEREST AND MOTIVATION:
This area measures the breadth and quantity of a student's interests and natural motivation for learning.

Please rate student performance based on the student's recent behavior. Read the skill sets listed under each learning area. Rate the student's performance. If a student's performance fluctuates and is inconsistent, mark the spectrum of performance by putting an X for each rating in all learning areas that apply.

Learning Strengths Profile	STRENGTH		N	BARRIER	
	1	2	3	4	5
MOVEMENT IMITATION 1-2 = Quickly picks up skills by watching someone demonstrate "how" to do the skill. Imitates a sequence of movements easily. 3 = Imitates a few new gross and fine motor actions accurately, but does well during familiar routines. 4-5 = Struggles to imitate motor movements well, but is beginning to imitate movements during favorite activities.					
TOUCH LEARNING 1-2 = Learns well by manipulating and building with objects. Connects to learning in a "hands on" way. 3 = Responds positively to many touch and texture learning activities, but does not always engage in the activity for long. May have a few strong touch preferences (i.e. tags removed from clothing.) 4-5 = Becomes very distracted in learning situations when texture or "hands on" activities are presented, either craving or resisting the activity.					
VISUAL LEARNING 1-2 = Learns quickly and accurately by watching videos or animated teaching of a subject. May enjoy visual puzzle games (i.e. Wheel of Fortune, crossword puzzles). 3 = Responds to visual learning activities as long as they are clear and concise without too much "busy" background. Responds to visual information that is familiar. May have a few strong visual preferences (i.e. font size) 4-5 = Struggles to organize and understand visual information without support and responds best to highly structured visual information presented in small chunks. Needs consistent repetition to learn visually. May crave visual stimulation, but has trouble making sense of it or avoids visual stimulation all together.information presented in small chunks.					
MOVEMENT LEARNING 1-2 = Actively engages in routine movement activities without fear or over-excitement. 3 = Engages actively in movement activities for a short time or with adequate preparation. 4-5 = Avoids movement activities and quickly disconnects from a group when movement is a part of learning or play.					
SELF-REGULTAION 1-2 = Able to self-calm following an exciting or upsetting event without supports or intervention. 3 = Sensitive to new experiences and events, but handles them well with supports and preparation. 4-5 = Difficulty calming down, even with supports, or has difficulty "waking up" to participate in daily routines and learning activities.					
AUDITORY LEARNING 1-2 = Actively engages when listening to a story or lecture, "tunes in" easily and can accurately remember details. Actively remembers chants, songs, poems, or details. 3 = Remembers some details from conversations or lectures, but needs notes or other supports to remember accurate details. 4-5 = Struggles to understand and remember what he/ she hears. Needs consistent repetition to respond to auditory information. Responds inconsistently or disproportionately to environmental sounds.					
NATURAL INTEREST AND MOTIVATON 1-2 = Has a variety of interests, hobbies, and liked activities. Screen time (computer, video games, TV) stays in balance with other recreational activity. Student is interested in learning about a variety of topics and has healthy social connections. 3 = Has strong preferences about favorite things, but will actively engage in new activities that are presented. 4-5 = Demonstrates limited interest in activities outside of select favorites. Over-focuses on screen time (computer, video games, TV) to the point that it negatively impacts learning and social relationships.					

PRIMARY LEARNING STRENGTHS PROFILE

Student Name:	Date:
Student's Date of Birth:	Person Completing form:
Grade Level/School:	Relationship to Student:

The Learning Strengths Profile is a big picture method of capturing a student's individual approaches to learning and interacting. A parent/ caregiver, teacher, or therapist can complete a Learning Strengths Profile for a student. The Learning Strengths Profile is most effectively utilized with students who have a developmental performance level of 5-6 years through adolescence.

The Primary Learning Strengths Profile is a flexible tool that can be used to identify patterns of learning that are positive and strength based. Strength areas identify a child's most effective and efficient methods of learning (i.e. visual learning, auditory learning). It is designed to quickly identify strength areas that can be used when introducing new learning or social experiences as well as barrier areas to be avoided in those situations. The Primay Learning Strengths Profile can also be used to confirm patterns of dysfunctional learning in order to support, teach, and adapt learning situations for a student's best performance and success in learning.

Once all areas are completed, a student's learning strengths will emerge. Strength areas should be used to introduce new learning, expand social interaction, and highlight strength based performance. To increase a child's motivation for learning and natural reinforcement for learning, parents and teachers can build learning experiences and instruction around the identified learning strength areas. Barrier areas will identify learning areas that need support and treatment attention. Identified barrier areas indicate that the student is not processing that type of learning effectively and efficiently for learning purposes and, therefore, should not be used as a primary method of introducing new learning material. Barrier areas should be used with "old" learning for review of information that is already mastered. Once a student is successfully using strengths for new learning and is successfully reviewing information using a variety of senses to aid generalization, a plan to increase flexibility in learning can be designed to capitalize on strengths while incorporating weaknesses.

Learning Areas:

MOTOR IMITATION:
The ability to accurately or functionally copy a motor movement or position. This area investigates how a student watches and learns.

TOUCH LEARNING:
The ability to register and discriminate incoming sensory information through the skin and respond appropriately. This area investigates how a student engages in hands-on learning.

VISUAL LEARNING:
The ability to register and discriminate incoming sensory information through the skin and respond appropriately. This area investigates how a student engages in hands-on learning.

MOVEMENT LEARNING:
TThe ability to actively engage in motor movements safely and productively, not escalating into hyperactivity, but remaining self-controlled during movement. The ability to modulate motor and sensory processing information during movement activities. This area investigates how a student moves and learns.

SELF-REGULATION
The ability to become excited or active and then calm back down. The ability to calm after being upset. The ability to process social-emotional information. This area investigates self-calming.

AUDITORY LEARNING:
The ability to listen and understand spoken language and environmental sounds and then respond appropriately. This area investigates how a student listens and understands.

NATURAL INTEREST AND MOTIVATION:
This area measures the breadth and quantity of a student's interests and natural motivation for learning.

Please rate student performance based on the student's recent behavior. Read the skill sets listed under each learning area. Rate the student's performance. If a student's performance fluctuates and is inconsistent, mark the spectrum of performance by putting an X for each rating in all learning areas that apply.

Primary Learning Strengths Profile	STRENGTH		N	BARRIER	
	1	2	3	4	5
MOVEMENT IMITATION 1-2 = Imitates motor positions and movements easily. Imitates 2-3 step movements easily. 3 = Imitates a few detailed motor actions accurately. Imitates multiple motor actions within familiar routines. 4-5 = Struggles to imitate movement well at all or is beginning to imitate 1-2 actions involving an object in the context of play.					
TOUCH LEARNING 1-2 = Enjoys hands-on learning projects and responds positively to touch interaction. 3 = Responds positively to hands-on activities, but does not always actively engage in the activity for long. May have a few strong touch preferences (i.e. tags removed from clothing, etc.) 4-5 = May respond inconsistently or have a strong reaction to touch and textures in activities. May crave touch excessively or resist touch and texture interaction frequently.					
VISUAL LEARNING 1-2 = Likes to watch and learn. Able to look at visual information, remember it, and respond appropriately. 3 = Inconsistently responds to visual information, but is able to respond to visual cues during familiar routines. 4-5 = Struggles to understand what he/ she sees. Needs consistent repetition to respond appropriately. May crave visual stimulation, but have trouble making sense of it or avoid visual stimulation all together.					
MOVEMENT LEARNING 1-2 = Actively engages in movement activities in a safe way without fear and without escalating into hyperactivity. 3 = Sensitive to new events or movement activities, but handles them well with supports and preparation. 4-5 = Avoids movement activities and seems disconnected to that type of play or becomes excessively hyper with movement. Needs supervision for safety..					
SELF-REGULTAION 1-2 = Able to self-calm following an exciting or upsetting event without supports or intervention. 3 = Able to calm following an event when provided with supports or intervention. Child is sensitive to new events, but hands them well with supports and preparation. 4-5 = Struggles to calm down even with supports or child has difficulty "waking up" to participate in daily routines and seems disconnected. Needs supervision for safety due to poor safety awareness.					
AUDITORY LEARNING 1-2 = Listens and understands well. Readily responds to spoken language and environmental sounds appropriately. 3 = Inconsistently responds to new language and sounds, but responds consistently within familiar routines. 4-5 = Struggles to understand what he/ she hears. Child needs consistent repetition to respond appropriately. Needs supervision for safety.					
NATURAL INTEREST AND MOTIVATON 1-2 = Demonstrates a variety of interests. Interested in investigating new toys and activities. Seeks out or takes advantage of opportunities to engage in play with people and things in most situations. 3 = Has strong preferences about favorite things, but will actively engage in new activities that are presented. 4-5 = Demonstrates limited interest in activities outside of a limited selection of favorites. Over-focused on playing alone to the point that it negatively impacts learning and social relationships. Rigid play skills and interests.					

CHAPTER 10 DEEPER JOURNEY TO APPLICATION

The Deeper Journey portion of each chapter is set up to provide application and reflection questions or to help support group discussion regarding the information in the related chapter.

1. Complete The Learning Strengths Profile for your child. What are your child's strengths? Think through how you can capitalize on your child's strengths at home:

Think through how you can capitalize on your child's strengths related to school work:

2. What are your child's barriers? Are they overshadowing his strengths? How are they affecting your attitude and the attitudes of teachers toward your child?

Name one new way you can support your child in an area where he struggles in order to allow his strengths to shine more fully:

CHAPTER 11

"Do not train a child to learn by force or harshness; but direct them to it by what amuses their minds, so that you may be better able to discover with accuracy the peculiar bent of the genius of each."
-Plato

USING THE LEARNING STRENGTHS PROFILE TOOL

Now that the areas in the Learning Strengths Profile have been described, let's look at how to best use the form. Anyone who knows a child well can use it. However, you may start into this form and get stalled because it will challenge what you have noticed about a child.

This tool forces you toward a deeper understanding or a new perspective about a child and how he learns. If you begin to fill out the form, but find that you don't really know the answers, the areas that you struggle to rate will be the same areas you should target for observations in learning situations. Grow your knowledge about how the child responds in those situations.

Some teachers and parents like to pencil in their first "X" (guess) to rate an area, and then wait for a week or two before filling in their "final answer." Many children do not respond in the same way each day. Some days are higher "skill" days than others. If that is the case, put an "X" in each area that applies to your child's responses. This will show you his range of responses in a category. You may have one or more categories that have two or more "X's," showing the spectrum of how the child fluctuates in ability on a day to day basis. It is preferable to have the range of the child's performance reflected so you can see the fluctuation.

When you have finished rating the child and the profile is complete, look at the broad overview of the child's performance. Is he consistent in his performance, where you find one "X" to represent each category definitively? In that case, regardless of skill level, the child is presenting in a fairly straightforward and predictable manner during day to day interactions. That is a strength.

Is your child inconsistent in his performance, where you find multiple "X's" to represent one, or many, categories? In that case, it becomes even more important to continue investigating the child's specific learning profile, because that range of performance indicates that the child's struggle in specific learning and interaction situations is acute and stressful. The more you learn about his specific strengths in learning and interacting, the more you can begin to build on those strengths to grow them.

IDENTIFYING STRENGTH AREAS USING THE LEARNING STRENGTHS PROFILE

Once you have finished rating each area, notice the "X's" that are on the far left. Sometimes this will include the "3/ Neutral" box, and sometimes it will primarily include only the number 1 and 2 columns. This is the child's primary area of strength performance in daily learning and interacting. Some children will have multiple strength areas, indicating their personal is flexibility in learning and interaction. Others will have a primary area that emerges as a strength to build upon.

> **When you introduce new learning activities, make sure that you are incorporating the child's primary strength areas into the introduction of a topic or the child's first opportunities to practice a new task. You want new learning activities to always be tackled from a point of his greatest strength and most accurate processing abilities.**

When new learning is approached and introduced in a strength-based way, the child will naturally be taking in more accurate information. He will also tend to begin learning more comprehensively and effectively because he is approaching learning using the best tools he has. He will automatically be more inclined to enjoy learning and begin building more confidence in learning because he is more successful. Remember, we repeatedly choose things we enjoy if we have a choice.

If learning becomes **fun** for a child, he will naturally begin to choose to engage in more of it! If he is naturally more successful when engaging with the learning material, he will be more inclined to stick with it and apply the subject more readily in situations. At this point, you can congratulate yourself! You have just identified the pathway to increasing a child's motivation for learning, based on engaging him in the way his body is currently set up to learn best. For example, if social skills is something you are looking to support in his development, then you want to plan play dates and interaction that incorporate his learning strengths and avoid his weakness. The play date and interaction that meets both of those criteria will have the best chance of being successful and building a great memory for him and for you.

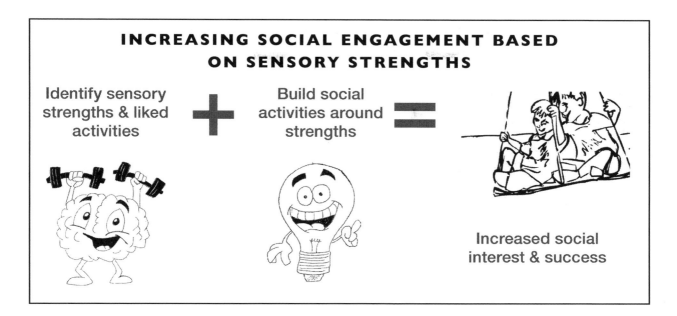

INCREASING SOCIAL ENGAGEMENT BASED ON SENSORY STRENGTHS

Identify sensory strengths & liked activities **+** Build social activities around strengths **=** Increased social interest & success

IDENTIFYING BARRIER AREAS USING THE LEARNING STRENGTHS PROFILE

Identified barriers will likely confirm what you already suspect or know about a child's barriers to learning. You probably won't have large amounts of new information regarding the areas in which a child is really struggling on a day to day basis. However, look closely at behavior patterns and disruptive or undesirable behaviors alongside the barriers, and then begin to analyze the connection between the two. What you discover about the connection between the behavior patterns and the learning patterns will give you insight into what may be fueling the perfect storm for unproductive behavior to occur.

Barrier areas are the areas that you target for support and for purposeful development of skills. These are the first areas where extra time and resource support will yield the most effective positive impact on performance. These are the first areas to target for enriching growth. The barrier areas are areas to support and develop with subtle "under the radar" work, sandwiched between the fun learning-strength moments. By using this method, you capitalize on the child's strengths to take in information most effectively for learning, while you simultaneously maximize learning potential by addressing barrier areas.

Once a learning concept has been introduced in a strength-based way, and the child begins to show some productive work with the concept, then ***review and practice of the new skill can be completed using an activity that targets working in a barrier area.*** You are taking a concept he understands and providing supported practice learning in his non-dominant learning style in order to increase his generalization skills. This type of process in learning will create a more flexible learner and will increase a child's ability to adapt to a teaching style in the future that is not perfectly aligned with his specific learning style.

The rest of this chapter will illustrate what The Learning Strengths Profile can do for a child. I share several profiles, each one with different strengths and different skill levels. I have chosen children with mild to significant impairment (and corresponding diagnoses) as examples, but please remember that this tool works for typically developing children as well.

MOTOR IMITATION IS KEY
APPLYING THE LEARNING STRENGTHS PROFILE TO CONNOR

Connor came to see me at eight years old. He was in the second grade. He was diagnosed with autism and ADHD. Connor's mother was concerned about his lack of success socially and about how much he was struggling in the classroom to attend and learn. His birthday was coming up the next month and she wanted to plan a fun birthday party that would be successful. His birthday the year before had been a disaster, where he left to go cry in his closet while the other children played. It was heart-wrenching to hear his mom relate that birthday story and her fears for the coming birthday. It was painful to watch the emotions cross her face at having to relive the last birthday while worrying about this coming birthday.

She said, "Birthdays are supposed to be fun. I'm just hoping to live through this one."
Connor had been in therapies most of his life, including ABA (Applied Behavior Analysis), speech therapy and occupational therapy. Connor's mom and I decided to use The Learning Strengths Profile alongside her other therapies and assessments. We planned to use the results to problem solve, related to her greatest worries for Connor, and to use the results to make practical plans for his birthday and the classroom. See his profile below:

Learning Area	Strength Area 1	2	Neutral 3	Barrier Area 4	5
Motor Imitation	X				
Touch Learning		X	X		
Visual Learning		X	X	X	
Movement Learning		X	X		
Self-Regulation Skill			X		
Auditory Learning		X	X	X	
Natural Interest & Motivation				X	

He had some inconsistencies in his performance, but his strength was in motor imitation. His related strengths included:

- Specific touch/ hands-on learning activities
- Occasional visual learning activities (His mother made a note that he enjoys learning from videos, but struggles with busy visual worksheets.)
- Occasional movement learning activities
- Occasional auditory learning (His mother made a note that his auditory learning is so varied that he'll remember conversations from when he was 3 years old and will recite parts of movies, but cannot always repeat and carry out simple instructions.)

My first advice for Connor and his family was to make sure that new learning activities should be introduced by showing him how to complete the activity, relying minimally on verbal instructions or pairing them with an action and using specific purposeful verbal and visual cues. Offering an opportunity for hands-on touch learning would enhance his ability to "work with" the new information.

In planning for Connor's birthday, given Connor's delayed social skill development, I asked him and his mom to invite only one or two kids with whom he already had an established relationship. (Last year, they had tried 10+ kids and families.) Next, we set up a LEGO theme for the party, because LEGOS was one of his top 5 favorite things, and because that was an activity that was predictable, yet provided the possibility for interaction time. LEGOS also lend themselves to being a good photo moment to capture the fun memory of the birthday.

We discussed avoiding social situations where he might have trouble self-regulating: no Jump Mania time for the party. No blow ups in the yard. No Chuck E. Cheese or Incredible Pizza game rooms for the party. No balloon-popping games or piñatas for the party. No high-alerting or combative activities. (This is why we ruled out Star Wars as a theme for his party, even though it was higher on his list of favorites than playing LEGOS.*). I explained that these activities may sound fun initially and are traditional birthday activities, but would likely end up in fighting or a melt-down, sabotaging Mom's dreams for a beautiful memory and budding friendship.

I am happy to report that the LEGO birthday party was a success. He enjoyed the party, asked to have his friends spend the night (which had never happened before), and had scheduled another play date with both friends before the day was over. All of the boys enjoyed having their pictures taken with their LEGO creations and were still referring to the party and their fun months later.

*Star Wars= light sabers = mock battles = real battles.

As we analyzed Connor's classroom behaviors and performance, we noted that it was helpful that he had defined preferences for activities in the classroom, and he was able to clearly identify non-preferred activities. (This came out when talking through his Natural Interests and Motivation.) However, he demonstrated a limited ability to naturally explore and investigate, both in the classroom and at home. He stuck to his routine and did not vary from it. He struggled to be open to new ideas. His limited repertoire of activities was exacerbating his tendency to perseverate* and over-focus on his few favorite things. His limited repertoire of liked things directly contributed to his difficulty relating socially with others, because there were few things to connect over. His tendency to strongly resist new and unfamiliar learning situations was interfering with his compliance during class. His tendency to resist new and unfamiliar games was interfering with his ability to try out a friend's ideas at recess.

Connor struggled with inconsistent movement learning performance. When his profile was compared with his motor skills (based on a standardized motor test or developmental chart), it became evident that, though he was able to perform practiced motor tasks (like copying from the board) with age appropriate skill, he struggled more with coordination and compliance during active movement learning times, especially in new environments.

He demonstrated limited attention, interest, and motivation for completing specific motor tasks (such as written expression/ journal activities). Therefore, he demonstrated limited endurance and cooperation during those activities. (Many of his behavior situations were related to avoid-escape triggers in order to get out of or avoid non-preferred learning tasks.)

Connor struggled with specific, yet intense sensory triggers, which influenced his inconsistent performance in multiple areas. His mother was able to identify the types of visual learning that he responded to best (video/animated visual examples, as well as the types of visual learning that tripped him up (visually busy worksheets). Likewise, she identified that his auditory skills were also inconsistent. He could remember specific conversations and movie lines that interested him, but he often struggled to accurately follow through with or repeat simple directions.

The key to jump-starting Connor's progress lay in the Natural Interests and Motivation portion of his profile. Do you see what I saw? His lack of natural interest and motivation is his most significant barrier. Connor was at risk for anxiety and depression issues, which were overshadowing his performance strengths and abilities on a daily basis.

*To perseverate is to repeat something insistently and repetitively. Perseverative actions can feel compulsive, intense, and almost involuntary. They are often self-calming rituals for kids. Redirecting or replacing this type of pattern can be challenging if you don't have a good list of favorites to work from. You have to find something enticing enough that it feels just as good as the perseveration.

As interaction with his family ensued, this area was the key to changing his entire situation. With focused support of his strengths, combined with an effort to expand his repertoire of interest and motivation, Connor began to take significant strides forward. His mother reported amazement that by simply studying his profile, she was better able to "read" him, interact with him, and adapt learning situations for greater success.

A HANDS-ON LEARNER
APPLYING THE LEARNING STRENGTHS PROFILE TO BARRY

Barry was a thirteen year old adolescent who came to see me following a two-year pattern of being in and out of residential care due to aggressive behavior. He had a diagnosis of Oppositional Defiant Disruptive Bx Disorder, ADHD and Intellectual Disability. In partnering with his family and team of professionals, we discovered some "out of the box" strategies that helped set him up for some success. See his profile below:

Learning Area	Strength Area 1	2	Neutral 3	Barrier Area 4	5
Motor Imitation	X				
Touch Learning	X	X			
Visual Learning				X	X
Movement Learning			X	X	
Self-Regulation Skill				X	
Auditory Learning				X	X
Natural Interest & Motivation			X	X	

He is an obvious "hands-on learner." His eyes light up when he is given a hands-on work project to complete. He can stack a cord of wood quickly and successfully. He can work a 12-14 hour day in the hay field. What he can't do is sit still at his desk to successfully complete worksheets. He also struggles to listen to lectures in class and learn information accurately by just listening. Fortunately, his family and professional team had already determined a few of the special supports he needed to succeed in the classroom and he had an aide available in the classroom for assistance as needed.

We discovered that, though the team had identified that he needed one-on-one assistance at times, he was primarily receiving instructions by listening to an adult tell him what to do or by reading instructions at the top of a worksheet or assignment. In tracking behavior referrals and acting out, we found that a majority of his acting out was for the function of avoiding assignments in the classroom. This made sense to me when I found out how those assignments were introduced to him. No one was **showing** him how to complete the assignment – they were relying on his weaknesses to start into the most challenging kind of work for him. It was a recipe for the perfect storm to begin brewing.

Barry described that he constantly took tests where he was expected to get a 70 and he kept getting a 69. He reported that the school was nice and let him retake one of his tests and he scored a 69.9%, but never got his 70. His mother and one of his therapists reported that he exaggerated and had a developing pattern of lying. However, it was true that he was consistently failing tests.

I was most interested in Barry's story because it gave me his perception. In this situation, his perception was his reality. I explained it to his family and therapist this way:

> *Imagine that you came to work this morning and I agreed to pay you $50,000 at the end of the day if all 30 things on a to-do list were completed. At the end of the day, you had completed 29. I put on my compassionate face and told you I was so sorry that I couldn't pay you today because you didn't complete the 30 tasks, but I looked forward to you coming back tomorrow to try again. How many days of working hard, but falling short, would you invest? How would showing up day after day for that experience begin to affect your self-confidence?*

What I learned from Barry is that, from his perspective, he was showing up day after day, only to just barely miss the expectation mark and no matter how hard he tried, he could never "make the grade."

Our first and most effective strategy was to focus on ensuring that all instruction to new learning material was provided by showing Barry instead of telling him or having him read instructions. This one change significantly affected his behavioral referrals.

Another strategy we used to help support Barry included tapping into his natural interests and motivation, including recognizing and providing more opportunity for Barry to plug into activities related to his outdoor interests, such as Boy Scouts. We also noted that most of his feedback about his performance came from the areas in which he was weakest, namely, his grade card. So, we expanded his grade card to include more of his strength areas including wood working/shop, farm skills, and nature/physical labor. We also looked closely at more traditional strategies that modified the educational expectations to better match his intellectual abilities. (He was attempting to keep up with his peers and complete grade level work, but he did not have grade level abilities.) I told his team that I was hopeful that the next time I saw Barry, he would be able to report that a 60 was expected to "make the grade" and he rocked a 69!

Success breeds success. When a student successfully surpasses expectations because those expectations are strategically set to be attainable, the student builds confidence and is more likely to meet the next challenge also.

A VISUAL LEARNER
APPLYING THE LEARNING STRENGTHS PROFILE TO KENDAL

Kendal is an eight year old boy who came to see me about sensory processing difficulty affecting his performance at home and at school on a daily basis. He was identified as a gifted and talented student and accelerated from first to third grade. He had a 504 Plan* in place to support his academic performance, including use of a scribe during testing and testing in a separate room from his peers.

He responded well to his acceleration, but continued to struggle with organizational skills. He struggled to pace himself during work and finish on time. He had poor endurance for daily tasks. He struggled when a task couldn't be completed during one sitting and did not make plans for finishing the work. (He would forget to come back and finish.) He struggled with overall time management. See his profile below:

Learning Area	Strength Area 1	2	Neutral 3	Barrier Area 4	5
Motor Imitation	X				
Touch Learning			X		
Visual Learning	X	X			
Movement Learning		X	X		
Self-Regulation Skill		X	X		
Auditory Learning		X	X		
Natural Interest & Motivation				X	

* A 504 Plan provides needed accommodations for those with physical and learning disabilities based on a federal civil rights statute. It is derived from section 504 of the Rehabilitation Act of 1973 that prohibits discrimination based on disability.

Kendal worked best if he had a visual cue or visual instructions to read. He responded well to a visual schedule and visual to-do list where he could look ahead to transitions that were coming, checking off work that was completed and highlighting work that he needed to return and finish. He struggled to list favorite things and benefited from purposeful expansion of his favorites. For him, this included taking pictures doing fun activities and having them posted on a bulletin board in his room. This positively affected his overall motivation. His teacher reported that once the recommendations were implemented, he had a much easier time engaging in a wider variety of topics with his classmates.

A MOVEMENT LEARNER
APPLYING THE LEARNING STRENGTHS PROFILE TO CARA

Cara was a six year old girl experiencing increasing symptoms of ADHD (though not diagnosed), sleep disturbances, some emerging aggressive tendencies, and general learning difficulty in the classroom even though she tested with average intelligence. See her profile below:

Learning Area	Strength Area 1	2	Neutral 3	Barrier Area 4	5
Motor Imitation	X				
Touch Learning			X		
Visual Learning			X		
Movement Learning	X	X			
Self-Regulation Skill			X	X	
Auditory Learning			X		
Natural Interest & Motivation				X	

Cara excelled at sports and gymnastics. She was able to attend to directions and receive coaching well in those situations. She loved drama and acting activities, but she struggled to sit and attend and complete worksheets in the classroom. Cara did not actually have ADD/ADHD. She had a strong kinesthetic learning style and kept trying to engage her "natural" strength in learning in the classroom but wasn't successful.

Once her teacher began to give her more movement opportunity, she began to engage much more readily in class. She was given the opportunity to help the teacher pass out papers, run errands to the office, and escort other students between classrooms between periods of sitting work. She was given the option of pacing in the back of the room while listening as the teacher taught new material or when she was reading to the class. She was also provided with a sit-n-fit junior disc in her seat to give her a balance/wiggle option that engaged her core muscles during seated activities. These changes made a big difference in her school life.

THE AUDITORY LEARNER
APPLYING THE LEARNING STRENGTHS PROFILE TO CARMEN

Carmen was a five year old girl referred from her counselor. She was diagnosed with Disruptive Behavior Disorder. She had a history of feeding sensitivity and GERD/severe reflux. See her profile below:

Learning Area	Strength Area		Neutral	Barrier Area	
	1	2	3	4	5
Motor Imitation	X				
Touch Learning			X		
Visual Learning		X			
Movement Learning			X		
Self-Regulation Skill			X	X	
Auditory Learning	X				
Natural Interest & Motivation			X		

Carmen demonstrated a clear strength in auditory learning. She struggled at times with over-reacting and did not always control her body movements well. She benefited from auditory cues (auditory scheduling) where a specific chime, song, or noise cued her into a coming transition. She benefited from auditory instructions paired with visual cues to show her how to apply the directions she was listening to. Out-patient therapy helped her finish working through her specific touch and movement sensitivity and triggers (many related to her feeding sensitivities and past medical history).

SOMETIMES IT IS ABOUT RECOGNIZING THE BARRIER
APPLYING THE LEARNING STRENGTHS PROFILE TO JACE

Jace was a ten year old boy who was referred to me with depression and a growing negative pattern of interaction with others. See his profile:

Learning Area	Strength Area 1	2	Neutral 3	Barrier Area 4	5
Motor Imitation	X				
Touch Learning		X			
Visual Learning		X			
Movement Learning		X	X		
Self-Regulation Skill			X		
Auditory Learning		X			
Natural Interest & Motivation				X	X

Jace demonstrated adequate learning performance skills. He had an average IQ. Though he had decent grades, his teacher described him as distracted and disengaged. He wasn't actively making friends. He demonstrated an increasing pattern of snapping at other children verbally, calling names, and playing alone. He was technically able to learn through movement, touch, and listening; however, he wasn't actively engaging in most learning activities.

The key to his profile was identifying how much he was struggling with natural interest and motivation. His list of liked activities was limited to screen time: computer games, video games, and watching television. He could not think of any other activities he liked to do and his parents had allowed him to engage solely in those things often, trying to go with what was making him happy.

By knowing this pattern, Jace's parents and I set out to purposefully expand his number of liked activities and we kept a notebook of his progress. Before long, Jace's symptoms were much more manageable, and he was actively engaging more readily in both classroom activities and interaction with peers.

EARLY LEARNERS
APPLYING THE PRIMARY LEARNING STRENGTHS PROFILE TO JOY

Joy was a two year old girl who came to see me during her multi-disciplinary autism assessment. She was diagnosed with autism. See her profile:

Learning Area	Strength Area 1	2	Neutral 3	Barrier Area 4	5
Motor Imitation			X	X	
Touch Learning		X			
Visual Learning		X			
Movement Learning		X			
Self-Regulation Skill					X
Auditory Learning					X
Natural Interest & Motivation					X

Joy was struggling to engage in age appropriate play skills and showed developmental skills around 10 months of age. She was struggling to progress from there and preferred repetitive play with a few favorite toys. She was sensitive to new activities, experiences, people, and environments. She struggled to "tune in" to her environment and learn from it. We identified that Joy would benefit from new learning opportunities built around touch, visual, and movement learning, but that she would be easily distracted or disinterested if the topic of learning and interaction was not connected to something she liked. She needed a treatment plan centered around acquiring motor imitation skills and expanding her repertoire of liked things in order to build her ability to learn through her other senses more readily.

APPLYING THE PRIMARY LEARNING STRENGTHS PROFILE: SAMSON

Samson was a one year old boy diagnosed with a chromosomal anomaly and pervasive developmental delay. See his profile below:

Learning Area	Strength Area 1	2	Neutral 3	Barrier Area 4	5
Motor Imitation				X	
Touch Learning	X				
Visual Learning				X	
Movement Learning			X		
Self-Regulation Skill			X		
Auditory Learning				X	
Natural Interest & Motivation		X			

Samson had already been working in treatment for a period of time with an early intervention team who had goals centered around motor imitation and motor skill development. However, he was not making quick progress, and so he was referred for a consult for insight into how to stimulate progress.

By identifying that he responded well to touch learning, the team was able to refocus Samson's interaction with toys, expanding his opportunity for touch experiences. His team worked to expand from cause-effect toys in his environment to tactile sensory play in shaving cream with cars (working for motor imitation in play) and work in the pool and bathtub with water and bubbles and toys. This information, combined with the fact that Samson was interested in a variety of new/ novel toys helped his team make sure they had a wide variety of different types of novel toys and activities during each treatment session to best harness his motivation and attention. This helped his team jump-start treatment with him and begin making more progress.

INCREASING SOCIAL INTERACTION SKILLS

You can use The Learning Strengths Profile to help you plan social play dates and group interaction that lends itself to creating good feelings and memories for a child. If you are looking for a "social hook" that will aid a child in making and keeping a friend, take time to study the child's profile while looking at the concept below. Possibilities should begin to emerge in your social planning.

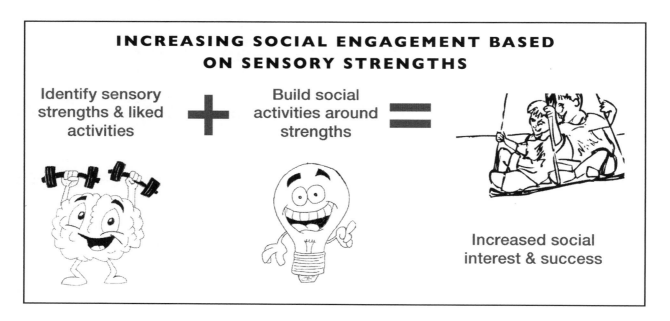

WRAPPING IT UP

At this point, you have some tools to begin analyzing a behavior, identifying the core function of that behavior, and determining what is maintaining the behavior. If the behavior is positive and you want to increase it, you add to the positive things that are reinforcing the behavior. If the behavior is a problem, identify the desired behavior that you are expecting and make a plan to replace the undesired behavior pattern with desired behavior. Knowing a child's strengths in learning can make implementing a positive behavior plan exponentially more successful.

You also have a new tool and framework to start using to identify a child's strengths and barriers in learning. You have the process for increasing a child's desire to learn and harnessing motivation so that it works in your favor and to benefit the child. The list of a child's favorite things, his personal carrots, will become your personal treasure chest. The great thing about this treasure chest is the more you use the gold, the more you grow the gold. What a great investment plan toward a child's future!

The Learning Strengths Profile enables you to more easily confirm problem behavior patterns and identify sets of barriers to better anticipate stressful situations for a child. Once stressful situations are identified, you can either avoid them until his skill builds in those areas, or enter them with careful planning and supports so he is more successful.

You have the keys to begin strategically setting the stage for successful social interaction, building a child's interest in interacting with others. You now have new keys to aid you in building fun memories and positive interaction for your child with his peers.

A child in stress has difficulty learning. You have new tools to help you look at your child's learning profile to see where he is stressed more clearly. You have new tools to help you make a plan to move from stress into a more positive learning opportunity. You now know to start with a strong motivator and build activities around that strong motivator. You know to make a list of your child's favorite things and purposefully work to expand that list in order to increase motivation for learning. You know to plan to move into a "new" opportunity that expands learning through multiple senses once your child is experiencing success. You know to provide movement as regular brain food every day. You also know to provide an opportunity for practice and repetition, especially for linear learners. You know that successful performance brings with it feelings of competence and that success breeds success.

By strategically setting up an environment or activity for purpose-driven learning, you enrich the environment and enable a child to successfully stack the "building blocks" in the pyramid of learning. Successful activity directs attention to progress and away from weaknesses. Now, you are ready for specific tools that can help you create and enhance your win-win situation for even greater success.

CHAPTER II DEEPER JOURNEY TO APPLICATION

The Deeper Journey portion of each chapter is set up to provide application and reflection questions or to help support group discussion regarding the information in the related chapter.

1. Complete The Learning Strengths Profile for your child.

2. Discuss your child's strengths and relate them to his list of liked activities and interests. Give specific examples.

3. Discuss your child's barrier areas and relate them to specific situations where he has avoided challenging situations.

4. What area represented in The Learning Strengths Profile do you need to learn more about? List it and then begin to brainstorm the best source of additional information that can help your child.

CHAPTER 12

"Each child is an adventure into a better life –
an opportunity to change the old pattern and make it new."
-Hubert H. Humphrey

PROBLEM SOLVING

Understanding your child's strengths based on The Learning Strengths Profile is a key to setting the stage for positive change. In addition, many parents that I work with are interested in how to support and problem solve in the area of identified barriers.

Sensory processing is relevant internally to each of us, but measured and overt through behavior. Therefore, treatment strategies built upon solid behavioral and sensory processing work will be the most effective strategies. Remember that behavior and sensory are two sides of the same coin, and make sure that you are looking at both when you plan for supports and skill building.

Also remember that small doses of meaningful activity where learning is achieved by doing something fun rewires the brain. Neurons that fire together, wire together. Your goal is to provide repeated positive experiences, engaging the senses in positive learning, to create lasting forward progress and change.

In this chapter, I have listed a few key components related to skill building in specific areas. Please understand that this is not a comprehensive list of skills or strategies in any area. The purpose of this section is to get you started and to provide information to facilitate discussion among parents and teams whose goal is to wrap around a specific student and plan for progress. This section is meant to be one resource, not an exhaustive resource, in that discussion.

This chapter is written with the preschool through grade school student in mind, but specific areas such as visual processing and auditory processing can directly apply to much older students as well.

This chapter is set up to aid problem solving related to a specific area of need identified in The Learning Strengths Profile, either to support progress in an area where the child is struggling or to enhance utilization of a strength area. If you do not need activity or support ideas in these areas, I recommend you skip to Chapter 13 to learn more about sensory diet.

MOTOR IMITATION

If motor imitation is a barrier area, it means that the other areas of visual learning, auditory learning, touch learning and movement learning are also barrier areas,* indicating that a child significantly struggles to take in accurate information through his senses and apply it to learning. When that is the case, building the skill of motor imitation becomes the most important section of most individual education plans. Before success will be significantly achieved in visual learning, auditory learning, touch learning and movement learning, motor imitation skills need to be in place.

Motor imitation skill builds in a systematic way. You can partner with a behavior analyst for a treatment called ABA* to address this area more comprehensively as needed. An overview of motor imitation skill development, listed from early skill to advanced skill, is listed below. A few examples are provided for a frame of reference, but the opportunities are as endless as your creativity.

- Imitation of and response to facial expressions (i.e. smiling in response to adult smile) and relational interaction. (Though this skill develops first in typical development, it will likely not be the first motor imitation skill to develop for those with Autism Spectrum Disorders.)
  - Smiling
  - Waving
  - Blowing kisses

- Motor imitation with an object in play
  - Zooming cars down a ramp
  - Hopping a toy chicken into a toy barn
  - Flying a toy plane through the air

- Motor imitation with 2 steps using an object in play
  - Using a toy wand or stick to move a toy frog into reach and then hop it to the pretend water
  - Having a toy plane hop along the runway and then fly through the air
  - Having a doll ride on top of a pretend car and then lay down to pretend sleep

*Limited motor imitation skill always limits other learning areas, but the amount of limitation varies per child.

*ABA is Applied Behavior Analysis. In this context, ABA therapists focus on shaping socially significant behaviors in order to support developmental progress.

- Motor imitation with an imaginary object in play
  - Using a banana for a pretend phone and having a conversation
  - Using a play hammer as a pretend microphone to sing with or as a pretend fork to eat with
  - Using small LEGOS as food to feed a baby doll

- Motor imitation for positioning and gross motor simple movement
  - Imitating standing and then bending over to touch toes
  - Imitating an army crawl and then tummy time position (prone on elbows)
  - Imitating shoulder shrugs and various arm positions

- Motor imitation during familiar daily routines
  - Imitating taking off jacket and hanging it up on a hook
  - Imitating brushing teeth
  - Imitating taking dishes over to the sink for washing

- Motor imitation during non-routine tasks
  - Imitating the positions for learning a new motor game such as holding hands to play Red Rover
  - Imitating a dance move to a new song
  - Imitating crumpling a piece of paper to make a fake snowball

- Motor imitation during fine motor play and work
  - Imitating drawing a circle and then face using a pencil and paper or index finger in shaving cream
  - Imitating touching each finger to thumb (finger opposition task)
  - Imitating hand and finger positions such as imitating a finger play sequence

TOUCH LEARNING

Touch learning has two skill development components: fine motor development and texture work development. The following strategies and activities are not in developmental skill order. For more resource in this area, consider consulting your child's teacher or occupational therapist. (Also, numerous resources are available related to this area on the Internet.)

For the child working to tolerate textures:
- Play in textures - see texture play in the Tool section of this book for more specifics
  - Smooth
  - Gritty
  - Goopy

- Sand
- Water
- Rice or Bean Play (Hide objects in the rice/ beans and dig for them.)

- Finger paint work

- Fidgets: used between texture play activities as a grounding activity
  - squishy ball
  - texture to rub or squeeze, etc.

- Taking shoes off can be calming and can help to refocus.

For the child who craves touch to the point that it interferes with daily activities:
- Velcro attached to sides of chair or underside of desk in classroom (It is a discreet fidget to rub while listening. It stays quiet and it stays in one place.)

- Fidgets:
  - squishy ball
  - texture to rub or squeeze, etc.

- Enough daily movement—moving at least 60 minutes per day! (Opportunities to walk and run errands can go a long way in helping to set this student up for success.)

- Weighted vest/heavy denim jacket/pressure vest to help improve focus, attention, calming, and self-regulation skills (This requires an onsite OT to determine the appropriate size of the vest, weight, and wearing schedule.)

- Opportunities to use play dough or clay while discussing ideas or "thinking" (This can be a great "break.")

For the child working to attend to detail in touch learning:
- Identifying objects hidden in a box or sock by feel only (no looking)

- Matching objects hidden in a box or sock (Look at an object outside of the box or sock and match it by feel to find the one hidden in the box or sock without looking.)

- Identifying shapes/letters drawn on hand or back

- Using manipulatives to teach a lesson (It helps to make concepts tangible and aides in understanding. Worksheets are the supplement, not the "meat."

Performance on worksheets only reflects a portion of learning. Don't allow them to dominate grades.)

- Touching each finger to the thumb and other simple hand/ arm exercises to get the hand and mind more prepared for writing tasks (The goal of this exercise is to increase oxygen to the brain for producing better written work.)

General touch considerations:
- Consider keyboarding as an alternative method for written assignments as opposed to 100% handwriting. Think through the goal of the assignment. Is the goal handwriting or content? If the goal is content, give options for delivery of their best work (i.e. typing).

- Cursive handwriting is sometimes the answer for those that struggle with printing work. It tends to flow easier and helps with spacing problems by requiring space between words only, not words and letters.

- When handwriting instruction and tutoring is possible, access it. Handwriting stimulates thinking and memory retention in those that master it. It is a skill worth mastering when mastery is possible.

VISUAL LEARNING

Visual learning is a primary method used in most classrooms for communicating information, so if a child struggles with visual learning, accommodation often needs to be made. Consultation with an optometrist, behavioral optometrist, or occupational therapist is often helpful in planning for any accommodations or modifications.

For the child who is working to tolerate visual experiences:
- Start with a comfort level. (Attempt to lower light levels: soft light, reduced clutter in the environment, etc.) Build inviting opportunities using themes and objects from your child's list of favorite things with the goal of expanding his visual learning without triggering his over-sensitivity.

- Limit visually busy worksheets. (Strive for plenty of margin, clear and concise information on the worksheet.)

- Consider use of a slant board for reading and some writing assignments. (This can support visual motor processing, posture, and attention.)

- Use incandescent lighting versus fluorescent lighting when possible. (Fluorescent lighting can have an excitatory effect.)

- Consider using light blue or pastel colored paper versus white paper. (White paper tends to reflect more light and is harder, more straining, on the visual system for some students. Pastel colors can be more calming.)

- Simplify. Simplify. Simplify. De-clutter the environment. (Everything has a place. Everything should be in its place.)

- Use color to match subjects. (For example, Reading = red folder and red book cover and red notebook; Science = green folder and green book cover and green notebook.)

For the child who craves visual input to the point that it interferes with daily activities:
- Flashlight games help to hone attention skills

- Play ball games /balloon games

- Use hide and seek games with people and/or objects

- Play "I spy"

For the child working to attend to detail in visual learning:
- Use 3D to 3D matching games

- 2D to 3D matching games

- 2D to 2D matching games

- Use single inset puzzles

- semi-inset puzzles

- interlocking puzzles with expanding number of pieces

- Use activity books with hidden pictures, "I spy", matching, same/different, word/symbol searches, etc.

- Play Connect Four, Tic-Tac-Toe, and Dots and Boxes/Square It types of games

- Promote visual memory with shapes. (Look at a card and then find the matching card when that card is removed.)

- Promote visual memory with letters/numbers/shapes. (Look at letter number or shape and then draw it on a marker board following a few seconds of delay.)
    - Add conversation during the delay.

    - Add motor tasks during the delay.

    - Add sequences of letters, numbers or shapes.

- Play "Go and Find" games. (Show an object or picture and have the child go and find the example hidden in the room.)
    - Add "go and find" in one of multiple rooms

- Use puzzles. (Visual puzzles and thinking puzzles to help stimulate thinking. These can be simple but very effective.)

General visual considerations:
- A picture or something visually pleasing can be used to represent positive experiences, memories and thoughts. (It can help to boost motivation and success. Adults keep them at desks, and it helps kids to get to keep one at theirs, too.)

- When possible, use a vertical surface (such as writing on the marker board or blackboard) to help strengthen visual-motor skills and endurance.

MOVEMENT LEARNING

Movement learning is all about motor control and coordination. For more information, consult a physical education teacher, physical therapist, occupational therapist or personal trainer for more information.

For the student who is working to engage in movement activities:
- Begin with walking. (Take family or educational walks focusing on increasing endurance.)

- Utilize music and movement games or fitness strategies. (i.e. Zumba, Pilates, Yoga, etc.)
- Utilize obstacle courses. (Begin with simple obstacles and motor challenges and increase the challenge.)
- Use mid-line crossing strategies. (See the Tool section of this book for a handout.)

For the student who engages in movement to the point that it interferes with daily activities:

- Make sure this student is getting enough movement built into his day, followed by grounding activities to help him calm and focus for learning.

- Utilize jumping games /dancing games/climbing games/balancing games

- Use digging activities.

- Try squishing with pillows for calming.

- Utilize a sit-n-fit/balance disc cushion in chair to engage core muscles and help focus attention in class.

- Bounce on a therapy ball.

- Do wall push-ups.

- Chew gum.

- Engage in "work" games that include pulling/pushing/lifting.

- Play "freeze" games and games that require balance and holding a specific position for brief periods of time.

- Provide opportunities to get up and move around the classroom. (Large muscle movement can help calming and self-regulating: standing up, running an errand, walking across the room, etc.)

- Carry weighted items to and from the office or between classrooms, such as a package of unopened paper or books. (This can be helpful for calming and to prepare to focus. Large muscle activation and using muscles increases oxygen flow to the brain to help support concentration and mood).

- Climb up/down stairs for a specific task makes for a quick "oxygen break to the brain."
- Engage in jumping jacks, stretches, jogging, or jumping in place every 20 minutes for up to 30 seconds.

- Provide a standing option for desk work or reading. (Standing can improve attention, decrease distractibility, and enhance blood flow to the brain.)

- Take a walk and discuss ideas. (Walking increases oxygen flow to the brain and can stimulate thinking.)

- Provide a Sit-n-Fit Junior as a chair cushion for those that need to bounce or wiggle in their chair. (This can engage core muscles and promote attention and focus for some students.)

- Replace a student's chair with a therapy ball (with a ring stand base) or ball chair. (This increases core strength which supports attention development and focus. Vertical movement is also thought to positively affect mood and emotional development.)

- RECESS! Never take away recess. (The need for physical activity throughout the day cannot be stressed enough for all students. Brainstorming alternatives to taking away recess for consequences and creating alternative plans for discipline is very helpful. Recess is vital and should be totally off limits to take away as a punishment.)

- Engage in clapping rhythm games and chants to help aid memory retention.

- Add a motor movement (such as bouncing on a ball) to memory work. (This can support memory and focus.)

For the student who is working to build movement learning skill and coordination:
- <u>Ready Bodies, Learning Minds</u> by Athena Oden (Oden, 2004) is a good motor lab programming resource.

- Practice specific motor tasks and set up opportunities to build skill through community sports programming.

- Consider personal training/physical education instruction/physical therapy/ occupational therapy resources.

SELF-REGULATION

Self-regulation skill develops through having adequate motor control, as well as specific training. This training can be provided through a counselor, psychologist, social skills program, or teacher. Though there are many programs developed to aid in self-regulation, one of my favorite programs is the <u>Alert Program</u> by Mary Sue Williams and Sherry Shellenberger. (Williams & Shellenberger, 1996) Again, one of the most important first steps is making sure that the student has enough built-in movement during his day. (See the Movement Tool in this book for more information.)

- Teach fast/slow/quiet/loud/soft/hard and begin using those terms to describe behavior and explain expectations. For example, asking a child to "slow down and use quiet, soft movements."

- Teach a child that he is the boss of his body and can control his actions.

AUDITORY LEARNING

Auditory learning is an important part of learning in most classrooms. If your child struggles with auditory processing, help can be found in consultation with a speech and language pathologist, an audiologist, or an occupational therapist.

For the child who is working to tolerate auditory information in the environment:
- Provide opportunities for auditory breaks and teach supports for when he gets overwhelmed. (Ask, "How can he help himself?" He can plug his ears, walk away, use noise-cancelling headphones, etc. This helps you identify needed supports and tools. Teach him to begin answering the question, "How can I help myself?" to build his independence and problem solving.)

- A student may prefer headphones (with or without instrumental background music) to support focus and attention while working. The headphones tune out natural auditory distractions in the environment.

- Provide multiple ways that support him in predicting what is going to happen in his environment, especially related to auditory events.

- Use social stories to help him predict what auditory events might happen and what he can do to help himself when he feels stressed about them. (Gray, 2010)

- Use clear and concise instructions for those that struggle to follow directions and remember to **show** students what to do when they struggle to listen and understand.

- Use songs and chants to help aid memory retention.

For the child who craves auditory input to the point that it interferes with daily routines:
- Use auditory scheduling where background music signals specific work and play times. For example, use dance music for free/recess time, instrumental music for writing work time, and other liked music (i.e. country, jazz, gospel, etc.) for other daily routines.

- Clearly define boundaries regarding when a child can vocalize or talk and when it is quiet time. Make sure the child knows when the next opportunity to vocalize or talk will be when you enter a quiet time. When introducing this technique, make sure you don't make quiet times too long or the child will have difficulty adhering to the schedule. Consult a behavior analyst if implementing this technique is difficult.

For the child working to develop auditory-motor skills:

- Play "Gossip"/telephone games.

- Play motor games that have a "go and do" component, requiring short listening and doing tasks. (This is similar to the visual "I spy" game listed above, but with verbal instructions instead of visual matching.)

- Play "Simon Says" games.

- Listen to books on tape, with questions following.

- Play auditory figure ground games. (Listen for specific sounds with competing background noise.)

- Engage in music and movement activities with directions for actions.

- Present information using a combination of verbal and non-verbal cues (such as pictures).

- Use single-step instruction when possible, as opposed to multiple-step instruction.

- Use visual lists of words or pictures to help him know what is coming next. (He likely struggles to anticipate what is coming next in his day and may miss vital auditory cues meant to alert him to change that is coming.)

- Give supports for expressive language. (He may have higher receptive skills than expressive skills because expressive language skills will often break down when he needs to remember and organize auditory information and then provide an accurate verbal response. He may have a general idea of the concept receptively, but not have enough information to form an articulate and accurate verbal answer.)

- He may have trouble providing definitions. His definitions may be simplistic or tangential.

NATURAL INTEREST AND MOTIVATION

This is one of the most important areas addressed in The Learning Strengths Profile and is also the most common barrier identified by this tool. In the Tool section of this book, multiple strategies are provided to address this barrier, including expanding a child's list of favorite things, creating a Uniquely You Notebook, and a journal technique to help focus thoughts.

GENERAL CONSIDERATIONS

Below are some ideas for strategies and modifications that might generally apply to a student, especially a student struggling with poor written expression work:

- Use prone positioning as an alternative to desk work. Have students lie on the floor for prone reading/writing work (drop down and read time). The prone position is good for anchoring/calming, focusing and directing attention. It also helps students visually, as there are fewer distractions when looking down at a book versus sitting at a desk. The book is also well-positioned for maximum visual accommodation and distance for the eyes.

- If possible, dedicate a "sensory corner" in the room where there is carpet, a bean bag, and a weighted blanket or lap pad (and other fidgets and tools as needed). This is an alternative "thinking" space that can be used to finish assignments.

- Use frequent breaks to refocus and de-stress. Adults take regular breaks to refocus, and we need to teach children how to do this instead of simply zoning out.

- Shorten assignments when appropriate.

- Allow extra time, especially for students who "beat to a different drum" or need more time to process and think. Pushing them will stress them and be counter-productive in many situations.

- Create moments of positive laughter to release endorphins. After all, learning is fun... right?

EXPANDING SKILL BETWEEN THE SENSES

Once you have focused on individual senses, the goal is to begin expanding communication between senses. Choose a learning concept to teach and link it to something that is interesting to your child. Present the new information using your child's strength areas. Then begin to expand your child's understanding and generalization of the concept using additional senses, working toward multi-sensory learning.

By reviewing "old" information using a variety of senses, you are allowing opportunity for the sensory processing pathways that might not be as strong to strengthen and develop without risking as much misapplication of the information, because the concept is already familiar.

The child already has a conceptual framework to more accurately interpret any "spotty" messages (remember **The Cell Phone Reception Principle**). Over time, using this type of review method to expand into multi-sensory processing, you will help grow your child's learning flexibility and "whole brain" learning and connection skills.

The Deeper Journey portion of each chapter is set up to provide application and reflection questions or to help support group discussion regarding the information in the related chapter.

1. In what areas does your child need you to provide support?

2. What skills does your child need to learn in the barrier areas you identified?

3. What modifications or adaptations need to be considered to help create an appropriate learning environment at home or at school for your child?

4. List current team members that need this information in order to support your child:

5. List additional people you might need on your team:

6. List research topics about which you need to gather more information. What are your next research questions on your quest to identify the information and supports your child needs to thrive?

CHAPTER 13

*"Nothing you do for children is ever wasted.
They seem not to notice us, hovering, averting
our eyes, and they seldom offer thanks, but what we
do for them is never wasted."*
-Garrison Keillor

SENSORY DIET

What is a sensory diet? Chances are if you have investigated sensory processing or any type of sensory dysfunction, you have heard the term "sensory diet." A sensory diet is a set of purposeful daily activity options that are designed to feed the nervous system, right at the level and intensity that the child needs. A sensory diet is individual. It contains some activities that are foundational to learning and good for all kids. You will find the first activities I recommend in the Tools Section of this book. A sensory diet also contains some specific work, whether it is sensory input or skill development work that will be very specific to your child's individual learning ability and skill set.

Just like we eat nutritious food multiple times per day to provide energy for our bodies to use, a sensory diet provides enriching sensory activities to provide energy, calming, and motivation. In essence, healthy eating plus healthy activity is just what a body needs to put the brain and body in an optimal state for learning and interaction.

SENSORY DIET - WHAT IS THAT?

Healthy eating + Healthy activity
=Just what the body needs

Just like we wouldn't skip meals for three days and then "catch up" with one large meal on the fourth day, one weekly time of therapeutic activity, such as a therapy session, will not be enough nervous system food for the week. When a child is experiencing learning or developmental stress, a sensory diet must be consistent and regular to provide enough nervous system nutrition to keep the body in balance.

When the body is sick or stressed, good food nutrition can make a significant difference in how the body copes and bounces back from illness. The same is true of the activities we provide for the nervous system. When the body is stressed, with atypical developmental patterns, trauma, or anxiety, we must be more purposeful, more consistent and more thoughtful about the activities and the combination of activities we provide for it. Just as we would be purposeful and thoughtful about meal choices and the combination of the foods we put together when recovering from a physical illness, so it is with sensory diets. The more stress and trauma, the more thought, support, and consistency is needed.

Occupational therapists, teachers, physical therapists, speech and language therapists, music therapists, psychologists, counselors, and behavior therapists are a few of the professionals that you might encounter or pursue partnership with as you explore what your child's sensory diet needs to look like. These professionals will help to support his optimal ability to effectively and efficiently take in information and respond well.

The goal of a good sensory diet is for it to be so ingrained in the daily structure and routine of a person's life that it does not stand out as "special." It just happens in the background of the day to support daily function. It doesn't have to include fancy equipment or therapy exercises per se, but it can include those as needed.

A consistent, solid sensory diet will provide a child with expanding coping skills, with the goal that when the child becomes stressed, agitated, or overwhelmed with a challenge, he begins to know what to do to help himself in that situation. He eventually develops the additional skill of planning for those times ahead of time.

There is a suggestion in the Tool Section of this book, Tool #6, that suggests creating a laminated visual cue card with lists of helpful activity choices for your child. As your child develops tried and true sensory calming, sensory alerting/"get ready to learn" strategies that work for him, this card can be updated to represent the activities that work best for him when he is stressed or struggling.

The visual cue card can be updated or changed as needed, but begins to provide a very effective tool for your child to use regularly. For some kids, just being able to picture the card in their minds and know that they can pull the card out as a resource is all that is needed. The card may never leave the backpack, but it is available if the child needs it for support and its existence means that the child is able to think through options for coping in times of stress.

CHAPTER 13 DEEPER JOURNEY TO APPLICATION

The Deeper Journey portion of each chapter is set up to provide application and reflection questions or to help support group discussion regarding the information in the related chapter.

1. List the activities that are currently a regular part of your child's week:

2. List additional activities that are needed to provide adequate brain food for your child:

3. What is your plan for incorporating the new activities into your child's day?

4. Review the Tool Section of this book and then record behavioral changes you notice as you utilize the tools:

TOOL SECTION

SECTION 4

TOOL SECTION

*"Perseverance is the hard work you do after you get
tired of doing the hard work you already did."*
-Newt Gingrich

TOOLS: TIME TO START DOING

Now that we have a framework in place, it's time to start **doing**. The doing part is my favorite part! I am a passionate advocate for therapy, especially occupational therapy, and I agree with Annie, a nine-year-old girl wise beyond her years (remember Annie and her bird Jingle?). She said, "Everyone needs OT. Just some people get to get it!"

So true, Sweet Annie. So true.

Before we get into the nuts and bolts of what to be doing, please remember that these activities are targeted to children that are preschool-aged through late grade school. (Many of them are applicable to children younger or older, especially when adapted). Many of them can be adapted to be applicable to children younger or older. I will also share a few tips along the way for those of you with children outside this target age range. Remember as you read that these tips are written and targeted to those ages. They are also written with the assumption that if you have children with medical complications (heart conditions, GERD/ acid reflux, severe digestive conditions, etc.) or physical disabilities, you will consult your team of professionals for individual help in applying each of these strategies and adapting them specifically for your child.

As we start into the topic of what we will purpose to do to stimulate development for a child, there is a truth we must digest:

Therapy won't change your child's life.
What you <u>learn and apply</u> from therapy sessions will change your child's life.

Taking your child to weekly therapy, even multiple sessions and different types of therapy multiple times per week, will not change your child's life forever. It may be fun for your child. He may look forward to therapy. (Hopefully he does!) Your therapist may grow to love and have a strong relationship with your child. But the fact is that 30 minutes or one or two hours per week won't be dynamic enough to create new, lasting connections in the brain. There is simply not enough skill repetition practice time in one setting once or twice per week to dramatically effect performance and to stimulate development.

Let me clarify: What **you** as the parent or caregiver will learn in those sessions—**what you apply to your child's daily routines**—will change your child's life forever! The power lies in what you build into your daily life. There is no such thing as a one-time "fix" or "miracle pill." Even if your child is on a medication that helps to support his natural chemical balance for self-regulation, behavior management, attention, or anxiety, it will be helpful for your child to have options for coping when the medication is waning in its effectiveness throughout the day. The activities in this section are what I prescribe as the foundation to set the stage for progress, whether the purpose is enrichment (in an attempt to avoid more formal therapies), preparation for best progress in therapy treatment, or as a support to or alternative to medication intervention.

I encourage you to learn and apply new tools, so that they can begin to support your child. It can be overwhelming to learn a new language and walk the purposeful path of consistently providing those new tools. It is worth your time and attention. The extra attention and time you invest now will set your child up to blossom into all he can be. I promise that the time taken to discover his learning style (and gifts and talents) and get to know him for the delightful being he is will pay off.

When you apply yourself to this journey of taking the time to put a framework for **doing** in place, and taking the time to diligently get to know your child's unique sensory processing strengths and barriers, you are ahead in your efforts to effectively support his development. The commitment to do is the first step in this **doing** process.

ON THE FLIP SIDE

Some of you are struggling, but "therapy" is not your answer. For some of you, studying this information and beginning to apply the tools that we will cover in this chapter will get you jump-started to progress without formal intervention. My hope is that the following information is helpful, whether you are preparing for therapy, or whether you are attempting to enrich your home activities to the point where formal therapy is not needed. Either way, the activities in this section are exactly where I suggest you start.

PURPOSEFUL INTENTIONALITY IS KEY

Being purposeful in your planning is one key to success. Interacting with your child and spending quality time will be valuable, but planning purposeful opportunities for your child to thrive is even more valuable. Another component to success is being intentional. Being intentional means setting the tone of the interaction. I have heard Elaine Hall, the producer of <u>Autism: The Musical</u>, say,

"Intention is like your compass – it keeps you on track and further defines your purpose."

Intention is the way you show up in the interaction. It is **how** you interact with your child, not just what you do. It is all about your attitude. You can be going through the "right" motions and doing the "right" things and not make much progress, because the intentional tone of the interaction is off and confusing to the child. For example, an adult can use a syrupy sweet, soft tone of voice, but if her words are unkind or her interaction is passive-aggressive, the child might become distrusting and less engaged in learning than before. Therefore, I encourage you to be intentional in your actions and attitudes. You can be the facilitator to start the change you'd like to see.

FIRST WORK

You might be saying, "I'm ready to **act already**!" If so, then you are ready for tools. This entire section is dedicated to bringing you the foundation of "first work" that I recommend for every child, whether in my own home or in the clinic or in the classroom.

There are numerous resources available that give option after option for building fine motor skills or developing attention. The first strategies that I suggest are the basics. They are the foundation that stays in place to support your child's development. Other fun activities can then be added to the foundation. You may do many therapeutic and fun activities, but if your child's body is not primed to receive them efficiently and effectively, they are simply...not as effective. We are going for "**bang for our buck**" here, our *time buck*. If your life is like my life, you don't have time to just try a few fun things just because they are fun. You need the heavy lifters in place first that are going to set the stage for **everything** to be more fun.

You will notice that these first activities are pretty simple to implement. They are flexible and can be adapted and added to most children's games and activities. They can be seamlessly applied to your child's favorite activities. Do you remember the list of "favorites" that you made earlier? It's time to use it!

The brain is wired to engage more fully in liked activities than in non-preferred activities. Suppose you are listening or watching information that is boring to you. For me it would be something like quantum physics or racing statistics or how a piece of machinery works. If we hooked electrodes up to my brain in that situation, we would see a handful of red dots indicating brain activity during that time. Now, let's say we change the subject to one that I am very passionate about. For me that would be something like children and learning styles or sand volleyball. Now, we would watch as **hundreds** of red lights indicated brain activity, connection, and processing of that information.

Not only do we engage more fully when we are interacting with interesting things, but also any other pieces of information that are chained to that interest get more fully processed as well. Let's say that I can't memorize my spelling words, but I love throwing a football, playing tennis, and other hands-on learning. If I work on spelling words with Mom, Dad or a peer (who can spell well) **while** I am throwing a football and make it a fun game (such as "keep away" from the incorrect spelling), I can have fun throwing the football **and** learn my spelling words. In addition, I could learn spelling rules (made into football chants that rhyme since most spelling rules rhyme anyway). After that, I might sit down to work with spelling in another hands-on way, such as finding word strips hidden in theraputty or play dough, identifying which are spelled correctly and which are spelled incorrectly. Next, I might write a paragraph (using my spelling words) in which each word I spell correctly earns me time doing a favorite activity with Mom or Dad. I bet I learn more spelling that week.

Your biggest job is taking the therapeutic DOING exercise, motion or position that I present below and tying it into the things your child is **already doing and loves to do**. This is key! I suggest that you spend extra preparation time observing and making a good plan to provide opportunities with a new therapeutic twist. It will pay off! This is also the stage where you need to gather data (what your child is already doing and what he likes to do) and make a list of the things you plan to encourage him to do (to expand his list). Brainstorm with your support network, including other parents and professionals about how you can connect those two pieces creatively.

These tools are also applicable to the classroom. I know teachers that use these in their early preschool classes and teachers that use these principles with middle school and high school students. Many teachers keep a checklist in their classrooms to ensure that opportunities are readily available in their classroom sometime during the day.

TOOL #1: POSITION FOR FUN LEARNING

Refer to the Position for Fun Learning Handout. Make a copy of it. Put it on the refrigerator or up on the wall in your child's play space to remind you to incorporate developmental positions into your child's daily routine.

Developmental positions are the positions that we find occurring naturally in typical early development that set a child up for developmental next steps. They are a core part of the foundation for learning and help set the stage for progress. When a child increases his ability to maintain a developmental position, it demonstrates an increase of core strength. Progress in this area helps to support the child's development in the areas of motor planning and coordination, attention, self-regulation/ self-control skills, fine motor skills, visual perception skills and eye tracking skills, hand dominance and bilateral coordination.

The Position for Fun Learning Handout outlines the three primary developmental positions of tummy time, tall kneeling, and hands and knees positions. It gives a short list of activity ideas beside each position. You will notice that the handout targets preschool and grade school uses of the activities. I will describe how to translate this principle for middle school and high school students, but I want you to really understand the foundational use of the developmental positions first.

Sometimes, I tailor an activity around the position. If I know one of my kids needs to practice a specific position, I brainstorm a rewarding activity that can be done in that position. I then offer that rewarding activity tied to the developmental position. Other times, I look at what my kids are doing and ask myself, "Can that be done in tummy time, tall kneeling, or hands and knees and still be fun, appropriate, and safe?" If the answer is yes, I encourage my kids to use one of those positions.

For example, I am passionate about encouraging kids to reap the benefits of the tummy time position. I also recognize that it is hard work, especially when a child first starts into it. So, I encourage parents to reserve things like a favorite toy, even the Nintendo DS, for this time. This is where the list of favorites comes in handy. Look on the list and find a favored toy or activity and provide it during tummy time.

Remember, building muscle and stability is hard work. Your child may only tolerate this position for about 30 seconds with good alignment. You may see him kick a knee out to the side so that he shifts his weight out of the "straight/midline" position. You may see him slump down and "hang" where his ears drop down beside his shoulders in this position. You may see him insist on propping his chin on his hands in this position. All of these are signs that he REALLY needs to work in this position because he can't hold it correctly and his muscles are screaming at him, "I've never had to work like this before!" You may see some resulting behavior from your child that reflects what his muscles are screaming at him. This just means that we have the muscles' attention! Our goal is to wake them up and teach them to do their job. We have accomplished step one when we see that behavior. They are definitely awake!

Don't overdo it at this stage. If this is your child and his muscles are not used to working this hard, ease into this step throughout a week. Introduce tummy time with a **_SHORT AND SWEET_** approach where your goal is good alignment for 30 seconds to 2 minutes. Don't push much beyond that the first week. Short, accurate motor positioning will be more effective for developing good posture, alignment and motor work habits than one daily session of overdoing it with faulty patterns. This is a very important stage.

Tummy time is a developmental position that often feels like a "magic pill" to me. Tummy time supports the development of shoulder and arm stability, which in turn allows hand development (and handwriting skill) to flow naturally. It supports attention development as the body learns to stabilize in a "quiet" position so that the eyes and ears can be supported to gather accurate information and attend readily to new information. It supports visual scanning and the development of eye tracking/scanning skill as it helps the body develop neck stability and allows the perfect distance for the eyes to focus well.

The added bonus for visual processing work in this position is that the most exciting thing on the floor where your child is doing tummy time is probably the reading or visual work that you've placed in front of him. He will naturally be able to focus more readily in this position, especially after his muscles wake up and support him. You will begin to see a difference in your child's skills when he can maintain this position well and comfortably for at least 5-7 minutes. I find 5-7 minutes to be a therapeutic threshold where these muscles are now on the body's learning team and beginning to do their job in the background to support the progress of other skills (like those listed above).

Tummy time is also what I call a **grounding** position from a sensory processing perspective. For example, when a child is a big mover, often he is not good at processing that movement well. He experiences a poor sense of his body's position in space after movement activities. For example, he might come in from recess "hyped up" and not necessarily ready to focus and work. By **grounding** him after his involvement in movement activities like having him do weight bearing/proprioceptive work, my goal is to help him re-establish his position in space and re-establish his internal understanding of where his body ends and the world begins. It also helps **ground** him for better quality of movement and better processing, which in turn prepares him for better reactions to his world. It helps his nervous system calm down to give the best response that he can following movement activities and to be more organized in his processing than when he moves straight from a movement/alerting activity into the next thing in his daily routine.

APPLYING DEVELOPMENTAL POSITIONS AND MOVEMENTS TO THE OLDER STUDENT

Once you understand how developmental positions support core strengthening and help to connect the brain into effective movement and learning, you will start seeing them everywhere. You will find that Yoga, Pilates, Crossfit, Zumba, Aerobics, and most other popular and effective exercise classes are designed to build core strength, beginning with developmental positions and expanding into cross lateral movements. You can look at exercise videos, exercise posters, and exercise classes and find the ones that spend the most effective time developing these positions and movements. It's really that easy.

Sometimes, we forget that tummy time positioning is very effective for older students, too. There is not always an appropriate way to offer studying opportunities in the classroom where students have a place to lie on their stomachs to study, but I have seen it accomplished by some creative teachers. Working with students individually to build up tummy time endurance is applicable in almost every situation.

I have received a couple of phone calls from college students in their freshman and sophomore years that were former clients of mine when they were children and adolescents. The phone calls begin with a panic about how they are sure they are going to fail the semester because they can't seem to remember anything. They are overwhelmed and developing major anxiety and they are certain their parents are going to flip when they flunk out. My first question is often, "Tell me how you are studying. Are you ever using tummy time?" It's often met with silence.

They are in a new environment and didn't naturally carry one of their most effective study tools with them to the new environment. They forgot about effective positioning for studying. Each time, we have reviewed tools they know such as finding a quiet place, reading chapters in chunks (in a tummy time position), finding a study group to review information **after** having looked at it, reading into a voice recorder and listening to it while lying on a bed or running, and making sure they are moving enough every day.

I am pleased to report that in each situation, I received a report at the end of the semester that "all is well." Their strategies are working again (when they use them). One college student expressed that the tummy time positioning changes everything so that he can focus and absorb information. He had been trying to study primarily in the library because that's what he thought was expected in college. It wasn't working for him. He has ADHD, and he was more distracted by who was at the library and what they were working on than getting his own work done. By finding a quiet place where he could get in a position to really focus, his studying time was more effective. He could then be social in his study group and make new connections because he had a foundation of knowledge to start connecting to.

That same smart boy was not sure he would get to go to college at one point because his struggle with sensory processing was a significant barrier to consistent learning in the classroom. Good for him and for his family for working so hard to give him the tools he needed to succeed and follow his dreams!

a note about tummy time:

I am often asked, "Are there any times when tummy time is not a good idea?" For typically developing children and adolescents who struggle with mild to moderate sensory processing difficulty, I have not run into a time when tummy time and developmental/core strengthening work has not been effective. I have never seen it in 15+ years.

However, if your child has a medical issue such as a heart problem, a severe respiratory/lung issue, GERD (gastroesophogeal reflux disease), or significant reflux of any kind, your child is the exception to this rule. Typical motor development may be compromised by the medical needs that your child is experiencing. Things need to be adapted for your child to work forward in motor development without exacerbating those medical concerns. In this case, I recommend consulting with an occupational therapist or physical therapist to help you look at your child's unique medical symptoms and precautions and adapt strategies like tummy time. The shoulder and neck strength he builds will support future learning activities.

Tummy time can be adapted to provide weight bearing through the arms, but no pressure on the tummy such as leaning on a mat or table in a hands and knees position or a elbows and knees weight bearing position. It can be challenging to encourage hands and knees work if the child has never been in a prone weight bearing position—those muscles don't know how to do their job and so the child may resist that position. A child with this type of medical condition subconsciously protects his chest and stomach area. This often requires therapeutic support to work through, but it is time well spent to help effective sensory processing and learning pathways develop.

POSITIONING MAKES A DIFFERENCE!

Positioning can make a positive difference in the way a child attends to and takes in information. The following are three developmental positions that can be used to support learning. They are a core part of the foundation for learning and help set the stage for forward progress. When a child increases his or her ability to maintain and utilize one of these positions, it demonstrates an increase of core strength. Progress in this area helps support the child's development in the areas of attention, self regulation/self control, fine motor skills, visual perception skills and eye tracking skills, hand dominance and bilateral coordination.

After a child has mastered using the developmental positions, he is ready for advanced core strengthening work. Use this worksheet to bridge the gap between developmental positions in play and more advanced balance and movement coordination. After your child has mastered the core strengthening program, then he is ready for general classes such as Yoga, Pilates, Zumba, and other group exercise workouts.

CORE STRENGTHENING
BUILDING A LEARNING FOUNDATION

Core strength is widely recognized as vital for developing posture, but core strength also provides the background foundation for skills, such as:

- **Reflex Integration**: The body is designed for voluntary movement and coordination skills to naturally surpass the body's automatic, less immature, movement patterns. Core strength is a vital part of this natural process.

- **Establishing and Maintaining Attention**: Core strength allows a child to focus energy and attention in an outward focus, on a given task, as opposed to using energy and attention to maintain body positions and perform routine motor tasks. When core strength is weak, tasks become more labor intensive for a child.

- **Visual Perception**: Core strength helps to provide stability through the head and neck to allow the eyes to take in accurate visual information for visual processing. Weak core strength often correlates with weak eye muscles and difficulty with eye coordination skills. The child will still scan, but the task is more labor intensive for the eye muscles and the eyes will often fatigue much more quickly.

- **Visual Motor Response**: Just like with visual perception, core strength is important for visual motor skills. It aids the eyes in taking in accurate information and supports the body as an effective motor response is formed. When core strength is weak, children often have difficulty with visual motor and visual motor sequencing tasks.

- **Static/Stationary Balance Skills**: Core strength provides the stability for the arms and legs to develop coordinated movement skills. It is also the foundation for balance skills such as standing on one foot.

- **Body Position Sense Processing**: Core strength provides the basis for efficient proprioceptive processing (body position sense). It provides the stability and the foundation for processing that allows a student to sit in his chair without wiggling or falling out of the chair. It also supports the development of coordination skills and results in more graceful, purposeful movements.

TOOL #2: MOVEMENT... EVERY DAY

As our culture changes and becomes more electronic and grows in convenience, movement is no longer as naturally built into our day. Therefore, we must make sure it is **purposefully** built into our day because we were designed to move. Movement is an essential foundation for learning to occur.

Carla Hannaford is a scientist who has studied how our bodies learn. I recommend her book: Smart Moves: Why learning is not all in your head. (Hannaford, 1995) In this book, she explains the neuroscience behind movement and how it is an essential foundation for learning. If you step back and analyze your child's day, you may be shocked to realize how little your child is actually moving throughout the day. Do you remember the earlier discussion about movement?

> "Sensations, movements, emotions and brain integrative functions are grounded in the body. The human qualities we associate with the mind can never exist separate from the body."
>
> --Carla Hannaford, Ph.D.
> *Smart Moves*

Many of our American classrooms are designed around the next seated activity the child is going to do. Though most of our elementary kids still get to go out for recess at least one or two times per day, many of them don't really know what to do at recess, and so they stand around. Have you watched a child with a learning disability stand around, kicking rocks at recess? Just because there is an opportunity for movement doesn't mean children naturally know how to grasp the opportunity and make the most of it. Most of them need direction.

Once given direction, you see groups of kids begin to grow comfortable going outside with a group of peers. They are more productive as they begin to strike up a basketball game, soccer game, kickball game, four square game, jump rope game, tetherball game, etc.

If you are an observer at recess, you may find that some of the kids who are struggling the most in the classroom don't know what to do with their recess time. They struggle the most relationally, and so they are not naturally included or drawn in by the other kids. It is not because the other kids are unkind, but because there is probably a history of the other kids inviting that child and that child not having the skills to gracefully enter the group and maintain his place in the play.

The play deteriorates and the child is either ejected from the group, and the group moves on, or the child withdraws himself from the group because it is stressful for him.

Some of the best support services in the school setting can be provided on the playground where aid is given to assist a struggling child in experiencing a productive recess time. This is well spent support time as it often sets that child up for a better afternoon of learning. The aide may be teaching play skills one on one, teaching the child how to play tetherball or kickball or basketball or jump rope. Then the aide will transition into a coaching role with the child, such as in a small group interaction to successfully participate with peers in what he has been taught.

How is your child moving throughout the day? Is it enough?

A child needs at least 60 minutes of quality movement time each day. Is your child getting that? An hour is minimal. Even better is two hours. When was the last time you took a walk as a family? When was the last time you ran a mile with your child? When was the last time you rode bikes together or played tennis together?

There are hundreds of ways to get your child moving. I have listed a few recommendations in the box below. There are additional benefits that you may experience as you work toward ensuring that your child has been moving enough during the day, especially if you purpose to spend some time moving with him.

You will find that when you move and play together that you grow in relationship together. You will find that you enter a new level of relationship and influence in your child's life. You may feel a difference in yourself also. You will become more balanced emotionally, handle stress more effectively, and become more productive. If you try it, you will never go back!

The purpose of putting movement into your day is to feed your nervous system so that it is ready to learn, not to put your nervous system under sports performance pressure. This concept also applies to athletes. If you are a parent of an athlete, where is your child moving during the day where the purpose is to provide **good nervous system food**, not high pressure motor performance? Where is the **fun** movement in the day? Find it, build it in, and you will be on your way to higher motor performance and higher learning performance.

If you read through those examples and thought, "Yes, he would do all of those and still not be done moving," this means that you have a child who is craving movement, but not necessarily processing it well. Your child likely has trouble attending to learning for long periods of time without a break. He may be formally diagnosed with ADHD or may have a **Sensory Modulation Disorder,** meaning he has trouble responding well to sensory information in a way that matches the nature and intensity of the situation.

Daily movement is even more essential for this child than it is for the typical population. Building in 1 or 2 hours of purposeful movement is especially important for this child. Do you remember way back in the beginning of this book when I described the child with a behavior problem who was using his recess time to spin at school and then had trouble learning in the afternoon? He was moving, but the movement was not feeding his system in a way that was most effective for him.

If you take a look at the types of movement activities your child is naturally choosing, it might be as if he is eating cookies nutritionally. It is food and he likes it, but it is not providing him with great nutrition. Replace the **cookies**. Give him better movement options and you may be surprised at how much that helps. In other words, **bouncing off the walls** doesn't count as his movement activity for the day.

---

a note for families of children with autism and other developmental disabilities...
I find that an organized movement piece is often one of the first things to fall to the wayside in the midst of busy therapy schedules and the other interventions that you may be working to fit into the day. Make sure you purposefully take a step back at times to make sure this piece isn't forgotten. Consistency with this piece will help all of your other therapies and strategies work better for you.

TOOL #3: MIDLINE CROSSING / CROSS LATERAL MOVEMENT

The left side of your brain controls the motor movements on the right side of your body, and the right side of your brain controls the motor movements on the left side of your body.

Information is exchanged between the two halves of your brain on a super highway called the **corpus collosum**.

When one side of your body, such as your arm, reaches across (past) the middle of your body, the two sides of your brain communicate and coordinate information. That coordination of information between the two halves of the brain is a key to the brain's ability to process information well and contributes to the body's ability to execute a graceful response to the information. The more practice the brain has with processing in this way, the faster that super highway runs. Better coordination of information results in faster processing speed and accuracy.

The goal is to give your child every opportunity to be able to process information to the best of his ability. Priming that speedway with motor movement practice, especially practice in coordinating information between the two sides of the body, is one of the best ways to begin to support better and faster processing. Midline crossing exercises or cross lateral movement is one tool to stimulating that pathway.

Refer to the midline crossing handout on the adjoining page for specific instructions and ideas on how to incorporate midline crossing into your child's everyday activities. Remember for older children and adults, it can often be as simple as regularly participating in exercises, such as Zumba that includes cross lateral movements.

Is crawling really that important? Can my child skip it and just start walking?

I regularly get this question when I travel and speak. I have a set of articles from popular parenting magazines published since 2000 that have put forth the idea that it is ok if your child skips crawling because most children start walking around the same age whether they crawl or not. That data is probably true.

Is crawling present in development just to propel us into walking?

My opinion is no! First, let me say that I have never met an accomplished athlete (collegiate or professional) that skipped crawling, and so I do think that practice on your knees sets a child up for smoother coordination and a more firm foundation for building sports coordination.

Crawling is perhaps the first time in development where you are truly practicing **whole brain learning** and coordinating information consistently between the two sides of the brain in a sustained activity. The nerves that carry information on that super highway (the **corpus collosum**) are experiencing myelination, which allows them to develop into faster communicators across that bridge. It is my belief that this first practice sets a child up with a firm foundation for all other processing skill development to be built upon. Eventually, all sorts of information will travel across that **corpus collosum bridge**—and the information will become increasingly complex.

The more practice the brain receives in supporting information processing for "simple" motor purposes such as crawling, the more it is prepared to face the heavier demands placed on it to process future information, such as speech and academics. Crawling and other coordinated motor movements prime the pump for other forms of processing that occur later in development. This is why many speech therapists have begun to pay more attention to motor positioning and motor movements when they are addressing speech delays. They recognize the importance of the motor foundation to help support speech development.

So what do you do if your child skipped the crawling stage and is now experiencing sensory processing and learning problems? Build midline crossing back in, daily and purposefully. It will be awkward for the child at first because that bilateral coordination of using both sides of the body (and brain) to work together has not gelled developmentally for the child, and you've found a **crack in his developmental foundation**. The great news is that children's brains are incredibly plastic (flexible and formable) and resilient.

When the brain is given the opportunity to experience the **just right opportunities**, it's like giving the brain organic food when it has been surviving on junk food. The body begins to mature, heal itself, and take steps forward into healthier processing and healthier brain-body connection. Your child begins to benefit immediately. Just like it can feel good to provide your child with healthy food to eat, it can feel good to know you are providing your child's brain with the opportunities it needs to build patterns for learning. This in turn helps a child begin to show more of what he knows, which increases his performance at home and at school.

MIDLINE CROSSING

What is Midline Crossing? Midline crossing happens when one body part actively crosses over the center of the body in a movement.

Why is midline crossing important? Midline crossing engages both halves of the brain in "communication" so the whole brain works together to accomplish the movement. This type of "whole brain communication" is foundational to faster and more efficient processing skills—for motor, sensory, and all "academic" information.

TOOL #4: TEXTURE WORK

The skin is the largest organ in the body. It accounts for a portion of the body's ability to accurately take in information and give back good information. I use texture and motor coordination work (Tool #3 and Tool #4 in combination) as a beginning step in helping children who have difficulty showing what they know as they begin to increase their performance output. For example, if a child struggles with getting his thoughts on paper, but is able to verbally express his thoughts, I start with texture and motor coordination work. He may be hiding pennies in theraputty or play dough and then reaching across midline to put the pennies he finds in a cup beside him. He may be lying in a tummy time position on top of a coffee table while bearing weight through his hands (which are positioned on the floor) while he uses a finger to scoop shaving cream and "mark" specific plastic cards that are scattered in front of him. (This activity combines texture work, motor coordination, tummy time/weight bearing, and visual scanning skills.) Whatever I have him doing, it will be connected to something on his list of liked things or something he has expressed interest in during therapy time.

My goal is to give his body practice taking in touch information and coordinating that information into a motor response. Initially, he simply tolerates the texture input and forms the motor response. (This is what is described above.) I will then work toward activities that require him to accurately interpret what he feels from his hands and then form a motor response. For example, a more advanced activity might be reaching into a bag and feeling for an object that matches the picture he is looking at and then writing down the name of the object after he has found it. I might use my finger to draw a shape or write a word on his back and he has to draw it/write it on a marker board in front of him and then tell me something about it.

The first step to this process is to use the texture handout on the adjoining page to begin engaging in regular, purposeful touch learning. Regular texture work-play not only begins to support your child's creativity and love of exploring a texture, but also helps to build a foundation for fine motor skill and self-calming skill development. In addition, many children become more interested in expanding their thoughts and ideas as they engage in this sort of work. Their motor and sensory processing systems begin to better support their thinking skills, and then those skills can more naturally grow. The texture handout will systematically walk you through introducing texture play, beginning with dry textures and working toward wet textures and mixed textures.

Texture play is not just for the young child. It is also applicable to the older student or adult. How many of you find something to fidget with or play with in a meeting? Look no farther than a professional's office to find texture activities. I love to walk through Brookstone and other office toy stores and look at all the newest touch and fidget wonders. Funky pens and pencils, massage chairs, and toys that make impressions and pictures by moving magnetic shavings or metal pins are very fun stuff indeed. We are never too old to provide nutritious input for our nervous systems.

I firmly believe that daily texture work with a substance like theraputty or play dough or clay significantly increases fine motor production quality, fine motor endurance, and a student's ability to get his thoughts onto paper. One of my personal research utopia moments will be when there are multiple studies that show this to be directly linked. I am waiting for there to be such overwhelming evidence of the link between texture work and hand strengthening and handwriting skill development that texture work becomes a daily part of every elementary education routine.

INTRODUCING TEXTURE PLAY

Enjoying texture plays a key role in a child's ability (and motivation) to explore the world around him. The guidelines below outline a method of introducing texture play. The levels are listed in order from what is typically easiest to hardest for most children. When you encounter an activity that your child resists, think about the texture components and which "level" they may fall into. Once that is determined, you may begin working at the level just before the targeted activity level and then eventually begin to re-introduce the activity your child resisted. Another strategy would be to break the resisted activity into parts and reintroduce the activity in small parts to build up to the full activity.

TOOL #5: EXPANDING THE LIST OF FAVORITE THINGS

By now you know I feel a list of favorites is vital to planning for progress for any child. The first goal is to expand that list. If the list has enough items already, your goal becomes enhancing and enriching the depth of the experiences on that list. By focusing on expanding a child's list of favorite things and enhancing them, you are increasing your basket of **carrots** (rewards) for hard work. You are also increasing quality of life, increasing the opportunity for anticipating fun ahead, and increasing a child's ability to engage fully in an activity or moment for shared fun with you or a peer.

If you are a parent of a child with autism spectrum symptoms, this type of work should be purposefully interwoven into all of your treatment plans from now on. This becomes connected to work that helps your child share enjoyment with others, engage in joint attention to things, show things to another person for the purpose of communicating about it, and shift his attention to include another in something he enjoys.

If you are a parent of an adolescent, this list will be especially helpful to you as you work to support your adolescent's skill development and social development. Adolescence can be a time when it is harder for parents and children to strengthen relational connections if they were not strong prior to adolescence. This area of work can become a key to strengthening relationship with your adolescent, communication, and can enhance your influence in your teen's life.

TOOL #6: WHERE ARE THE VISUAL SUPPORTS?

Rarely do I find a case where some visual scheduling or visual aids are not helpful. For young children, it can be as simple as a list of pictures indicating the flow of a routine, or visual choices that they can pick from for an activity opportunity or a reward choice. For older children and adolescents, especially those with auditory processing issues, a written checklist that details expectations, a routine, or a job list trumps verbal requests and prevents arguments and partial or poor task completion. It can be a strategy that helps to defuse stress, especially communication stress.

Schedules can be used to represent the activities in a week or in a month, the activity flow of a day or of part of a day, or specific functional routines such as a bathroom routine, dressing routine, or mealtime routine. It is OK to have multiple different visual aids and schedules that work together systematically. For example:

- A bathroom routine hanging in the bathroom.
- A dressing routine hanging in the bedroom.
- A setting the table routine or meal time rules in the kitchen.
- A picture of organized school supplies to show where items belong in a desk or bedroom.

As your child learns new coping skills and has a growing list of things he can do to help himself (after implementing Tool #8), I recommend a laminated card with a list or visual symbols (to represent his options for self help with sensory activities that are good fits for him). Keeping a copy of this card in the car, mom's purse, student's backpack or pocket, student's desk, teacher's desk, and in the kitchen or living room at home means that you can support him in helping himself and in making a sensory smart choice when he needs to—even if he is becoming stressed.

For older children and adolescents, also consider teaching how to make to-do lists, shopping lists, color-coded assignment calendars to show homework, due dates, and tests, and how to use computer and phone calendars and list apps.

TOOL #7: BRING ON THE MUSIC

Music is powerful! It bypasses our natural avenues for taking in information through "regular" pathways in the brain and often enters through our Limbic System, which is tied to our emotions. There is little that is more powerful than emotion. Using music for therapeutic change is like a secret weapon. It's powerful!

Imagine that you've had a full day of hard work and realize that important company will be at your house in two hours. You need to clean house and make meal plans before the company arrives. You scurry home, and it is quiet at your house. Chances are, if you leave it quiet, you may get part of what you need to get done, but you might also take a nap! If you turn on spa-like, relaxing music, you may be calm when your company comes, but your work may not be done. However, if you turn on your favorite up-beat, dance-party music, you can probably whip the house into shape, have your dinner prepared, and switch to the calm music right before the company arrives so that they get the impression that you had all day to prepare for them after your nap and you were not stressed at all! (Or that magic fairies clean your house and do the rest of your work for you, too, so that you get to relax most of the day.) Either way, you get my point. Music can work for us to motivate us in ways few things can.

I refuse to do a gym workout without great music. It is torture otherwise!

Think through the musical atmosphere at your house. What music is calming to your child? Are you playing it when the whole house needs to support a "calming/ regrouping" time after school or before bedtime? What music is **fun** for your child and motivating? When are you dancing, laughing, clapping? Can music enhance those times? Does your child need the house to be quiet during homework time so that he can concentrate, or does he need instrumental music (no words please) in the background when he is studying to focus best? Find out.

Music can support and enhance our ability to engage in daily routines. It can be especially important for the developmentally delayed child or the child who is cognitively challenged. We often provide visual schedules, but we often don't think of providing auditory cues in preparation for a transition or of providing an auditory schedule. I find that auditory cues are powerful.

For example, I worked with a severely developmentally delayed young lady with autism and cerebral palsy, including significant cognitive challenges. Auditory scheduling was significant to her progress. She was struggling to remain calm and attend at meal time. Eating was very challenging for her, and she became distracted and agitated easily during meal time. As a result it was a stressful instead of enjoyable time for the family. She loved bath time as it was very relaxing to her. She loved dancing and was most relational during that type of interaction.

We used music to help cue her into what kind of "time" it was during the day. Instrumental, calm music was played during meal times and at bath time. The music would turn off about 3-5 minutes before transitioning to another "time" in the day, cueing her that a change was coming. New music, such as preschool sing-along music, then indicated "get-ready-to-work" time and included clapping rhythms and chanting preschool learning favorites. Academic goal work followed that "get ready to work" preschool music. Her favorite country dance music signaled it was recess/dance/free play time. Lullaby music signaled rest, relaxing, massage, and stretching time. It worked wonders for her ability to anticipate transitions, cooperate with the routine, and calm to enjoy meal times with her family.

There are many popular auditory training tools available in the therapy world now that are built on the science of creating a strong learning loop between the auditory system, the movement system and the visual system:

See it. Say it. Hear it. Do it.

The science is solid. Whether you build in music and movement for learning by using the tools and framework provided here, or add to it with specialty therapy tools and equipment, make it a priority to pay attention to that learning loop in your child's daily life.

TOOL #8: THE UNIQUELY YOU NOTEBOOK

Do you remember the *Uniquely You Method of Learning* from Chapter 7? Each child has a unique set of preferences and approaches to learning, based on his personality, sensory processing abilities, cognitive abilities, and past learning experiences. I recommend creating a *Uniquely You Notebook* that represents your child's unique preferences, strengths, and learning style. The purpose of this notebook is to track what you know about your child, as well as the progress he makes.

I use a three-ring binder for my own children. The first half of the binder includes pages highlighting that child's strengths, personality traits, and character qualities. This includes a *Learning Strengths Profile*, the *List of Favorites* for that child, and a few pictures that capture that child at his best. The second half of the binder includes specific communication regarding that child's learning progress, including grade cards, progress reports, and other paperwork organized by grade or age. It also includes a current plan for supporting that child's progress at home, including developmental skill-based progress, character work, and concepts that my husband and I are targeting to reinforce and teach that child. At the back of each binder, I have also included a section on developmental and medical history for that child.

Parents who have designed a **Uniquely You Notebook** report that teachers and other professionals are very appreciative of the information in that notebook and that it is used regularly to support their child. Some parents who have a child in multiple therapies also include a section for the therapists to write notes back and forth to increase the communication and collaboration between therapies. They also add a tab for each individual therapy so that a copy of the progress notes can be quickly and easily accessed by parents or other members of the team during treatment.

The look of each notebook is unique and based on that parent and child's personality and style, but they all have one thing in common. They are a treasure-trove of information about that child. The notebook supports faster progress as it provides information from past teachers to new teachers. The notebook provides a tool that supports collaboration between professionals to support better intervention and more targeted planning for progress. The notebook also provides background information and a frame of reference for specialists who are focused on providing consultation or specific treatment for your child, which can set the stage for them to hone their advice more specifically for your child.

TOOL #9: JOURNAL TIME

I use the Journal Time strategy when children are worrying, focusing on the negative, struggling to talk about the positives of their day, and struggling with sleep. This worksheet is designed to be copied and made into a journaling notebook. The smaller space at the top of the worksheet is designed to hold worries, mess-ups, and negative experiences that happened during the day or week. The larger space is designed to refocus on the positive things that happened, the life lessons that were learned and can be positively applied from now on, and the things the child is looking forward to in the coming weeks or months. By utilizing the space in this way, it visually gives the child perspective on how to encapsulate his worries and focus less on his worries and negative thoughts than the positives in his life.

The journal page can be a parent-child activity, where the areas are discussed, and then the child writes or draws pictures to represent his thoughts. The parent can be the scribe and write or draw to represent the high points of the discussion. The focus during this time is not written expression skills. The focus is a symbol, word, sentence, or picture that helps get thoughts down on paper so that the child does not have to worry about them anymore. The focus is also in expressing worries and negative thoughts in order to refocus on the positive or the lesson learned, instead of dwelling and getting "stuck" in the negative experience or feelings about the experience.

TOOL #10: PROBLEM SOLVING THE BEHAVIOR-SENSORY WAY!

This worksheet can be used to apply all of what you have learned in this book. It is designed to provide a clear and concise representation of behavior principles, including the following:

- You will have a place to list the learning strengths you have identified in The Learning Strengths Profile, as well as place to list the barriers to learning that you have identified in The Learning Strengths Profile.

- The ABC's of behavior where you will identify and describe problem behavior specifically and then identify antecedents that might be contributing to the perfect set-up for the behavior, as well as consequences that are reinforcing the behavior.

- Identifying Favorites/Repertoire of Reinforcement where you will list your child's favorites for quick reference as you plan how to move forward into more positive behavior patterns. You will identify whether you need to begin a campaign of purposefully expanding this list. You will also have a list of your first *carrots*, as you begin to work to build motivation related to the behaviors you will identify that you need to teach.

- You will answer the question: What do you want the child to be doing? (As you now know, this is one of the most important questions you can answer, because it highlights what you need to specifically teach.)

- You will identify one behavior (or more) that you are targeting to increase for more positive interaction and performance.

- You will outline any plans or key people needed to teach the behaviors you have identified.

- You make a place to note any additional insights your team has when thinking through and discussing the behavior and sensory findings.

- The worksheet also summarizes findings in a Positive Response Plan that includes a behavioral plan. This section will include the following:
    - Specific behavior plans and strategies
    - Specific team members responsible for implementing the plan
    - Specific sensory-motor plans, including plans for coping skill development and self-regulation skill development and specific team members responsible for teaching these skills

- Additional team members that are needed, based on identified work to be completed or any team members that were not present for the discussion that will need to be filled in.

FIRM FOUNDATION FOR LEARNING

Using the assessment and planning tools in this book combined with the action tools provided in this section will lay the foundation for progress and help you start on a strategic pathway to supporting your child in positive progress and positive sensory and motor learning. This is the first step. When this foundation is laid, the next steps of specifically addressing individual pockets of sensory dysfunction, skill deficits or behavioral issues are much more doable and successful!

APPENDIX

SECTION 5

TOOL #1-A
POSITION FOR FUN LEARNING

Positioning can make a positive difference in the way a child attends to and takes in information. The following are three developmental positions that can be used to support learning. They are a core part of the foundation for learning and help set the stage for forward progress. When a child increases his or her ability to maintain and utilize one of these positions, it demonstrates an increase of core strength. Progress in this area helps support the child's development in the areas of attention, self regulation/ self control, fine motor skills, visual perception skills and eye tracking skills, hand dominance and bilateral coordination.

As you engage in the developmental positions shown below, remember that the position is the important part. You can utilize any game or reinforcing activity that fits your child and so don't limit yourself to the ideas supplied here. Tummy time is the most popular position for learning of the three below.

TUMMY TIME: Lie on your tummy – up on your elbows.

Remember!   » No propping your chin on your hands

» Keep your legs as straight as you can stretched out behind you

Activity Ideas
- Reading a book
- Playing play dough games
- Playing Sticker games
- Using manipulatives/blocks
- Playing board Games
- Drawing games
- Watching TV/playing video games

TALL KNEELING: Position yourself up tall on your knees.

Remember!   » Do not sit down on your heels, stay up tall on your knees

Activity Ideas
- Tossing a ball back and forth
- Bouncing a ball to a person
- Bouncing a ball to the wall
- Drawing/painting on an upright surface
- Playing games in front of a low table or couch

HANDS AND KNEES: Position yourself in hands and knees.

Remember!   » Hold your tummy up and flat and keep your feet on the floor

Activity Ideas
- Tossing a ball back and forth
- Bouncing a ball to a person
- Bouncing a ball to the wall
- Drawing/painting on an upright surface
- Playing games in front of a low table or couch

TOOL #1-B CORE STRENGTHENING
BUILDING A LEARNING FOUNDATION

Positively Sensory!

Superman/Prone Extension Activities:

- Work on arm position first: hit a rolled or tossed ball with both hands or with alternating hands.
- Work to maintain head, chest, and arms in correct position between hits with the ball.
- Work into maintaining the full position with arms, head, legs
- Work in short bursts (1-15 seconds) and focus on increasing QUALITY of the position and then increase how long the child can hold it.

Popcorn/Supine Flexion Activities:

- Work on crossing arms over chest, bringing knees up to chest
- Encourage head tuck to complete the Popcorn position
- Work to maintain the position in short burst (1-15 seconds) and focus on increasing QUALITY of the position and then increase how long the child can hold it.

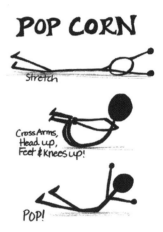

POP CORN

Stretch

Cross Arms, Head up, Feet & Knees up!

POP!

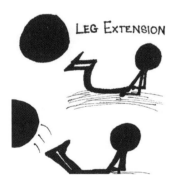

LEG EXTENSION

Leg Extension Activities:

- Work on leg extension exercises next with tossed or suspended ball
- Hips should flex about 90 degrees and feet remain off the floor
- Encourage head up with long neck for leg extension activity
- Encourage legs working together and then alternating.

Bridge Activities:

- Work on flat tummy (no sagging!) for short bursts (1- 15 seconds) and focus on increasing QUALITY of the position and then increase how long the child can hold it.
- When the child is able to hold the position with good alignment, begin lifting and straightening one leg at a time.

BRIDGE

Dog Activities:
- Begin with maintaining all fours and
turning head side to side while keeping balance.
- Then add lifting alternating arms
- Then add lifting opposite arm/leg together in an alternating pattern.
- This exercise can be connected to academic and visual scanning activities easily.
- Finally, add a head turn to lifting the opposite arm/leg together in an alternating pattern.

Bicycle Activities:
- This exercise is built upon the skills learned in Popcorn/ Supine Flexion work. Pull into a partial popcorn position initially and then touch one hand or elbow to the opposite knee in an alternating pattern.
- This exercise is good to use during memory or spelling work to help increase memory work and recall of information.
- This exercise also supports processing speed.

Tree Activities:
- Begin teaching standing on one foot by supporting the child at the hip joint and then fading your support to finger-tip touch. When the child can maintain balance on one foot with finger-tip touch for 10 seconds, you are ready to move to the next step.
- Encourage the child to place his hands on his hips or stretched out to the side while standing on one foot.
- Encourage him to maintain balance skills for increasing periods of time, building to at least one minute.
- Make it harder by repositioning the flexed leg into an abducted/angle position with the foot resting on the opposite knee.
- Make it harder by repositioning the hands touching above the head.
- Build tree strength in the new positions to at least 60 seconds.
- Work on dynamic balance by standing on one foot and reaching with arms to complete a task or reach down to the ground to pick up objects.

BRING IT ALL TOGETHER
Bring it all together by adding academic information into the exercises and activities. Add visual motor and eye scanning tasks while the head is in the supported, steady position. Add auditory motor tasks. Add sequencing and memory tasks.

TOOL #2: MOVEMENT...EVERY DAY

As our culture changes and technology temps us to be more sedentary, movement is no longer as naturally built into our day. Therefore, we must make sure it is purposefully built into our day because we were designed to move. Movement is an essential foundation for learning to occur.

A child needs at least 60 minutes of active movement per day. An hour is minimal. Even better is two hours. You will find that when you move and play together, you grow in relationship together. There are hundreds of ways to get your child moving. I have listed a few recommendations here to get you started.

- Taking a walk with family or friends
- Swinging
- Ripsticking/ Skateboarding
- Crawling Games
- Canoeing/ Kayaking
- Dancing
- Riding Bikes
- Swimming (pool games)
- Tennis
- Rocking in a Rocking Chair
- Group exercise instruction: Pilates, Zumba, Crossfit, Yoga, Tae Kwon Do, etc.

- Zip lining
- Jumping on a trampoline
- Gymnastics/ Tumbling
- Hopscotch
- Climbing
- Roller Skating
- Vacuuming

The purpose of putting movement into your child's day is to feed his nervous system so that it is ready to learn, not to put the nervous system under sports performance pressure. This concept also applies to athletes. If you are a parent of an athlete, where is your child moving during the day where the purpose is to provide good nervous system food, not high pressure motor performance?

The goal? Find fun motor opportunities and engage in them...every day.

TOOL #3 MIDLINE CROSSING

What is Midline Crossing? Midline crossing happens when one body part actively crosses over the center of the body in a movement.

Why is Midline crossing important? Midline crossing engages both halves of the brain in "communication" where the whole brain works together to accomplish the movement. This type of "whole brain communication" is foundational to faster and more efficient processing skills—for motor, sensory, and all "academic" information.

What do I DO? Incorporate midline crossing into regular routines or new activities. There are a few activities listed below to help jump start your routine. As your child attempts to reach across the body, watch for turning of the body/trunk to where midline crossing does not actually occur—make sure the arm or leg passes TOTALLY across the center of the body.

ACTIVITY IDEAS:

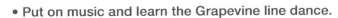

- Put on music and learn the Grapevine line dance.

- Put objects in a container by placing the container on one side of the child and the objects on the other.

- Place puzzle pieces to each side of your child and have him reach with the opposite arm to get a puzzle piece and put it in the puzzle.

- Place legos or blocks to each side of the child and have him reach with the opposite hand for the pieces that he wants.

- Practice batting a soft ball or balloon. Keep both hands on the bat throughout the swing. Be sure to ensure the safety of others in the area.

- Practice golfing with a soft ball or balloon and a plastic golf club or stick. Be sure to keep both hands on the club throughout the swing. Be sure to ensure the safety of others in the area.

- Reach over the opposite shoulder to get a sticker, bean bag, pencil/crayon, napkin, puzzle piece, game piece, etc. to complete an activity.

- Kick a ball to the side by kicking across the front of the body.

- Plan Exercise that has cross lateral movement. (i.e.: windmill exercises)

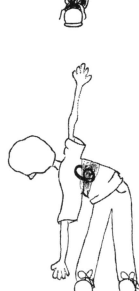

TOOL #4 INTRODUCING TEXTURE PLAY

Enjoying texture plays a key role in a child's ability (and motivation) to explore the world around him. The guidelines below outline a method of introducing texture play. The levels are listed in order from what is typically easiest to hardest for most children. When you encounter an activity that your child resists, think about the texture components and which "level" he may fall into. Then begin working at the level just before the targeted activity level. Eventually begin to re-introduce the activity your child resisted. Another strategy is to break the resisted activity into parts and reintroduce the activity in small parts to build up to the full activity.

REMEMBER TO HAVE FUN

<u>Textures Present</u>: Child uses tools to work with textures
Goal—Initiate touching a texture and tolerate the texture being present in play, not necessarily to touch it.

<u>Dry Play</u>: 1 texture
Goal—Child is able to play (with hands) in 1 dry texture at a time for a variety of dry textures.

<u>Dry Mixed</u>: 2 or more dry textures
Goal—Child is able to mix 2+ dry textures for an activity or game and actively touch the mixed texture.

<u>Wet Play</u>: 1 texture
Goal—Child is able to play (with hands) in 1 wet texture at a time for a variety of wet textures.

<u>Wet Mixed</u>: 2 or more wet textures
Goal—Child is able to mix 2+ wet textures for an activity or game and actively touch the mixed texture.

<u>Mixed-Complex textures</u>: mixing wet & dry texture play
Goal—Mixing multiple combinations of wet and dry textures together for active play.

BASIC DRY TEXTURE PLAY

Beans
Cotton
Uncooked noodles
Sand/Moon Sand
Rocks

Rice
Velcro
Chalk
Flour
Fabric textures

*Transition texture: Play dough/clay/silly putty

BASIC WET TEXTURE PLAY

Shaving cream
Water
Pudding
Cooked noodles (mixed with butter or oil)
Peanut Butter (or other "spread")

Hair gel
"Slime"
Finger paint

EXTENDED ACTIVITIES

CHALK DRAWINGS
On multiple surfaces (paper, concrete, chalk boards, etc) encourage your child to draw multiple pictures, shapes, letters, etc. Ask him to tell you a story about the picture that was drawn.

SILLY FACES
• Markers (to draw the face)
• Paper (Construction/cardstock paper works best)
• Beans or buttons (for eyes)
• Noodles or cotton balls (for hair)
• Sand or rice (for a beard/hair)
• Twizzlers (for a smile)
• Craft glue (school glue may not hold it together)

Draw a simple picture of a face. Glue on various items to decorate.

Parent: "What do we see with?"
Child: "Eyes!" (Apply glue to the eyes and let your child put the beans in place.)
Parent: "What do we talk with?"
Child: "Mouth" (Apply glue where a mouth should be, and add the twizzler.)

MARBLE PLACEMAT:
• Shaving cream
• Food coloring (1+ colors)
• Paper plate
• Plain white paper
• 2-3 Q-tips

1. Prepare your white paper with your child's name or fun design. Darker ink shows up best.

2. Pour a large amount of shaving cream onto the paper plate. Spread into a thick layer over the plate.

3. Put multiple drips of food coloring onto the shaving cream. Using the Q-tip, allow your child to make a swirled design (do not mix the colors completely). Note: Food coloring will dye your clothes and hands if it comes in contact.

4. After mixing, place your white paper from step one FACE DOWN onto the shaving cream. Turn them over so the paper plate is on top and "squish" the plate down.

5. Remove the plate and wipe the shaving cream from the paper.

6. Once the paper is dry, laminate for safe keeping.

BUBBLE ART:
• White tissue paper
• Tape
• Food coloring
• Premixed bubbles

Tape a white piece of tissue paper to a window or bathtub wall. (You may also do this activity outside where things cannot be stained.) Help your child to mix several cups of bubbles and drops of food coloring.Using a bubble blowing wand, encourage your child to blow multiple bubble colors at the paper until it is totally covered.

TOOL #5: EXPANDING THE LIST OF FAVORITE THINGS

If we spend time identifying and building a list of favorite things (for a child or for ourselves), we are building toward a happier, more productive future. By increasing the repertoire of liked things, we build natural reinforcement into our daily lives.

You will want to know the things your child is passionate about so you can hook him into learning. You will want to regularly take inventory of his preferences and passions. Start by making a list of your child's favorite things and then work to expand them.

Favorite color.

Favorite food.

Favorite indoor activities.

Favorite outdoor activities.

Favorite "active" activities.

Favorite sedentary activities.

Favorite things to do alone.

Favorite things to do with friends.

Favorite things to do out in the community.

Favorite adventure idea.

Favorite vacation.

TOOL #6: WHERE ARE THE VISUAL SUPPORTS?

Embrace visual learning strategies in your environment by taking a week to review the visual supports in your life.

VISUAL SCHEDULING

For young children, use pictures to represent the flow of a routine.

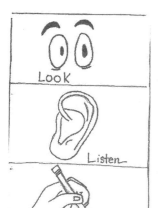

Be clear and concise. Don't make the schedule busy and visually cluttered.

Detail your routine or task steps, not the exact time it will happen. You want the child focused on what comes next, not distracted by the exact time it will happen while missing the sequence of the steps.

Decide whether you will use line drawings, actual pictures, or graphics. Then be consistent. Don't mix them up within the same visual schedule or visual aide.

The presentation should match the child's skill level and be appropriate for both his developmental age and his chronological age.

Schedules can be used to represent the activities in a week or in a month, the activity flow of a day or of part of a day, or specific functional routines such as a bathroom routine, dressing routine, or mealtime routine. It is ok to have multiple different visual aids and schedules that work together systematically. For example:

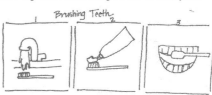

- A bathroom routine hanging in the bathroom.
- A dressing routine hanging in the bedroom.
- A setting the table routine or meal time rules in the kitchen.
- A picture of organized school supplies to show where items belong in a desk or bedroom.

For older children and adolescents, also consider teaching how to make to-do lists, shopping lists, color coded assignment calendars to show homework, due dates, and tests, and how to use computer and phone calendars and list apps.

TOOL #7 BRING ON THE MUSIC

Music is powerful! It bypasses our natural avenues for taking in information through "regular" pathways in the brain and often enters through our emotions. There is little that is more powerful than emotion. Using music for therapeutic change is like a secret weapon. It's powerful!

Music can support and enhance our ability to engage in daily routines. Providing auditory cues in preparation for a transition can be as helpful as visual scheduling.

Tips for using music:

Auditory cues to signal a transition: This can be as simple as a snap, a clap, a hand motion or a type of song (i.e. jazz, dance party, etc.) that signals a specific time such as "time to clean up", "time to move from one station or activity to another," "time to wake up and get ready for the day" or "free play time."

Using background music: Music can be used in the background for various activities since it lends itself to creating atmosphere and motivation (for most people). Calming music to influence concentration is generally instrumental, whereas music to motivate gross motor work is generally more upbeat with words to sing along to while you complete motor tasks.

Music to stimulate multi-sensory processing skill: Music is a great tool to increase multi-sensory processing skill, ability to filter information, and ability to attend and shift attention. The goal—creating a "see it/say it/ hear it/ do it" loop for learning.

1. Create an activity with a "see it/ say it/ hear it/ do it" loop. For example, start by drawing a shape on a marker board, covering it, and having the child name the shape and then draw it from memory. Work at this until the child can accurately remember and imitate drawing 5 basic shapes.

2. Next, use your finger to draw one of the shapes on the child's back. He will picture it in his mind, name it, and then draw it on the marker board in front of him.

3. Next, add background music (I usually use Beethoven) to the above sequence.

4. Next, use your finger to draw two shapes in relationship to one another on the child's back. He will picture it in his mind and then draw it on the marker board in front of him.

5. Next, switch from shapes to letters and words.

Auditory Sequencing activity:

1. Draw 2-4 shapes on the marker board. Give each shape a story name such as "The Day We Went Camping" or "The Boy Who Loved Exploring." After each shape has a story theme, use your finger to draw one of the shapes on the child's back. The child will add one or two details to the story. Then, draw another shape and the child adds details to that story. Once the child can keep the stories straight and remember the details in the story, begin mixing up the order of the stories by mixing up the sequence of the shapes you draw on the child's back.

2. I usually have instrumental music playing in the background during this activity.

TOOL #8: THE UNIQUELY YOU NOTEBOOK

Each child has a unique set of preferences and strengths and weaknesses, based on their personality, sensory processing abilities, cognitive abilities, and past learning experiences. A **Uniquely You Notebook** is a notebook that you create to reflect your child's personality, skills, talents, preferences, learning style, and learning history. The purpose of the notebook is to track what you know about your child, as well as the progress he makes. This will be helpful both for you and for the other teachers and adults in your child's life for a season.

I use a 3-ring binder. The first section of the binder includes pages highlighting my child's strengths, personality traits, and character qualities. This includes a **Learning Strengths Profile** and my child's **List of Favorites**, and a few pictures that capture the child at his best.

The second section of the binder includes specifics about the child's learning—awards, grade cards, progress reports, notes from parent-teacher conferences, and other paperwork organized by grade or age. It also includes a current plan for supporting the child's progress at home, including developmental skill-based progress, character work plans, and concepts that parents are targeting to reinforce.

The last section of the binder holds developmental and medical history for the child and any medical or therapeutic reports related to the child (such as a speech therapy evaluation).

Other sections or items to consider including in **The Uniquely You Notebook:**

1. A therapy section for collaborative notes between therapists or teachers if your child participates in therapies or special instruction courses.

2. A section to track progress for any individual therapies that your child participates in.

3. A medication history section if your child takes medication to track medication and the when the prescription was originally given, how it has worked, etc.

4. Memorable events such as cultural rights of passage in your family, first sports teams, first camping adventures, baptism, etc.

5. A set of questions that you ask every year or so and recorded answers along with a picture of the child at that age.

The goal is to create a notebook that reflects your child and can be a quick reference as you share facts with teachers, therapists, or other important people in your child's life. Regardless of how you design your notebook, it will be a treasure-trove of information about your child to support progress, collaboration between the adults that are investing in your child's life, and targeted planning for progress.

TOOL #9: JOURNAL TIME

The goal of Journal Time is to reflect on the day and look forward to fun things tomorrow. It is a tool that can be used to keep challenges and tough moments in perspective. Though it can be completed by a child independently over time, it is designed to be used as a parent-child tool where the child has support to complete the activity and reflect on it.

Worries, tough moments and challenges go in the small box in the upper left. Take a brief time to acknowledge them with the focus being on learning from them, not dwelling on them. Positive lessons and things to look forward to tomorrow or ways to positively apply what we learned today and use it tomorrow go in the rest of the space.

Acknowledge the past and the mistakes, remind your child that "mistakes are an opportunity to try a better way" and dwell on the positive that is to come.

My worries, challenges, and tough moments . . .

There were great moments today too. I learned . . .

Tomorrow, I'm looking forward to . . .

TOOL #10: PLANNING WORKSHEET

Child's Name:	☐ MALE	☐ FEMALE
	Grade level: _____	☐ Special supports/outside therapy

LEARNING STRENGTHS PROFILE (Strengths and Barriers) summary:

Behavior Analysis

Description of targeted (problem) behavior:

Function of Behavior: (check all that apply)

☐ Attention: (to get attention from preferred person)

☐ Tangible: (to get something "I want")

☐ Avoid/ Escape: (to avoid/escape something "I don't want")

☐ Sensory: (just because it "feels good")

IDENTIFY Set Up/Antecedents to Behavior:

IDENTIFY Favorites and Repertoire of Reinforcement:

IDENTIFY Consequences of Behavior:

Specific Targeted to teach: (What do you want the student to be doing?)   (What behavior do you want to increase?)

What is your plan to TEACH that behavior?

Positive Response Plan:

Strengths that will be used to facilitate positive change:

Barriers that will be supported and avoided in teaching strategies or behavioral instruction until acute stress resolves:

Behavioral Plan/Behaviors to be taught and targeted:

Sensory Supports Needed:

Who else needs to know and be invited to join the team? Plan for facilitating additional team members:

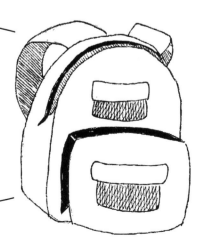

Remember that a child will use the most effective tool in his current

Response Backpack. If you want to change the response, you have to add

the better tool. What tool are you going to teach and encourage?

For positive results, we must REPLACE negative behavior with a "better way."

Tip #4, Amy's Top 10 Tips

LEARNING STRENGTHS PROFILE

Student Name:	Date:
Student's Date of Birth:	Person Completing form:
Grade Level/School:	Relationship to Student:

The Learning Strengths Profile is a big picture method of capturing a student's individual approaches to learning and interacting. A parent/ caregiver, teacher, or therapist can complete a Learning Strengths Profile for a student. The Learning Strengths Profile is most effectively utilized with students who have a developmental performance level of 5-6 years through adolescence.

The Learning Strengths Profile is a flexible tool that can be used to identify patterns of learning that are positive and strength based. Strength areas identify a child's most effective and efficient methods of learning (i.e. visual learning, auditory learning). It is designed to quickly identify strength areas that can be used when introducing new learning or social experiences as well as barrier areas to be avoided in those situations. The Learning Strengths Profile can also be used to confirm patterns of dysfunctional learning in order to support, teach, and adapt learning situations for a student's best performance and success in learning.

Once all areas are completed, a student's learning strengths will emerge. Strength areas should be used to introduce new learning, expand social interaction, and highlight strength based performance. To increase a child's motivation for learning and natural reinforcement for learning, parents and teachers can build learning experiences and instruction around the identified learning strength areas. Barrier areas will identify learning areas that need support and treatment attention. Identified barrier areas indicate that the student is not processing that type of learning effectively and efficiently for learning purposes and, therefore, should not be used as a primary method of introducing new learning material. Barrier areas should be used with "old" learning for review of information that is already mastered. Once a student is successfully using strengths for new learning and is successfully reviewing information using a variety of senses to aid generalization, a plan to increase flexibility in learning can be designed to capitalize on strengths while incorporating weaknesses.

Learning Areas:

MOTOR IMITATION:
The ability to accurately or functionally copy a motor movement or position.

TOUCH LEARNING:
The ability to register and discriminate incoming sensory information through the skin and respond appropriately.

VISUAL LEARNING:
The ability to understand and respond to what is seen.

MOVEMENT LEARNING:
The ability to actively engage in motor movements safely and productively, not escalating into hyperactivity, but remaining self-controlled during movement.
The ability to modulate motor and sensory processing information during movement activities.

SELF-REGULATION
The ability to become excited or active and then calm back down. The ability to calm after being upset. The ability to modulate social-emotional information.

AUDITORY LEARNING:
The ability to listen and understand spoken language and environmental sounds and then respond appropriately.

NATURAL INTEREST AND MOTIVATION:
This area measures the breadth and quantity of a student's interests and natural motivation for learning.

Please rate student performance based on the student's recent behavior. Read the skill sets listed under each learning area. Rate the student's performance. If a student's performance fluctuates and is inconsistent, mark the spectrum of performance by putting an X for each rating in all learning areas that apply.

Learning Strengths Profile	STRENGTH		N	BARRIER	
	1	2	3	4	5
MOVEMENT IMITATION 1-2 = Quickly picks up skills by watching someone demonstrate "how" to do the skill. Imitates a sequence of movements easily. 3 = Imitates a few new gross and fine motor actions accurately, but does well during familiar routines. 4-5 = Struggles to imitate motor movements well, but is beginning to imitate movements during favorite activities.					
TOUCH LEARNING 1-2 = Learns well by manipulating and building with objects. Connects to learning in a "hands on" way. 3 = Responds positively to many touch and texture learning activities, but does not always engage in the activity for long. May have a few strong touch preferences (i.e. tags removed from clothing.) 4-5 = Becomes very distracted in learning situations when texture or "hands on" activities are presented, either craving or resisting the activity.					
VISUAL LEARNING 1-2 = Learns quickly and accurately by watching videos or animated teaching of a subject. May enjoy visual puzzle games (i.e. Wheel of Fortune, crossword puzzles). 3 = Responds to visual learning activities as long as they are clear and concise without too much "busy" background. Responds to visual information that is familiar. May have a few strong visual preferences (i.e. font size) 4-5 = Struggles to organize and understand visual information without support and responds best to highly structured visual information presented in small chunks. Needs consistent repetition to learn visually. May crave visual stimulation, but has trouble making sense of it or avoids visual stimulation all together.information presented in small chunks.					
MOVEMENT LEARNING 1-2 = Actively engages in routine movement activities without fear or over-excitement. 3 = Engages actively in movement activities for a short time or with adequate preparation. 4-5 = Avoids movement activities and quickly disconnects from a group when movement is a part of learning or play.					
SELF-REGULTAION 1-2 = Able to self-calm following an exciting or upsetting event without supports or intervention. 3 = Sensitive to new experiences and events, but handles them well with supports and preparation. 4-5 = Difficulty calming down, even with supports, or has difficulty "waking up" to participate in daily routines and learning activities.					
AUDITORY LEARNING 1-2 = Actively engages when listening to a story or lecture, "tunes in" easily and can accurately remember details. Actively remembers chants, songs, poems, or details. 3 = Remembers some details from conversations or lectures, but needs notes or other supports to remember accurate details. 4-5 = Struggles to understand and remember what he/ she hears. Needs consistent repetition to respond to auditory information. Responds inconsistently or disproportionately to environmental sounds.					
NATURAL INTEREST AND MOTIVATON 1-2 = Has a variety of interests, hobbies, and liked activities. Screen time (computer, video games, TV) stays in balance with other recreational activity. Student is interested in learning about a variety of topics and has healthy social connections. 3 = Has strong preferences about favorite things, but will actively engage in new activities that are presented. 4-5 = Demonstrates limited interest in activities outside of select favorites. Over-focuses on screen time (computer, video games, TV) to the point that it negatively impacts learning and social relationships.					

© Amy Vaughan, OTR/L, BCP 2014   www.positivelysensory.com

PRIMARY LEARNING STRENGTHS PROFILE

Student Name:	Date:
Student's Date of Birth:	Person Completing form:
Grade Level/School:	Relationship to Student:

The Learning Strengths Profile is a big picture method of capturing a student's individual approaches to learning and interacting. A parent/ caregiver, teacher, or therapist can complete a Learning Strengths Profile for a student. The Learning Strengths Profile is most effectively utilized with students who have a developmental performance level of 5-6 years through adolescence.

The Primary Learning Strengths Profile is a flexible tool that can be used to identify patterns of learning that are positive and strength based. Strength areas identify a child's most effective and efficient methods of learning (i.e. visual learning, auditory learning). It is designed to quickly identify strength areas that can be used when introducing new learning or social experiences as well as barrier areas to be avoided in those situations. The Primary Learning Strengths Profile can also be used to confirm patterns of dysfunctional learning in order to support, teach, and adapt learning situations for a student's best performance and success in learning.

Once all areas are completed, a student's learning strengths will emerge. Strength areas should be used to introduce new learning, expand social interaction, and highlight strength based performance. To increase a child's motivation for learning and natural reinforcement for learning, parents and teachers can build learning experiences and instruction around the identified learning strength areas. Barrier areas will identify learning areas that need support and treatment attention. Identified barrier areas indicate that the student is not processing that type of learning effectively and efficiently for learning purposes and, therefore, should not be used as a primary method of introducing new learning material. Barrier areas should be used with "old" learning for review of information that is already mastered. Once a student is successfully using strengths for new learning and is successfully reviewing information using a variety of senses to aid generalization, a plan to increase flexibility in learning can be designed to capitalize on strengths while incorporating weaknesses.

Learning Areas:

MOTOR IMITATION:
The ability to accurately or functionally copy a motor movement or position. This area investigates how a student watches and learns.

TOUCH LEARNING:
The ability to register and discriminate incoming sensory information through the skin and respond appropriately. This area investigates how a student engages in hands-on learning.

VISUAL LEARNING:
The ability to register and discriminate incoming sensory information through the skin and respond appropriately. This area investigates how a student engages in hands-on learning.

MOVEMENT LEARNING:
TThe ability to actively engage in motor movements safely and productively, not escalating into hyperactivity, but remaining self-controlled during movement. The ability to modulate motor and sensory processing information during movement activities. This area investigates how a student moves and learns.

SELF-REGULATION
The ability to become excited or active and then calm back down. The ability to calm after being upset. The ability to process social-emotional information. This area investigates self-calming.

AUDITORY LEARNING:
The ability to listen and understand spoken language and environmental sounds and then respond appropriately. This area investigates how a student listens and understands.

NATURAL INTEREST AND MOTIVATION:
This area measures the breadth and quantity of a student's interests and natural motivation for learning.

Please rate student performance based on the student's recent behavior. Read the skill sets listed under each learning area. Rate the student's performance. If a student's performance fluctuates and is inconsistent, mark the spectrum of performance by putting an X for each rating in all learning areas that apply.

Primary Learning Strengths Profile	STRENGTH		N	BARRIER	
	1	2	3	4	5
MOVEMENT IMITATION 1-2 = Imitates motor positions and movements easily. Imitates 2-3 step movements easily. 3 = Imitates a few detailed motor actions accurately. Imitates multiple motor actions within familiar routines. 4-5 = Struggles to imitate movement well at all or is beginning to imitate 1-2 actions involving an object in the context of play.					
TOUCH LEARNING 1-2 = Enjoys hands-on learning projects and responds positively to touch interaction. 3 = Responds positively to hands-on activities, but does not always actively engage in the activity for long. May have a few strong touch preferences (i.e. tags removed from clothing, etc.) 4-5 = May respond inconsistently or have a strong reaction to touch and textures in activities. May crave touch excessively or resist touch and texture interaction frequently.					
VISUAL LEARNING 1-2 = Likes to watch and learn. Able to look at visual information, remember it, and respond appropriately. 3 = Inconsistently responds to visual information, but is able to respond to visual cues during familiar routines. 4-5 = Struggles to understand what he/ she sees. Needs consistent repetition to respond appropriately. May crave visual stimulation, but have trouble making sense of it or avoid visual stimulation all together.					
MOVEMENT LEARNING 1-2 = Actively engages in movement activities in a safe way without fear and without escalating into hyperactivity. 3 = Sensitive to new events or movement activities, but handles them well with supports and preparation. 4-5 = Avoids movement activities and seems disconnected to that type of play or becomes excessively hyper with movement. Needs supervision for safety..					
SELF-REGULTAION 1-2 = Able to self-calm following an exciting or upsetting event without supports or intervention. 3 = Able to calm following an event when provided with supports or intervention. Child is sensitive to new events, but hands them well with supports and preparation. 4-5 = Struggles to calm down even with supports or child has difficulty "waking up" to participate in daily routines and seems disconnected. Needs supervision for safety due to poor safety awareness.					
AUDITORY LEARNING 1-2 = Listens and understands well. Readily responds to spoken language and environmental sounds appropriately. 3 = Inconsistently responds to new language and sounds, but responds consistently within familiar routines. 4-5 = Struggles to understand what he/ she hears. Child needs consistent repetition to respond appropriately. Needs supervision for safety.					
NATURAL INTEREST AND MOTIVATON 1-2 = Demonstrates a variety of interests. Interested in investigating new toys and activities. Seeks out or takes advantage of opportunities to engage in play with people and things in most situations. 3 = Has strong preferences about favorite things, but will actively engage in new activities that are presented. 4-5 = Demonstrates limited interest in activities outside of a limited selection of favorites. Over-focused on playing alone to the point that it negatively impacts learning and social relationships. Rigid play skills and interests.					

© Amy Vaughan, OTRL/L, BCP 2014   www.positivelysensory.com

REFERENCES

A.Jean Ayres, P. (1979). Sensory Integration and the Child. Los Angeles, CA: Western Psychological Services.

Adlard, P., Perreau, V., Engesser-Cesar, C., & Cotman, C. (2003). Voluntary exercise differentially induces brain-derived neurotrophic factor across lifespan and protects agains behavioral depression. Society for Neuroscience, Poster Program #633.1, New Orleans, LA.

Allen, C. (2007). An action based research study on how using manipulatives will increase students' achievement in Mathematics. Marygrove College, November 3, 2007.

Amen, D. G. (2005). The Brain and Behavior: A Comprehensive Clinical Course on the Neurobiology of Everyday Life. Mind Works Press, Inc.

Bandura, A. (1971). Social Learning Theory.

Bear, M., Connors, B., & & Paradiso, M. (2006). Neuroscience: Exploring the Brain. Lippincott-Raven Publishers.

Bengoetxea, H., Ortuzar, N., Bulnes, S., Rico-Barrio, I., Lafuente, J., & Argandona, E. (2012). Enriched and deprived sensory experience induces structural changes and rewires connectivity during the postnatal development of the brain. Neural Plasticity, article 305693.

Benoit, R., & Benoit, J. (2010). Jillian's Story: How Vision Therapy Changed My Daughter's Life. Dallas, Texas: The P3 Press.

BrainFacts.org. (n.d.). BrainFacts.org. Retrieved January 12, 2014

Case-Smith, J. (2002). Effectiveness of School-Based Occupational Therapy Intervention on Handwriting. The American Journal of Occupational Therapy, 117-125.

Catania, C. (2013). Learning, 5th Edition. Sloan Publishing.

Character, V. I. (2011). VIA Me! Retrieved February 23, 2014, from VIA Me!: www.viame.org

Churchill, J., Galvez, R., Colcombe, S., Swain, R., Kramer, A., & Greenough, W. (2002). Exercise, experience and the aging brain. Neurobiological Aging, 23 (5), 941-955.

Daniels, M. (1982). The Development of the Concept of Selfactualization in the Writings of Abraham Maslow. University of Toronto Libraries.

Dewey, J. (1910). How we Think.

Dewey, J. (1916). Democracy and Education: An Introduction to the Philosophy of Education.

Dewey, J. (1938). Experience and Education.

Diamond, K. a. (1964). Effects of an Enriched Environment on the Histology of Rat Cerebral Cortex. Journal of Comparative Neurology, 111-120.

Ellis, B., Fisher, P., & Zaharie, S. (2004). Predictors of disruptive behavior, developmental delays, anxiety, and affective symptomatology among institutionally reared Romanian children. Journal of the American Academy of Child & Adolescent Psychiatry, 1283-1292.

Garrity, C. (1998). Does the Use of Hands-On Learning, with Manipulatives, Improve the Test Scores of Secondary Education Geometry Students?

Ginsburg, H. P. (1987). Piaget's Theory of Intellectual Development (3rd Edition). Pearson.

Gladwell, M. (2011). Outliers: The Story of Success. Back Bay Books.

Gladwell, M. (2013). David & Goliath: Underdogs, Misfits, and the Art of Battling Giants. Little, Brown and Company.

Goldstein, K. (1939). The Organism: A Holistic Approach to Biology Derived From Pathological Data.

Gray, C. (2010). The New Social Story Book, Revised and Expanded 10th Anniversary Edition. Future Horizons.

Greenspan, S. I., & Greenspan, N. (2010). The Learning Tree.

Hadjikhani, N., Joseph, R., Syder, J., & & Tager-Flusberg, H. (2006). Anatomical differences in the mirror neuron system and social cognition network in autism. Cerebral Cortex, 1276-1282.

Hannaford, C. (1995). Smart Moves: Why Learning is Not All in Your Head. Alexander, NC: Great Ocean Publishers.

Hein, P. G. (October 15-22, 1991). Constructivist Learning Theory. THe Museum and the Needs of People. Jeruselem, Isreal: Lesley College, Massachusetts, USA.

Hutcheson, L., Selig, H., & Young, N. (1990 January). A success story: A large urban district offers a working model for implementing multisensory teaching into the resource and regular classroom. Ann Dyslexia, 77-96.

Jensen, E. (2005). Teaching with the Brain in Mind, 2nd Edition. Association for Supervision and Curriculum Development.

Kazdin, A. (2008). Parent Management Training: Treatment for Oppositional, Aggressive, and Antisocial Behavior in Children and Adolescents. Oxford University Press, 2nd Edition.

Kazdin, A. (2012). Behavior Modification in Applied Settings. Waveland Press, Inc, 7th Edition.

Keays, J., & Allison, K. (1995). The effects of regular moderate to vigorous physical activity on student outcomes: a review. Canadian Journal of Public Health, 62-66.

Klin, A. (August 16-17, 2013). Mission Possible: Successful Treatment for Autism Spectrum Disorders. Springfield, Missouri.

Knoster, L. B. (2009). Designing Positive Behavior Support Plans. American Association on Intellectual and Developmental Disabilities, 2nd Edition.

Kochanska, G., Coy, K. C., & Murray, K. T. (July/ August 2001 ; Volume 72, Issue 4). The Development of Self-Regulation in the First Four Years of Life. Child Development, 1091-1111.

Koegel, R., & Koegel, L. K. (2012). The PRT Pocket Guide: Pivotal Response Treatment for Autism Spectrum Disorders.

Lobo, M. A., Harbourne, R. T., Dusing, S. C., & McCoy, S. W. (2013). Grounding Early Intervention: Physical Therapy Cannot Just Be About Motor Skills Anymore. Journal of the American Physical Therapy Association, January, 93 (1): 94-103.

Markakis, E., & Gage, F. (1999). Adult-generated neurons in the dentate gyrus send axonal projections to field CA3 and are surrounded by synaptic vesicles. Journal of Comparative Neurology, 406 (4), 449-460.

Meyer, M. (2008). Let Freedom Ring: A Collection of Documents from teh Movements to Free U.S. Political Prisoners.

Middleton, F., & Strick, P. (1994). Anatomical evidence for cerebellar and basal ganglia involvement in higher cognitive function. Science, 266, 458-461.

Miller, L. J. (2006). Sensational Kids: Hope and Help for Children with Sensory Processing Disorder (SPD).

Oden, A. (2004). Ready Bodies, Learning Minds. David Oden.

Ogden, S., Hindman, S., & Turner, S. (1989 January). Multisensory programs in public schools: A brighter future for LD children. Ann Dyslexia, 247-267.

Piaget, J., & Inhelder, B. (1969). The Psychology of the Child. Basic Books.

Pintrich, P., Zusho, A. W., & Eccles, J. (2002). The Development of Self-Regulation in Academics: The Role of Cognitive and Motivational Factors. A volume in the Educational Psychology Series, 249-284.

Ploughman, M. (2008). Exercise is brain food: the effects of physical activity on cognitive function. Dev Neurorehabilitation, 236-240.

Rath, T., & Conchie, B. (2008). Strengths Based Leadership. Gallup Press.

Reed, K. L., & Sanderson, S. N. (1999). Concepts of Occupational Therapy. Lippincott Williams & Wikins.

Rogers, C. (1961). On Becoming a Person.

Rogers, S., & Dawson, G. (2009). Early Start Denver Model for Young Children with Autism: Promoting Language, Learning, and Engagement.

Rogers, S., Dawson, G., & Vismara, L. (2012). An Early Start for Your Child with Autism: Using Everyday Activities to Help Kids Connect, Communicate, and Learn. The Guilford Press.

Roth, T. (2007). Gallup Press. Retrieved February 23, 2014, from Strengths Finder: www.strengthsfinder.com

Ruby Payne, P. (2005). A Framework for Understanding Poverty. aha!Process, Inc.

Shaywitz, S. (2005). Overcoming Dyslexia: A New and Complete Science-Based Program for Reading Problems at Any Level. Vintage Publishing.

Sutoo, D., & Akiyama, K. (2003). Regulation of brain function by exercise. Neurobiology of disease, 13 (1), 1-14.

Taub, M. B., Bartuccio, M., & Maino, D. (2012). Visual Diagnosis and Care of the Patient with Special Needs.

Tomoporowski, P. (2003). Effects of acute bouts of exercise on cognition. Acta Psychologica, 112 (3), 297-324.

Torgesen, J., & Barker, T. (1995). Computers as aids in the prevention and remediation of readily disabilities. . Learning Disabilities Quarterly , 76-88.

Trost, S. (2009). Active Education: Physical Education, Physical Activity and Academic Performance. San Diego State University: Active Living Research.

Trost, S., & Van der Mars, H. (2009). Why we should not cut PE. Educational Leadership, 60-65.

Van Praag, H., Kempermann, G., & Gage, F. (1999). Running increases cell proliferation and neurogenesis in the adult mouse dentate gyrus. Nature Neuroscience, 2 (3), 266-270.

Weinfeld, R., Jeweler, S., Barnes-Robinson, L., & Roffman Shevitz, B. (2013). Smart Kids with Learning Difficulties, Overcoming Obstacles and Realizing Potential. Prufrock Press.

Wikipedia. (n.d.). Wikipedia Foundation. Retrieved January 12, 2014, from www.wikipedia.com.

Williams, M. S., & Shellenberger, S. (1996). An Introduction to How Does Your Engine Run? The Alert Program for Self-Regulation. Therapy Works, Inc.

Wismer Fries, A., Ziegler, T., Kurian, J., Jacoris, S., & & Pollak, S. (2005). Early experience in humans is associated with changes in neuropeptides critical for regulating social behavior. National Academies of Science, 17237-17240.

Woo, C., & Leon, M. (2013). Environmental enrichment as an effective treatment for autism: a randomized control trial. Behavioral Neuroscience, 487-497.

Woo, C., Hingco, E., Hom, C., Lott, I., & Leon, M. (2010). Environmental Enrichment as a Potentially Effective Autism Treatment. Neuroscience Meeting Planner (p. Program No. 561.21.2010). San Diego, CA: Society for Neuroscience.

Zhang, L.-f., Sternberg, R. J., & Rayner, S. (2011). Handbook of Intellectual Styles: Preferences in Cognition, Learning, and Thinking. Springer Publishing Company.